American Heirloom

★★★ BABY ★★★

NAMES

American Heirloom

★ ★ ★ BABY ★ ★ ★

NAMES

CLASSIC NAMES TO CHOOSE WITH PRIDE

CHARLOTTE DANFORTH

NEW AMERICAN LIBRARY

NEW AMERICAN LIBRARY
Published by New American Library, a division of
Penguin Group (USA) Inc., 375 Hudson Street,
New York, New York 10014, USA
Penguin Group (Canada), 90 Eglinton Avenue East, Suite 700, Toronto,
Ontario M4P 2Y3, Canada (a division of Pearson Penguin Canada Inc.)
Penguin Books Ltd., 80 Strand, London WC2R 0RL, England
Penguin Ireland, 25 St. Stephen's Green, Dublin 2,
Ireland (a division of Penguin Books Ltd.)
Penguin Group (Australia), 250 Camberwell Road, Camberwell, Victoria 3124,
Australia (a division of Pearson Australia Group Pty. Ltd.)
Penguin Books India Pvt. Ltd., 11 Community Centre, Panchsheel Park,
New Delhi 110 - 017, India
Penguin Group (NZ), cnr Airborne and Rosedale Roads, Albany,
Auckland 1310, New Zealand (a division of Pearson New Zealand Ltd.)
Penguin Books (South Africa) (Pty.) Ltd., 24 Sturdee Avenue,
Rosebank, Johannesburg 2196, South Africa

Penguin Books Ltd., Registered Offices:
80 Strand, London WC2R 0RL, England

First published by New American Library,
a division of Penguin Group (USA) Inc.

First Printing, July 2006
10 9 8 7 6 5 4 3 2 1

⬛ REGISTERED TRADEMARK—MARCA REGISTRADA

LIBRARY OF CONGRESS CATALOGING-IN-PUBLICATION DATA:

Danforth, Charlotte.
    American heirloom baby names / by Charlotte Danforth.
        p.   cm.
    ISBN 0-451-21655-5
    1. Names, Personal—United States—Dictionaries.   2. United States—Biography—
Dictionaries.   I. Title.
    CS2375.U6D36 2005
    929.4'4'097303—dc22   2005015368

Set in Bembo
Designed by Eve Kirch

Printed in the United States of America

Acknowledgments

I would like to thank Anne Bohner, my editor at Penguin Group (USA) Inc., for her understanding and unfailing support throughout this huge project, and Rachel Boyman, who diligently watched over the many details. A special *thank-you* goes to John Talbot, my agent, who remained calm when I was feeling as panicked as a passenger who has taken over the controls of a crashing plane and talked me into a safe landing. And deep gratitude belongs to my friend Priscilla Adams of the Haddonfield New Jersey Friends Meeting—descendant of those great Quaker women who so changed American history—for intuitively sending me hugs, books, love, and boxes of candy just at the right moments when my spirit needed a lift.

Introduction

Welcome to a book that opens the pages of America's history to offer you the most prestigious, meaningful, and powerful names possible for your baby. Here you will find beautiful, strong, and honest names of American men and women who made their mark in our nation's past, demonstrated great acts of personal courage, accomplished important things in life, and have shone as beacons of inspiration. Their names evoke a heritage that should not be forgotten and values that can move future generations to create a better world. The purpose of choosing one of their names as your own baby's name is to build both the character of your child and the character of this nation. You will find:

Girls' names inspired by such outstanding women as:

The New Jersey Quaker and suffragist **Alice Paul**, born in 1885, who was imprisoned for fighting for women's rights, wrote the Equal Rights Amendment, and proved that one person can truly change the world.

A teenager who entered a battle against Mexico with Texas founder Stephen Austin, **Ann Raney Coleman**, born in 1810, who said, "The word *afraid* is not in my vocabulary, sir. I am one of the old Revolutioners of Texas."

The African-American **Althea Gibson**, a tennis superstar born in 1927, who overcame a poverty-stricken childhood to win Wimbledon's triple crown and integrated American tennis for both men and women.

A pioneer in women's rodeo, **Bertha Blancett**, born in 1883, who was the first woman to ride bucking broncos in competition and won fame as the "Champion Lady Rider of the World."

America's first African-American woman pilot, beautiful **Bessie Coleman**, born in 1892, who made history on September 3, 1922, as the first black woman to fly over American soil.

The legendary photographer **Dorothea Lange**, born in 1892, who shaped the direction of modern documentary photography, and once said, "You put your camera around your neck along with putting on your shoes, and there it is, an appendage of the body that shares your life with you."

Considered the greatest woman athlete of all time, **Mildred "Babe" Didrikson Zaharias**, born in 1914, who was once asked if there was anything she did not play; she replied, "Yeah, dolls."

A Savannah native whose home is now a museum, **Juliette Gordon Low**, born in 1860, who became the founder and first president of the Girl Scouts of the USA.

A Paiute Indian princess, Tocmetone ("Shell Flower"), or **Sarah Winnemucca**, who was born into a great family of Paiute leaders in 1844 and fought for her people's rights.

The first woman to run for president of the United States—in 1872!—**Victoria Woodhull**, born in 1838, who could not even vote for herself because women didn't have the right to vote.

Boys' names inspired by such men as:

The historian, writer, and curator **Arturo Alfonso Schomburg**, born in 1874, who vowed to combat racial prejudice by providing proof of the extraordinary contributions of peoples of African descent to world history.

The signer of the Declaration of Independence **Benjamin Rush**, born in 1745, who made groundbreaking discoveries about yellow fever, cofounded the Pennsylvania Hospital, helped found Dickinson College, and was the most famous doctor of his time.

The first African-American patriot to be killed in the Revolution, **Crispus Attucks**, who gave his life for his country on March 5, 1770, when British Redcoats fired on a mob of colonists.

The lawyer **Francis Scott Key**, born in 1779, who wrote the words of "The Star-Spangled Banner" while watching the bombardment of Fort McHenry in Baltimore Harbor during the War of 1812.

One of the creators of the U.S. Constitution, **Gouverneur Morris**, born in 1752, who fought for American Independence and a government for all the people that was stable and sound enough to last forever.

The Native American Olympic great **James Francis "Jim" Thorpe**, born in 1887, who is considered by many to be one of the most versatile athletes ever born—and has a town named after him in Pennsylvania.

A New York City native, **Jonas Salk**, born in 1914, who is the creator of the Salk vaccine, which eliminated polio as a threat to children.

A humanitarian, he insisted that the vaccine belonged not to him but to the world.

The trapper, scout, Indian agent, soldier, and authentic legend of the West **Kit Carson**, born on Christmas Eve in 1809, who was known for his humility and implacable courage.

The black genius **Langston Hughes**, born in Joplin, Missouri, to a family of abolitionists, who became the poet laureate of Harlem and influenced a generation of writers.

The first black baseball player in the major leagues—in 1884!—the African-American **Moses Fleetwood Walker**, born in 1856, who studied Greek, French, German, Latin, and math at Oberlin College and attended the University of Michigan law school.

One of the fiercest believers in liberty ever born, **Samuel Adams**, born in 1722, who organized the Boston Tea Party and is called the Father of the American Revolution.

The famous Charlestonian **St. Julien Ravenel**, born in 1819, who designed the torpedo cigar boat, called the *Little David*, which helped defend Charleston, South Carolina, during the Civil War—and developed the torpedo as a weapon.

Why American Heirloom Names . . . Why Now?

Creating a nation's character

Whether at peace or war, American men and women today are concerned with creating a society that reclaims our nation's ideals of independence, self-sufficiency, compassion, can-do spirit, equality, and self-determination. But we live in a time beset with difficult challenges and threats to, as Thomas Jefferson wrote and the Declaration of Independence promised us, "life, liberty, and the pursuit of happiness." One of the greatest of those threats is ignorance about who we are and what our nation's heritage truly is. The poet and philosopher George Santayana wrote, "Those who do not remember history are doomed to repeat it." More tragically, for Americans living now, those who do not remember our history are doomed to lose it, perhaps forever.

One effective way to keep alive the ideals we cherish is to choose American heirloom names for our children. Naming a child after a significant historical figure has always been a way for cultures to memorialize and honor the great people in their societies. Sadly, Americans have forgotten this tradition over the past fifty years. Instead, during recent decades, the most popular names of American children, such as Jennifer, Amy, Madison, Aiden, Michael, and Christopher, have no association with any living human being. They are trendy, anonymous, and ubiquitous—names that don't rock the boat—but they fall far short of what names can do for children besides helping them "fit in." And popular contemporary names don't do what names that promote values have the innate power to do: shape a society. As a result, our authentic American past is dying, our present is chaotic, and our future is jeopardized.

Passing on our beliefs

The names found in *American Heirloom Baby Names*, a very different kind of baby name book, represent American heroes, American values, and real-life people whose deeds make us proud of our past. They include, as does the American melting pot, men and women from all walks of life, from all ethnic groups, and from a wide spectrum of professions. Most of these people overcame great personal hardship to succeed, and all of them possessed immense personal courage to accomplish what they did. The names in almost every case belong to people in history, except for recent presidents and First Ladies, and have withstood the test of time. They include all the signers of the Declaration of Independence, pathfinders, trailblazers, and famous firsts in various fields.

Names Have Power: Why Choosing Your Baby's Name Is One of the Most Important Decisions You'll Ever Make

Great expectations

No one had to tell total strangers who encountered a child named Abigail Smith Adams, Dorothy Quincy Hancock, George Herbert Walker Bush, George Washington Carver, or Martin Luther King, Jr., that they were meeting someone of substance—because their names alone made that clear. And in each case the child fulfilled the expectation that he or she would amount to something special.

The building of self-esteem

One of the first formative elements in creating the adult that a child will become is his or her name. Each time a name is uttered, it announces to the world a child's ethnic background, economic class, and social identity. While some or all of the elements in this perception may in fact be false, names themselves form a powerful image for others, which sets up expectations about what the bearer of a name is like or what he is capable of doing. For example, name a boy Samson or Bruno and he is expected to be strong and perhaps belligerent—but not particularly intelligent. Name a girl Kaitlyn or Jennifer and she is expected to be feminine and popular—but not to join a university's physics department. Test this out for yourself by choosing a name and then visualizing the person you associate it with. Try it again by asking others what kind of person they see when you say it. You'll find that most people conjure up the same image you do.

Also, names have the power to help form children's conceptions of themselves—images often influenced by how the world initially reacts to them. A name can establish a positive self-image and become one of the first influences in establishing strong self-esteem. (A poor name choice can also be a hindrance, and something a child has to overcome!) One of the ways a parent can be sure a name will help, not hurt, a child is to choose one that belongs to someone they admire. The name may belong to an esteemed family member or acquaintance. Or it can be an American heirloom name, one chosen because it can provide a source of pride and embodies the values you want to teach your child to embrace.

Consider the different experiences of these two hypothetical children. One, when asked her name, replies, "My name is Samantha Roberts." That's an attractive and appealing name. Perhaps she will get a response, something like, "Oh, do you have a nickname?" or "Do people call you Sammy?" The reaction of the person to the child is positive, although somewhat condescending, and gives the impression that the child is "cute."

The other, when asked her name, replies, "My name is Anne Sullivan Roberts." And she might add, especially if speaking with an adult, "I was named after Helen Keller's teacher, who was a pioneer in teaching disabled children." This name is also attractive, appealing—and impressive. It indicates prestige, a sense of history, and parents who prize education, empathy, and an individual's will to attempt and achieve what some called impossible. The response to the child's statement might be, "That's very interesting," or "Why did your parents name you after her?" And if asked, the child can discuss Helen Keller and the accomplishments of Anne Sullivan, or "Teacher," as she was called. The child might mention the play about Anne Sullivan called *The Miracle Worker*. From the very first, an *expectation* is set up that this child is from a family of quality, has intelligence and goals, and deserves respect. From the very first, the child is proud of her name and has a powerful role model to help form her own character.

And yes, it all begins with a name.

Naming ceremonies and birthday rituals

A formal naming ceremony to confer a name upon your child is vitally important. It sets up, in a public forum, the way you want the world to react to and interact with your child. For many American parents this ceremony is a christening or a bris. But if you do not belong to an organized religion, it is important to create your own ritual with family and friends. And in every case, whether you choose an American heirloom name or the name of a beloved family ancestor, it becomes a time to tell the story of the forebear whose name you chose, to explain why you picked that person, and to talk about the qualities you hope to instill in your child. And from that day on, the people present will be predisposed to respond to and think about your child in the way you have helped to shape.

On every birthday, you should repeat this part of the naming ceremony. A birthday then becomes more than a time for material gifts: it becomes a spiritual event that memorializes and celebrates your child's being and tells again the story of his or her name. The positive impact on your child's self-esteem of reciting the story of her name is enormous. If it is possible, a child's birthday is also the perfect time to visit a place associated with the child's name. The memories created and the lessons learned will stay with your child throughout her life.

For example, avid outdoorsmen and -women might choose **Davy Crockett**, after the celebrated hero, warrior, and backwoods statesman, as the first and middle names for a child. (They might modify the name to David from Davy, or simply use Crockett as a first name. *See below*, **First names, last names, combination names, or initials**.) Davy Crockett has been said to embody the spirit of the American frontier; his life is fascinating, and his death is especially heroic. Telling his story can be moving and inspiring—and a trip to the Alamo, where he died, would be an unforgettable experience for a child and his family.

In-depth education and a lifelong passion

Another benefit of choosing an American heirloom baby name is that it reinforces the idea that parents don't need to wait for schools to educate their children. Teaching about our past and the values most important to us must begin at home. Your child's name can be a catalyst for this. Giving your child an American heirloom name is often the start of a lifelong passion for the period, the profession, and/or the place associated with your child's name. For example, women were some of the Old West's most interesting pioneers. One of my favorites is **Nellie Cashman**:

Called the Angel of Tombstone and the Angel of the Cassiars. Feisty and fearless, Nellie lived the life of a miner in towns and settlements from Arizona to the Klondike. She ran boardinghouses and restaurants, built churches and hospitals, and risked her life on several rescue missions. One of her most famous missions: traveling for seventy-seven days through a bitter winter with six men and pack animals laden with supplies to rescue one hundred desperately ill miners.

From learning about Nellie Cashman, your child may be motivated to investigate the pioneer days of Arizona, Alaska, and the Klondike. You and she can read about women in the Old West. Your family and your daughter together can visit mining sites in several states, discover how to pan for gold, explore frontier sites and ghost towns, and even take the trip of a lifetime to Alaska and the Klondike. Is there any child on earth who wouldn't like to run behind a dogsled? And can you imagine the delight and pride of a child who can say, *I am the namesake of Nellie Cashman, the Angel of the Cassiars!*

How to Use This Book

Finding the right name

American Heirloom Baby Names gives you many avenues for finding the best name to fit your values and your child. Each entry includes a short biography of the outstanding man or woman, including their birth date and death date, and touches on the highlights of their life, personal qualities, and contributions. Here is a sample of the entry for Philadelphia's favorite son, Benjamin Franklin:

Benjamin Franklin (1706–1790) was a patriot, author, inventor, printer, and Founding Father. Born in Boston, he spent most of his life in Philadelphia. His achievements are as varied as they are impressive: he founded America's first public library, the Library Company of Philadelphia, as well as the country's first scholarly society, the American Philosophical Society. He founded the University of Pennsylvania and was a cofounder of the Pennsylvania Hospital. His experiments with electricity are the stuff of legend, and the stove he invented is still used more than two hundred years after his death. He negotiated an alliance between France and the United States during the Revolution, helped to create the Declaration of Independence, and helped to write the Constitution. Poor Richard's Almanack *is perhaps his best-known work, though he wrote several books, including an autobiography. When Benjamin Franklin died, George Washington proclaimed that the country had lost "a genius, a philosopher, a scientist, a noble statesman, and its first citizen."*

When you narrow your selections down to a few potential names for your child, please take the time to read more deeply into the life of the hero you choose. Remember that heroes are all real people and not fictional characters, and real people are far from perfect—we all have weaknesses and we all make mistakes, even the greatest among us. But it is important that you know enough about the person so there are no big surprises that upset you!

For example, **Thomas Jefferson** was a brilliant thinker, a wonderful leader, and without doubt instrumental in creating a nation that was founded on the belief that "All men are created equal." After all, he wrote the Declaration of Independence—and risked his life to do so. Any child can feel proud to bear his name. But you as the parent should be aware that Thomas Jefferson was a slave owner, and did have children with at least one of those slaves. Does that detract from his world-changing accomplishments? No, it does not. But it does mean he could have made better choices, especially as a young man.

First names, last names, combination names, or initials

Once you decide on a name, you have many ways to use it. You can choose the noteworthy man or woman's first and last name as your child's first and middle names. For example, if your last name is Hamilton, and you have always admired the African-American businesswoman and philanthropist **Madame C. J. Walker**, you can choose her real name, which was Sarah Breedlove, to make the name Sarah Breedlove Hamilton. Or you can create the name C. J. Walker Hamilton. (Initials are a fun way to update and modernize American heirloom names.)

On the other hand, you might like the effect of using just a last name for your child's first name, although this seems to work out better for boys' names. For instance, if you admire the musician and composer **Edward Kennedy "Duke" Ellington**, you can use Duke Ellington as first and middle names, or just Ellington as a first name. Again, if your last name is Hamilton, your baby would be Duke Ellington Hamilton or Ellington Hamilton.

And don't forget that many people have more than one middle name. While more than two can become a burden for a child, you can create some exciting names by using first, middle, and last names before your own surname. For example, you might choose the American president **Lyndon Baines Johnson**; the World War II general **George Smith Patton**; the African-American nursing pioneer **Adah Belle Thoms**, or the writer and abolitionist **Harriet Beecher Stowe**. Any of these names preceding your own surname will carry clout and sound chic as well.

A few words of caution

Here are some things to watch for:

- Always make sure your child's initials don't spell anything derogatory.

- Test to see that the name isn't a tongue twister; it should be easy to say.

- Don't choose a name that might provoke teasing or stereotyping. For example, either **Orville** or **Wilbur Wright** are terrific role models—evoking the qualities of perseverance, creativity or invention, and a passion for flying. But in urban areas, both Orville and Wilbur might sound countrified (in the South or farm country, these first names would probably be accepted without a raised eyebrow), so be aware of regional differences when it comes to names. You can simply use Wright as a first name to create Wright [Your Surname], or modify his brother's first name, Wilbur, to Wil Wright [Your Surname]. You keep the spirit and take away any potential negative.

- Make the name gender appropriate. It is always hurtful to a child's self-image to have a girl's name if he is a boy, or a boy's name for a girl. Avoid making a name something a child has to defend or work against. Choose a name that gives a child a boost upward and does not become an obstacle to be surmounted.

The reward

You should get a great deal of enjoyment out of browsing through and reading *American Heirloom Baby Names*. You'll discover many heroic Americans you never knew about—many of whom are men and women the history books have excluded or overlooked. You should find several names that will excite your imagination and expand your horizons for yourself and your child. Discovering what our forefathers and -mothers had to overcome and the amazing things they accomplished—from saving lives to climbing mountains to making life-and-death medical breakthroughs—can spur us on to bigger dreams for our children and higher goals for ourselves.

And because there are many more great Americans than the ones in this book, your further reading can lead you down new educational paths, spark your curiosity, or ignite your creativity. For example, if you love art and admire artists, you can delve deeper into the history of American art, visit the terrific museums that exist in every city and every state, and discover schools, workshops, and working artists too. Similar roads will open up in nearly every field until you are walking in directions you never expected—and leading you and your child toward a future bright with hope and founded on values that provide strength and sure footing as you build a meaningful, fulfilling life!

★ ★ ★ ★ G I R L S ★ ★ ★ ★

★ ★ ★ ★ ★ ★ ★ ★ A ★ ★ ★ ★ ★ ★ ★ ★

ABIGAIL: from the Hebrew for father's joy. Abbie or Abby are the most common diminutives, but Gail could work, too.

Abby Morton Diaz (1821–1904), a social activist whose credo was "It is not life to live for one's self alone. Let us help one another," lectured on women's rights. A founder of the Women's Educational and Industrial Union, the Woman's Clubs, and the Protective Bureau, Abby also wrote children's books.

Abigail Smith Adams (1744–1818) was one of America's First Ladies. A trusted and influential political advisor to her husband, President John Adams, Abigail was ahead of her time with her ideas: she opposed slavery and believed in equal education for boys and girls. Her famous letters—pungent, witty, and vivid—detail life during the American Revolution. Abigail Adams, with its alliteration, is a powerhouse of a name. Her birthplace in Weymouth, Massachusetts, is open to the public from July 1 through Labor Day.

"We have too many high-sounding words, and too few actions that correspond with them." —Abigail Adams, in a letter

---

Abigail Scott Duniway (1834–1915) was born in a log cabin in Illinois. Abigail journeyed by covered wagon to Oregon when she was eighteen, and began publishing a weekly newspaper that espoused equal rights for women. Because of her efforts, women's suffrage passed in Idaho in 1896, in Washington in 1910, and in Oregon in 1912.

Abigail Powers Fillmore (1798–1853) became First Lady after Zachary Taylor died in office and her husband, Millard Fillmore, became president. Abigail was shocked to find that the White House had no books, so she founded the White House Library. She also insisted that the White House be fitted with indoor plumbing.

Abigail Kelley Foster (1810–1887), at a time when women did not speak in public, risked her safety to lecture crowds against slavery and, later, for women's suffrage. She and her husband, Stephen Symonds Foster, made their home in Worcester, Massachusetts, a stop on the Underground Railroad.

ADA, ADAH: from the Hebrew for ornament, and the English for prosperous.

ADA BEATRICE QUEEN VICTORIA LOUISE VIRGINIA SMITH (1894–1984) might be more of a mouthful than you're willing to bestow upon your daughter, but this redheaded African-American woman, nicknamed Bricktop, was one of the most famous celebrities of the 1920s. She took Josephine Baker under her wing, worked with Langston Hughes, was friends with F. Scott Fitzgerald, and was the inspiration behind Cole Porter's "Miss Otis Regrets." She told her story in *Bricktop: An Autobiography* (written with James Haskins).

ADAH BELLE THOMS (1870–1943) fought for African-American nurses to have equal opportunities. A graduate and later acting director of the Lincoln School for Nurses in New York, Adah was president of the National Association of Colored Graduate Nurses and won for blacks the right to serve as army nurses during World War I. Adah was one of the original inductees into the American Nurses Association Hall of Fame in 1996.

ADELAIDE: from the German for noble and serene.

ADELAIDE JOHNSON (1859–1955) was, among other things, the sculptor of the Suffrage Monument to the women's movement that stands in Washington, D.C. (visit it at the National Women's Party Headquarters). Her life work began with the exhibition of busts of Lucretia Mott, Elizabeth Cady Stanton, and Susan B. Anthony at the Woman's Pavilion of the 1893 World's Columbian Exposition in Chicago, and her sculpture of Anthony was used as the model for a postage stamp.

ADELLA, ADELLE: variations on Adelaide, from the German for noble and serene. Adele is another spelling.

ADELLA PRENTISS HUGHES (1869–1950) was founder of the Cleveland Music School Settlement and the Musical Arts Association, and was the first general director of the Cleveland Symphony Orchestra.

ADELLE DAVIS (1804–1874) is most famous for her bestselling books on nutrition (she wrote four, including *Let's Eat Right to Keep Fit*), but she was more than just a natural-foods pioneer. Davis received a master of science degree in biochemistry from the University of Southern California in 1938, and her groundbreaking ideas can be seen in the Zone Diet and the Atkins Nutritional Approach. She's the one who's credited with advising people to "Eat breakfast like a king, lunch like a prince, and dinner like a pauper."

ADINA: from the Greek for noble or adorned, and the Hebrew for delicate or slender.

ADINA DE ZAVALA (1861–1955) was a historian who helped to preserve the Alamo as a historic site. The founder of the Texas Historical and Landmarks Association, she also fought for the recognition of Tejano contributions to the history of Texas.

AGNES: from the Greek for pure.

AGNES DE MILLE (1905–1993) was instrumental in bringing ballet from the rarefied cultural heights to the popular stage. Among this choreographer's many works are *Black Ritual*, the first ballet performed by black dancers in a classical American ballet company; *I*, which included tap dancing; as well as some of Broadway's most enduringly popular musicals, including *Carousel*, *Oklahoma*, *Brigadoon*, and *Gentlemen Prefer Blondes*.

AGNES NESTOR (1880–1948) drew on her experience working sixty-hour weeks in a Chicago glove factory to become a labor organizer who worked for child labor laws, minimum wage, maternity health, and women's suffrage.

ALBERTA: from the German for noble and bright.

ALBERTA HUNTER (1895–1984), one of the great blues singers of all time, made her professional debut in Chicago but moved to New York to begin her recording career; "Tain't Nobody's Biz-ness If I Do" was one of her most famous hits. Alberta left the music scene in the 1950s, but she returned in the late 1970s and became a bigger star than before.

ALICE: from the Greek for truthful, and the German for noble. Similar to Elise or Alicia but not as fussy as either, Alice is a timeless name that has been shared by playwrights, feminists, artists, and high-spirited wits.

ALICE AUSTEN (1866–1952) was a photographer whose work of immigrants and laborers set the stage for documentary photography.

Thousands of her photographs are exhibited at the Alice Austen House on Staten Island.

ALICE CHILDRESS (1916–1994) was part of the Harlem Renaissance. A playwright whose best-known work may be *A Hero Ain't Nothin' but a Sandwich*, Alice won the Obie Award in 1956 for her play *Trouble in Mind*.

ALICE BROWN DAVIS (1852–1935) was a Seminole Indian chief who helped her people regain their land; the Seminoles won a settlement after her death.

ALICE LEE ROOSEVELT LONGWORTH (1884–1980), the daughter of President Theodore Roosevelt, was sufficiently high-spirited that her father once said, "I can either run the country or I can control Alice. I cannot possibly do both." Best remembered as a wit (she is one of the most quoted women of the last century), she also helped Jacqueline Kennedy restore the White House.

ALICE PAUL (1885–1977) devoted her life to the fight for women's rights. She was one of the key fighters to win for women the constitutional right to vote, and she also was the author of the Equal Rights Amendment.

ALINE, ALINA: from the Slavic for bright, and the Scottish for fair.

ALINE BERNSTEIN (1880–1955) was to Broadway and American theater what Edith Head was to Hollywood and movies. This visionary designer won a Tony Award in 1950 for the opera *Regina*. She was instrumental in establishing the Costume Institute at the Metropolitan Museum of Art, which she was the president of for the last nine years of her life.

ALTA: from the Latin for high or tall.

ALTA WEISS (1890–1964) was signed as a pitcher with a semiprofessional men's baseball team at the age of seventeen and became a sensation throughout the Midwest. In fact, she made enough money to put herself through medical school, and even after she began practicing medicine she continued to pitch until her early thirties.

ALTHEA: from the Greek for wholesome, or healer.

ALTHEA GIBSON (1927–2003) won acclaim for her athletic prowess, first on the tennis courts. She was the first African-American to win the Wimbledon singles title and the U.S. National title, and was named female athlete of the year two years in a row by the Associated Press. She also played professional golf and toured on the LPGA.

AMELIA: from the Latin for flatterer, and the German for hardworking. Looking for an alternative to the extremely popular name Emily? Consider Amelia. It has the same meaning, but the stress on the middle syllable enables it to pair with other names.

AMELIA JENKS BLOOMER (1818–1894) was a suffragist who lent her name to the "pantelettes" that came to be known as bloomers, but she was also the first woman to own and edit a newspaper for women. Called the *Lily*, the newspaper originally focused on temperance, but came to champion women's rights as well.

AMELIA EARHART (1897–1937), one of the world's most famous aviators, once said that "courage is the price that life exacts for granting peace with yourself." She must have known a thing or two about courage: Earhart was the first woman aviator to cross the Atlantic and, in 1932, set a transatlantic crossing record. In 1937 she set out to circumnavigate the globe, but after she and her navigator left New Guinea, the U.S. Coast Guard lost contact with them. Despite extensive searching, no trace of the plane was ever found.

AMELIA STONE QUINTON (1833–1926) fought for rights for Native Americans. She was the founder of the Women's National Indian Association, and her efforts helped to pass the Dawes Severalty Act, which made Native Americans citizens of the United States.

AMY: from the French for loved.

AMY MARCY BEACH (1867–1944) was the first woman composer whose work was performed by the New York Philharmonic Society; many of her works are available on CD.

AMY LOWELL (1874–1925) was a Pulitzer Prize–winning poet, biographer, and critic. Famously eccentric, she wore a pince-nez and smoked cigars, but no less an authority on American poetry than T. S. Eliot thought highly of her; in fact, Eliot called her "the demon saleswoman" who helped to popularize this literary form.

ANGELICA: from the Greek for angel, or messenger.

ANGELICA SCHUYLER CHURCH (1756–1815) was renowned for her beauty as well as her intellect and sensibility. The daughter of General

Philip John Schuyler and Catharine Van Rensselaer, Angelica married John Church, who was commissary general during the American Revolution, and she later became the confidante and friend of Alexander Hamilton and Thomas Jefferson. She was also the patron of many artists and writers. If you love the name Schuyler but want to avoid trendiness, pair it with a classic name like Angelica (or Catharine; see pages 20–21).

ANGELINA: from the Latin for angel.

ANGELINA GRIMKÉ WELD (1805–1879) grew up in Charleston, South Carolina, in a family that owned slaves. Influenced by her abolitionist older brother, she moved to Philadelphia and joined the Quakers and the Philadelphia Female Anti-Slavery Society, and became an outspoken crusader against slavery and an advocate of women's rights. She published a pamphlet entitled "An Appeal to the Christian Women of the South," which caused a sensation, and she further outraged clergy by speaking publicly at a time when women did not.

ANITA: from the Spanish for gracious.

ANITA LOOS (1893–1981) was a screenwriter (the first woman to do it full-time) who sold her first script at the age of nineteen. Her novels *Gentlemen Prefer Blondes* and *But Gentlemen Marry Brunettes* were international best sellers; the former became a movie starring Marilyn Monroe.

ANITA NEWCOMB MCGEE, M.D. (1864–1940) founded the Army Nurse Corps after seeing how urgently skilled nurses were needed during the Spanish-American War. After the nurses were enlisted, one surgeon remarked, "When you were coming, we did not know what we would do with you. Now we do not know what we would have done without you." Anita was also commissioned assistant surgeon general of the United States, and was awarded the Imperial Order for the Sacred Crown by the Japanese government for her work during the Russo-Japanese War.

ANN, ANNE, ANNIE: from the Hebrew for gracious. Whether you choose to spell this graceful name with or without the *e*, or choose Annie as a birth name rather than a nickname, there are plenty of role models from all walks of life.

ANN RANEY COLEMAN (1810–1897) once said, "The word *afraid* is not in my vocabulary, sir. I am one of the old Revolutioners of Texas." Her fearlessness predates the Texas Revolution: Ann arrived in Austin after a voyage where pirates ransacked the ship she was on; she survived by hiding in a closet. During the Battle of Velasco she helped to make bullets, then transported them by horseback to a hiding place fifteen miles away—and outran Mexican spies on the return. Ann later applied for a pension based on her role in the battle but was denied because she was a woman.

ANN LEE (1736–1784) was the founder of the Shaker sect, which taught that perfect holiness was attainable and that shaking and trembling were physical manifestations of sin leaving people's bodies. On a missionary journey, Mother Ann and some followers were whipped, clubbed, stoned, and dragged behind horses; she died as a result of injuries sustained in beatings. Shaker communities at Pleasant Hill, Kentucky; Pittsfield, Massachusetts; Canterbury, New Hampshire; Sabbathday Lake, Maine, and Mount Lebanon, New York, still stand as museums to this way of life.

ANN PRESTON (1813–1872) was a pioneering Quaker doctor. Rejected from medical school because she was a woman, Ann enrolled at the Female Medical College (later called the Woman's Medical College) of Pennsylvania. Barred from educational and medical societies because of her gender, Ann helped to found the Woman's Hospital in Philadelphia; she also established a school of nursing, and later became the first female dean at the Woman's Medical College.

ANNE BRADSTREET (c. 1612–1672) was born in England but emigrated with her husband to Massachusetts Bay Colony in the early 1600s. She is regarded as America's first poet.

ANNE HUTCHINSON (1591–1643) was an advocate of religious liberty and was one of the founders of the state of Rhode Island after she was banished from Massachusetts. There is a statue of her on the State House grounds in Boston, Massachusetts, and a memorial plaque at Boyd's Lane in Portsmouth, Rhode Island. The Hutchinson River and Hutchinson River Parkway in New York State were named after her.

ANNE MORROW LINDBERGH (1906–2001) wrote thirteen books, including the best-selling *Gift from the Sea*. She was an accomplished aviator in her own right as well as the wife of Charles Lindbergh. The first licensed female glider pilot in the United States, Anne was awarded the Hubbard Gold Medal for exploratory flying. Her book *North to the Orient* chronicled her and her husband's flights from Canada to Alaska, Japan, and China.

ANNE SULLIVAN (1866–1936) was christened Johanna but was never called anything but Anne (or Annie). This nearly blind woman gained fame as Helen Keller's governess and teacher. Using methods first tried by Samuel Gridley Howe, Anne taught Helen to communicate; when Helen went to Radcliffe College, Anne accompanied her, attending classes, helping her study, and offering encouragement. Her story has been told in the play and movie *The Miracle Worker.*

ANNIE JUMP CANNON (1863–1941) studied at Wellesley and Radcliffe Colleges before joining the Harvard College Observatory as an astronomer. She created the definitive system for classifying stars and stellar spectra that was adopted by the International Astronomical Union in the 1920s. She was awarded six honorary degrees, as well as the Draper Medal of the National Academy of Sciences.

ANNIE OAKLEY (1860–1926) was born Phoebe Anne Oakley Mozee in Ohio. By the time she was twelve she was such an accurate shot that she could shoot the head off a running quail. Though she stood only five feet tall, Annie rode show horses and bucking broncos as a vaudeville, circus, and rodeo performer. Greenville, Ohio, is home to the Annie Oakley Foundation and hosts an annual Annie Oakley festival, and her guns and letters are in the Nutley Historical Society Museum in Nutley, New Jersey.

ANNIE DODGE WAUNEKA (1910–1997) was the first woman elected to the Navajo Tribal Council. With a degree in public health, she worked to improve health care, particularly to lessen the risks of tuberculosis, and later was awarded the Presidential Medal of Freedom.

ANNA: from the Hebrew for gracious.

ANNA ELLA CARROLL (1815–1893) was a political writer, advisor to three presidents, and a strategist whose work was crucial to the Union army. The pamphlets she wrote helped to keep Maryland from seceding from the Union, and through the course of reporting on the war she uncovered information about the Tennessee Campaign, which helped the North to win.

ANNA BOTSFORD COMSTOCK (1854–1930), a naturalist, conservationist, and artist whose work *Handbook of Nature Study* is still in print nearly one hundred years after its initial publication, was the first woman to become a professor at Cornell University.

ANNA MARY ROBERTSON "GRANDMA" MOSES (1860–1961) began her career in her seventies; this beloved painter's work is on display at the Bennington Museum in Bennington, Vermont, as well as in the National Museum of Women in the Arts in Washington, D.C.; the Portland Art Museum in Portland, Oregon; and the Memorial Art Gallery of the University of Rochester in New York.

ANNIS: from the Hebrew for gracious.

ANNIS BOUDINOT STOCKTON (1736–1801) was the wife of Richard Stockton (one of the signers of the Declaration of Independence) as well as a poet. When the British invaded Princeton, Annis hid important documents, including the records of the American Whig Society. This act of bravery led to her being made an honorary member of the society.

ANTOINETTE: the French form of Antonia, from the Latin for praiseworthy. Nicknames may include Nettie or Toni.

ANTOINETTE LOUISE BROWN BLACKWELL (1825–1921) was the first American woman ordained as a minister; though she completed seminary in 1850, she was refused a degree and denied ordination until 1853 because she was a woman. A writer and public speaker who advocated women's rights, temperance, and abolition, she preached until she was ninety and wrote her last book at age ninety-three.

ARABELLA: from the Latin for beautiful altar. A name more common in England than in the United States, Arabella may be shortened to Ara, Belle, or Bella.

ARABELLA MANSFIELD (1846–1911) was the first American woman to become a lawyer. Born Belle Aurelia Babb, Arabella graduated from Iowa Wesleyan University in 1866 and was admitted to the Iowa bar three years later.

AUGUSTA: the feminine form of Augustine, from the Latin for majestic.

AUGUSTA SAVAGE (1892–1962) was a sculptor who founded the Savage School of Arts and Crafts in Harlem; she later became the first director of the Harlem Community Arts Center, which is the model for others across the country. The Augusta Savage Gallery in Amherst, Massachusetts, houses many of her works.

AYN: the Russian or Irish variation on Ann, Anya, or Enya.

AYN RAND (1905–1982) was born Alissa Rosenbaum in St. Petersburg, Russia, and arrived in New York in 1926 with fifty dollars to her name. After a brief stint as an actress, she wrote two Broadway plays, but she is best known for her novels *The Fountainhead*, which idealizes American individualism and man as hero, and *Atlas Shrugged*, which dramatizes major elements of Objectivism, her philosophy of reason, individualism, and capitalism. The Ayn Rand Institute is located in Irvine, California.

BARBARA: from the Latin for foreigner or stranger. Common nicknames include Barb, Bobbie, or Babs.

BARBARA PIERCE BUSH (b. 1925) is the wife of the forty-first president and the mother of the forty-third. As First Lady, Barbara adopted the promotion of literacy as one of her causes; the Barbara Bush Foundation for Family Literacy furthers her work to that end. In addition, she is a strong supporter of the Leukemia Society of America, the Ronald McDonald House, and the Boys & Girls Clubs of America.

BARBARA CHARLINE JORDAN (1936–1996) was a lawyer and the first black woman from the South to serve in the U.S. Congress, where she gained national renown during the impeachment hearings of President Richard M. Nixon. She was invited to be the keynote speaker for the Democratic National Convention in 1976, the first African-American to hold this honor. She resigned from Congress in 1978 because of a neurological illness, but was a professor of public affairs at the Lyndon Baines Johnson School of Public Affairs at the University of Texas at Austin until her death.

BEATRICE: from the Latin for blessed.

BEATRICE MOSES HINKLE, M.D. (1874–1953) founded the country's first psychotherapeutic clinic with Dr. Charles R. Dana at Cornell Medical School. Although she studied with Dr. Sigmund Freud in Vienna, she disagreed with Freud's belief that the female psyche was a derivation of the male psyche, and embraced the teachings of Carl Jung. One of the most famous female psychoanalysts of her time, she was also among the first to espouse Jung's theories and ideas. After retiring from the faculty of Cornell Medical College and the New York Post-Graduate Medical School, she moved to Washington, Connecticut, to fund a private sanatorium.

BELINDA: from the Spanish for beautiful.

BELINDA MULROONEY (1872–1967) was a rags-to-riches success story in the Klondike—not as someone who struck gold, but as someone who possessed the savvy to know what miners would need. She headed to

Juneau, Alaska, at age twenty-six with enough hot-water bottles and silk underwear that, after selling them to the miners, she was able to open a restaurant. She then opened a hotel, sold it, and built another—and lost her fortune when she married a phony French count. Four years later she established a bank in Fairbanks and made a second fortune.

BELLE: from the French for beautiful; it may be a nickname of Isabelle or Arabella.

BELLE BOYD (1844–1900) was dubbed "the siren of the South" by one biographer, and the more prosaic if somewhat more descriptive "Confederate spy" by another. Among her many feats were shooting and killing a Union soldier, spying on Union activities, running messages and information for Generals P. G. T. Beauregard and Stonewall Jackson, delivering medicines, and being arrested three times. After the war ended she had a career onstage and published her autobiography, *Belle Boyd in Camp and Prison*.

BELVA: from the Latin for beautiful view.

BELVA ANN BENNETT LOCKWOOD (1830–1917) holds the distinctions of being the first woman to plead a case before the U.S. Supreme Court and the second woman to run for president. A schoolteacher at age fifteen, she was almost fifty when she decided to attend the National University Law School; she had to appeal to President Ulysses Grant for the school to award her a diploma. She was admitted to the bar in Washington, D.C., at a time when it required an act of Congress to allow a woman to argue before the Supreme Court. She represented a black attorney, Samuel Lowrey, before the court and won for him the right to practice law. The National Equal Rights Party nominated her to run against Grover Cleveland in the 1884 presidential election.

BERNICE: from the Greek for bringer of victory.

BERNICE SHINER GERA (1931–1992) was professional baseball's first female umpire. Although she graduated from Florida Baseball Umpire School in 1967, she was barred from officiating at pro games because of arbitrary regulations until she filed a lawsuit. This suit opened doors for other women as well as men. Although Bernice only umpired one game professionally, she worked in community relations and promotions for the New York Mets from 1974 to 1979. A baseball trading card was issued in her honor, and her portrait, uniform, and pink whisk broom are on display at the Baseball Hall of Fame in Cooperstown, New York.

BERTHA: from the German for bright or famous. The French spelling is Berthe; Bert and Birdie are diminutives.

BERTHA KAEPERNIK BLANCETT (1883–1981) might sound like a stodgy old-fashioned name, but if you're looking for a role model who was fearless and bold, look no further. Bertha was the first woman to ride bucking broncos in rodeo competitions. After touring in Wild West shows, she moved to California with her husband and worked under contract to Bison Pictures. Visit the National Cowgirl Museum and Hall of Fame in Fort Worth, Texas, or the Museum of the American West to find out more about her.

BESS (BESSIE): a familiar form of Elizabeth, from the Hebrew for consecrated to God. Not as cutesy as Betsy or as casual as Liz, Bess is a diminutive for Elizabeth but a strong name in its own right—and if it's strength you're looking for, look no further than the women who've had this name.

BESS TRUMAN (1885–1982), though christened Elizabeth Virginia Wallace, was never called anything but Bess her whole life. This First Lady met her husband, Harry Truman, when she was five years old and he was six, but they didn't marry until 1919. As down-to-earth and no-nonsense as her name, Bess could hit a baseball as far as any boy as a child, and as an adult was considered one of the hardest-working First Ladies.

BESSIE COLEMAN (1892–1926), known as Queen Bess, was the first black woman to fly over American soil. She decided to become a pilot when her brother, who served in France during World War I, returned home with stories of female aviators in France. Unable to find anyone in the United States willing to teach a black woman to fly, Bessie went to France and got her license from the Federation Aeronautique Internationale in 1921. She returned to the United States and performed stunts and tricks in air shows, but was killed during a test flight.

BESSIE SMITH (1894–1937) was a blues singer who "let her soul do the singing," and put her life and troubles into her 160-plus recordings. Once stabbed during a performance, she chased her attacker for three blocks with the knife still in her side! Bessie was killed in a car accident, but it wasn't until forty-three years after her death that she got a proper tombstone, paid for in part by Janis Joplin.

BETSY: a familiar form of Elizabeth, from the Hebrew for consecrated to God.

BETSY ROSS (1752–1836) is known to nearly every schoolchild as the woman who sewed the first American flag, but she wasn't the type to stitch quietly in a corner. One of seventeen children, Betsy went to Quaker schools and apprenticed as an upholsterer; her husband and business partner was killed after he joined the militia. George Washington commissioned her to make the flag for the new nation in 1776, and Betsy made one design modification: her contribution was the five-pointed star (Washington's original design called for a six-pointed one). The Betsy Ross House is located at 239 Arch Street in Philadelphia.

BETTE, BETTY: a familiar form of Elizabeth, from the Hebrew for consecrated to God.

BETTE DAVIS (1908–1989) was known for playing strong characters, but she was indomitable offscreen as well. Bette was nominated for eight Academy Awards and won two of them, and she was the first female performer to be honored with the Life Achievement Award of the American Film Institute.

"My passions were all gathered together like fingers that made a fist. Drive is considered aggression today; I knew it then as purpose." —Bette Davis, in her autobiography

BETTY FORD (b. 1918) was born Elizabeth Anne Bloomer. Until the 1970s, breast cancer and drug addiction were taboo topics, and Betty Ford deserves a great deal of credit for making these illnesses part of the public discourse. After undergoing a mastectomy, Betty began to campaign to increase people's awareness of breast cancer and other women's health issues. She went public with her addiction to painkilling drugs in 1978 and entered a treatment center in California, and began speaking frankly about her addiction. In 1982 she founded the Betty Ford Center for Drug and Alcohol Rehabilitation. Betty Ford was awarded the Presidential Medal of Freedom in 1991 and the Congressional Gold Medal in 1999.

BILLIE: from the English for strong-willed; a familiar form of Wilhelmina.

BILLIE HOLIDAY (1915–1959), born Eleanora Fagan, overcame a terrible childhood to become one of America's greatest jazz singers. No stranger to racism, she was exposed to so much of it during a tour with the Artie Shaw Orchestra that she quit and returned to New York, where she recorded "Strange Fruit," a powerful, haunting song about lynching that never failed to move listeners. Other songs she made her own include "God Bless the Child" and "Lover Man." Despite her soaring career, Billie developed addictions to drugs and alcohol and died of cirrhosis of the liver at age forty-four. Her place in American music is honored at the Rock and Roll Hall of Fame and Museum in Cleveland.

BLANCHE: from the Latin for white.

BLANCHE WOLF KNOPF (1894–1966) might have been the assistant to Alfred A. Knopf when he founded his eponymous publishing company, but her meteoric rise was due to her passion, intelligence, and discerning taste rather than nepotism. The list of authors she published reads like a list of who's who of the twentieth century: André Gide, Thomas Mann, Simone de Beauvoir, and Sigmund Freud, as well as Langston Hughes and other writers of the Harlem Renaissance.

BRENDA: from the Irish for little raven; the feminine form of Brendan.

BRENDA PUTNAM (1890–1975) was an award-winning sculptor. Originally from Minneapolis, she studied at the Art Students League in New York City and at Washington, D.C.'s, Corcoran Art School, as well as in Florence, Italy. Her public commissions include a memorial to the women of Virginia in Lynchburg, the bas relief over the visitors' gallery in the United States House of Representatives, and a bust of Susan B. Anthony at New York University.

BRIDGET: from the Gaelic for exalted one. Alternate spellings and forms include Brigid, Brigit, Brigitte, Bergit, and Britt; Biddy and Birdie are common diminutives.

BRIDGET "BIDDY" MASON (1818–1891) was born a slave in Mississippi, but after her master took her to California, she successfully sued to win freedom for herself and her three children. She was one of the first black women to own land in Los Angeles, and the site of her home at 331 South Spring Street is now a park, where her life is commemorated in a series of plaques. She worked as a nurse and midwife, founded and financed the first black church in Los Angeles, founded fourteen nursing homes, and gave generously to the poor.

★ ★ ★ ★ ★ ★ ★ ★ **C** ★ ★ ★ ★ ★ ★ ★ ★

CAROLINE: a feminine form of Charles, from the French for strong. A bit more elegant than the variation Carolyn, Caroline has an old-fashioned air. Carolina is common in Spain and Italy, and Charlene has a French sound to it. Cara, Carly, Carrie, Caro, Carol, or Lina are used as nicknames.

CAROLINE LAVINIA SCOTT HARRISON (1832–1892) was the daughter of a professor at Miami University of Ohio and the wife of President Benjamin Harrison. She had a degree in music and taught music, painting, and home economics. As First Lady, Caroline was active in women's issues, had electricity installed in the White House, designed the china used at the White House, and put up the first Christmas tree in White House history. Johns Hopkins Hospital asked for her support in building a new wing, but she refused to help—until they agreed to admit women to their medical school. She died of tuberculosis while her husband was in office.

CARRIE, CARRY: familiar forms of Caroline.

CARRIE CHAPMAN CATT (1859–1947) was one of the visionaries responsible for women's rights, especially for the right to vote. She addressed Congress in 1892 at the request of Susan B. Anthony, speaking about the proposed suffrage amendment, and she succeeded Anthony as president of the National American Woman Suffrage Association. After ratification of the Nineteenth Amendment in 1920, she founded the League of Women Voters. Her childhood home is located in Charles City, Iowa; the Center for Women and Politics at Iowa State University is named after her.

CARRY AMELIA MOORE NATION (1846–1911) faced down mobs and was arrested thirty times as a temperance crusader—and she also inspired thousands of women to join the fight against alcohol. She and her followers smashed saloons and the liquor they contained with hatchets, hammers, rocks, and bats, unwavering in her belief that alcohol destroyed families. "Whatever she believes in she believes in with her whole soul, and nothing except superior force can stay her," noted one observer.

CARSON: from the English for son of Carr.

Carson Smith McCullers (1917–1967) published her first novel, *The Heart Is a Lonely Hunter*, when she was only twenty-three. This renowned Southern writer's other novels include *Reflections in a Golden Eye*, *The Ballad of the Sad Café* (which Tennessee Williams said was "among the masterpieces of the language"), and *The Member of the Wedding*. All are still in print. If you're thinking of names like Bailey or Madison for your daughter, consider Carson, another surname that's used as a first name.

CASSANDRA: a Greek prophetess in classical mythology whose warnings went unheeded. Cassandra may also be a feminine variation on Alexander. Cass, Casey, Cassie, and Sandy may be used as nicknames.

Cassandra Pickett Durham (1824–1885) was the first woman in Georgia to earn a doctor of medicine degree—at the age of forty-six. After seeing and experiencing hunger, deprivation, and the problems brought on by inadequate medical care during the Civil War, she went to medical school; her practice offered prenatal care, delivery, and nutrition to women.

CATHARINE, CATHERINE: from the Greek for pure. A timeless name that's both feminine and powerful, it's easy to imagine on a plate outside a corner office. With either spelling it's often shortened to Cathy; Cate and even Kitty are other alternatives.

Catharine Beecher (1800–1878) was the daughter of the famous preacher Lyman Beecher and the sister of Harriet Beecher Stowe and Isabella Beecher Hooker. Catharine opened the Hartford Female Seminary in 1825, and later founded women's colleges in Burlington, Iowa; Quincy, Illinois; and Milwaukee, Wisconsin. Her books include *A Treatise on Domestic Economy for the Use of Young Ladies at Home and at School* and a sequel, which she wrote with her sister Harriet, called *The American Woman's Home*; these books emphasize the importance of women's role in society and their work.

Catharine Littlefield Greene (1755–1814) was the wife of the Revolutionary War general Nathanael Greene. When the war ended they moved to a plantation in Georgia; there, after her husband died, Catharine rented a room to an enterprising Yale graduate named Eli Whitney.

Sources suggest that Catharine told Whitney he should build a machine to clean cotton and that she financed the machine's patent (women were not allowed to hold patents at the time) and manufacture.

CATHARINE VAN RENSSELAER SCHUYLER (1734–1803) was both a staunch supporter of the American Revolution and the wife of a famous revolutionary, Philip Schuyler. Immortalized in the painting *Mrs. Schuyler Burning Her Wheatfields on the Approach of the British 1777*, Kitty Schuyler did indeed burn her fields before fleeing Saratoga, preventing the British from harvesting the wheat. They retaliated by burning down her house.

CHARLOTTE: a feminine form of Charles, from the French for strong. Carlotta has a Latin flair and is common in Italy; Char, Carly, Charlie, or Lotta are common diminutives.

CHARLOTTE MIGNON CRABTREE (1847–1924), known as Lotta, was the first American entertainer to become a millionaire; when she was eight years old, she made more money in one night entertaining miners in California than her father made in four years of gold mining. She went on to become the most famous comedienne of her time before retiring to the East to paint seascapes. She left her estate to veterans, aging actors, music students, and animals.

CHARLOTTE PERKINS GILMAN (1860–1935) was a writer and feminist who was influenced by her great aunts, the Beecher sisters (Catharine Beecher, Harriet Beecher Stowe, and Isabella Beecher Hooker). Her best-known story, "The Yellow Wallpaper," was based on her harrowing mental breakdown and the subsequent "cure" following her daughter's birth.

CLARA: from the Latin for clear, bright.

CLARA BARTON (1821–1912), called the Angel of the Battlefield by soldiers during the Civil War, went on to found the American Red Cross. No mere figurehead, Clara traveled to sites of disasters on American soil to supervise relief efforts and aid victims; when she was seventy-nine, she went to Galveston, Texas, to help after the devastating hurricane of 1900.

CLARA BOW (1905–1965) was the original flapper—her slim figure and bobbed hair became the ideal standard of beauty during the Roaring Twenties, helped in no small part by her ability to project both sex appeal and humor. Clara started acting in her teens, and although she made fifty-eight movies in eleven years, she's perhaps best remembered for her starring role in *It*, which earned her the moniker "the It girl."

CLARA DRISCOLL (1881–1945) was the "savior of the Alamo." This Texas heiress contributed thousands of dollars to keep the Alamo convent from falling into the hands of a hotel firm; before her generosity, the mission church was the only part of the Alamo property that was state-owned. Clara left her home in Austin, Laguna Gloria, to the Texas Fine Arts Association, and established the Driscoll Hospital in Corpus Christi.

CLARIBEL: from the Latin for bright and beautiful. Clarabelle is an alternate spelling; Claribel could be shortened to Claire, Clara, Belle, or Bella.

CLARIBEL CONE (1864–1929) earned a medical degree from Women's Medical College and studied at Johns Hopkins University Medical School, but her real fame came as a patron of the arts. Part of the circle that included Gertrude Stein, Claribel and her sister, Etta, met Pablo Picasso and Henri Matisse. Over forty years of collecting, the sisters amassed what many consider to be the most important collection of modern art worldwide. Three thousand works from their collection were donated to the Baltimore Museum of Art; a second collection is located at the University of North Carolina in Greensboro.

CLARINA: a form of Clara, from the Latin for clear.

CLARINA HOWARD NICHOLS (1810–1885) wrote for a newspaper in Vermont before she and her husband moved to Kansas Territory. A suffragist who was friends with Susan B. Anthony and Elizabeth Cady Stanton, Clarina helped to draft her adopted state's constitution when Kansas entered the Union. Among the unprecedented rights granted to women under the new state's constitution were the rights to buy and sell property, to equal custody of children in divorce cases, and to vote in school elections.

CLAUDIA: the feminine form of Claudius, from the Latin for lame.

CLAUDIA ALTA TAYLOR JOHNSON (b. 1912) might not ring a bell; this First Lady has been known as Lady Bird since girlhood. Her passion for nature led her to create the First Lady's Committee for a More Beautiful Capital, and when she and her husband, Lyndon Baines Johnson, returned to Texas, she founded the National Wildflower Research Center in Austin.

CLEMENTINE: from the Latin for merciful.

CLEMENTINE HUNTER (1886–1988), born on the plantation that was reportedly the inspiration for Harriet Beecher Stowe's novel *Uncle Tom's Cabin*, worked as a cook at the Melrose Plantation, which was an artists' colony. Finding some paints and brushes a visiting artist had left behind, she asked permission to use them. The scene of a baptism she painted in 1940 on a window shade changed Clementine's life. Today she is regarded as one of the most important folk artists of the twentieth century.

CONSTANCE: from the Latin for steadfast. Constance was a "virtue name" popular among Puritans and colonial Americans; Connie is the most popular diminutive.

CONSTANCE BAKER MOTLEY (1921–2005) was a civil rights activist, state senator, lawyer, and judge. With a bachelor's degree from New York University and a law degree from Columbia Law School, Constance began her career as a law clerk with Thurgood Marshall at the NAACP Legal Defense and Education Fund. She assisted on the landmark *Brown v. Board of Education* case. She was the first black woman elected to the New York senate, and was the first woman and the first black Manhattan borough president. In 1966 she became the first black woman to be appointed as a federal court judge. Constance was inducted into the National Women's Hall of Fame, and in 2001 she received the Presidential Citizens Medal from President Bill Clinton.

CORA, CORRA: from the Greek for maiden.

CORA SLOCOMB, COUNTESS DI BRAZZÀ (1862–?) was convinced that a woman who was sentenced to death by the electric chair for murdering her abusive lover had not killed him intentionally. Cora took up her cause and organized an appeal, and she launched the first national campaign against the death penalty.

CORRA MAE WHITE HARRIS (1869–1935) was a novelist and writer from the South. She wrote ten novels that were serialized in the *Saturday Evening Post*, including *The Circuit Rider's Wife*, which was based on her own life married to an itinerant preacher.

CORETTA: a variation on Cora, from the Greek for maiden.

CORETTA SCOTT KING (1927–2006) first gained fame through her husband, the civil rights leader and Nobel Prize winner Martin Luther

King, Jr. During his career her focus was on rearing their four children, although she took part in many marches and events. After her husband's assassination, Coretta took up the torch, both to preserve his memory and to continue the work he began, and became active in other issues. She was an outspoken critic of capital punishment and an advocate for women's rights and lesbian and gay rights, as well as for civil rights. There is an award for excellence in children's literature that bears her name.

CORNELIA: the feminine form of Cornelius, from the Latin for fair and blond.

CORNELIA OTIS SKINNER (1901–1979) was the daughter of actors, so it isn't surprising that she was known for her witty plays and monologues. She began her career as an actress, then turned to writing one-act plays, dramas, and essays. *The Pleasure of His Company* was made into a movie starring Fred Astaire and Lilly Palmer.

★ ★ ★ ★ ★ ★ ★ ★ # D ★ ★ ★ ★ ★ ★ ★ ★

DEBORAH: from the Hebrew for bee. The spelling Debra became popular in the 1950s; Devorah is seen much less frequently. Deb and Debbie are the pet forms.

DEBORAH SAMPSON (1760–1827) fought for the American Revolution—as a soldier known as Robert Shirtliffe. For three years she successfully hid her sexual identity, despite being wounded twice; she was found out by a physician after she caught a fever, and was honorably discharged in 1783. Because Paul Revere sent a letter to Congress on her behalf, she received a pension for her years of military service.

DIXIE, DIXY, DICKSIE: from the American South.

DICKSIE BRADLEY BANDY (1890–1971) was a philanthropist and businesswoman. She and her husband marketed Southern crafts to Northerners, and their business grew large enough to become an integral part of the textile and carpet industries. Dicksie used the proceeds from her business to atone for atrocities committed against the Cherokees on the Trail of Tears.

DIXY LEE RAY (1914–1994) was a marine biologist and environmentalist. After earning her Ph.D., she joined the faculty at the University of Washington, served on countless scientific and government panels as an oceanography expert, became director of the Pacific Science Center, was appointed by President Richard M. Nixon to the Atomic Energy Commission, and served as the governor of Washington for a year. The United Nations awarded her the Peace Medal in 1973.

DJUNA: of unknown origin.

DJUNA CHAPPELL BARNES (1892–1982) didn't attain the same level of fame as her friends and contemporaries Edna St. Vincent Millay, Eugene O'Neill, and Henry Miller, but her writings have attained a cult status for their black humor and exploration of homosexual themes. In addition to several novels, including her masterpiece, *Nightwood*, Djuna wrote poetry and plays, and illustrated many of her works.

DOLLEY, DOLLY: a familiar form of Delores or Dorothy.

DOLLEY PAYNE TODD MADISON (1768–1849) was the fourth First Lady of the United States, renowned for her political savvy as well as being a charming, gracious hostess. When British troops neared Washington, D.C., in 1814, Dolley left her personal possessions behind and saved instead her husband's important papers and a portrait of George Washington that would otherwise have been lost.

DONNA: from the Italian for lady.

DONNA ALLEN (1920–1999) was an activist who worked on behalf of labor, peace, feminism, and civil liberties. After criticizing the execution of Julius and Ethel Rosenberg and founding Women's Strike for Peace, she was subpoenaed by the U.S. House Committee on Un-American Activities. She refused to testify in closed hearings and received a suspended sentence that was later overturned. Later she worked for the National Committee Against Repressive Legislation, which was instrumental in abolishing the HUAC. She was a founder of the Women's Institute for Freedom of the Press and of the Media Report for Women, as well as the author of numerous books on feminism, the media, and communications.

DORA: from the Greek for gift.

DORA KEEN (1871–1963) stood barely five feet tall, but her achievements belie her size. Dora was a mountain climber who led the first expedition to the Chugach Mountains in Alaska, where there is now a range named for her. She tackled mountains in North and South America as well as in Europe, and she traveled the world, too. It was on her second around-the-world tour that she died in Hong Kong.

DOROTHEA, DOROTHY: from the Greek for gift of God. Though it isn't as common now as it was one hundred years ago, Dorothy and its variations, including Theodora, are classic names that have stood the test of time. Common nicknames include Dot, Dottie, Dora, Dolly, and Dodie.

DOROTHEA LANGE (1895–1965) was a photographer whose images captured the human side of the Great Depression: families migrating west from the dust bowl of the plains, breadlines, strikes, and the homeless. Her photographs record Japanese Americans in camps during

World War II, as well as women working in the shipyards of California while the men served in the military.

DOROTHEA LYNDE DIX (1802–1887) was appalled by the conditions in prisons, asylums, and poorhouses, and worked on behalf of inmates and the mentally ill to improve treatment. She demonstrated that mental illness was treatable, changing the way this illness was—and still is—perceived. In addition to founding two hospitals, both of which are still in operation today, Dorothea was the superintendent of female nurses for the Union during the Civil War.

DOROTHY DANDRIDGE (1922–1965) began her career with a small role in *A Day at the Races* with the Marx Brothers. Although she was the first black woman to be nominated for an Academy Award for Best Actress, for her role in *Carmen Jones*, many consider her finest performance to be in *Porgy and Bess*, opposite Sidney Poitier; she was nominated for a Golden Globe for her portrayal of Bess.

DOROTHY DAY (1897–1980) is currently a candidate for sainthood. Combining social activism with faith, Dorothy worked to help women get the right to vote and for civil rights, and protested the Vietnam War. She was nearly killed by the Ku Klux Klan in the late 1950s, and was jailed several times, including at the age of seventy-five for picketing on behalf of farmworkers. She was a cofounder of the Catholic Worker Movement and wrote several books.

DOROTHY ROTHSCHILD PARKER (1893–1967) was known for her acerbic wit and biting satire. One of the regulars at the Algonquin Hotel's Round Table, Parker wrote short stories, screenplays, theater reviews, and poetry; her story "Big Blonde" won the O. Henry Prize in 1929.

★ ★ ★ ★ ★ ★ ★ ★ **E** ★ ★ ★ ★ ★ ★ ★ ★

EDITH, EDYTHE: from the English for rich gift. Though it's out of favor, Edith is a strong and classic name that lends itself to two terrific nicknames: Edie is traditional, but Dita has a Spanish flair.

EDITH HEAD (1898–1981), a costume designer, was nominated an amazing thirty-five times for Academy Awards in a career that spanned decades, and won eight times, for *The Heiress, Samson and Delilah, All About Eve, A Place in the Sun, Roman Holiday, Sabrina, The Facts of Life,* and *The Sting.* She created Mae West's gowns in *She Done Him Wrong,* Dorothy Lamour's sarongs in *The Jungle Princess,* and wardrobes for Grace Kelly in *To Catch a Thief* and *Rear Window* and for Kim Novak in *Vertigo.*

EDITH HOUGHTON HOOKER (1879–1948) was a suffragist and doctor who specialized in social work. She and her husband founded a home for unwed mothers and their babies; she also founded the Just Government League of Maryland and its publication, the *Maryland Suffrage News,* and held offices in the National Woman's Party.

EDITH KERMIT CAROW ROOSEVELT (1861–1948) was the second wife of Theodore Roosevelt. Renowned as a hostess, she was the first First Lady to hire a personal secretary to assist her.

EDITH SAMPSON (1901–1979) was the first black female judge in the United States. She left school at fourteen to work in a fish market, only to return to graduate from high school, the New York School of Social Work, and the John Marshall Law School. Appointed by President Truman as a representative to the United Nations, Edith worked for the State Department during the cold war.

EDITH WHARTON (1861–1937), who was one of America's foremost novelists, wrote more than thirty-two novels: *The House of Mirth, Ethan Frome,* and *The Age of Innocence* (for which she won the Pulitzer Prize for fiction in 1921) are perhaps her best-known works. The Mount, her home in Lenox, Massachusetts, is located at 2 Plunkett Street.

EDITH BOLLING GALT WILSON (1872–1961) was the second wife of President Woodrow Wilson. Although she was a close advisor to him before his stroke in 1919—she accompanied him to the Paris Peace Conference in 1918—Edith became even more influential during his period of recuperation. She determined which papers and documents he would review, as well as who would meet with him.

EDMONIA: a feminine form of Edmund, from the English for prosperous.

EDMONIA LEWIS claimed she was born in 1854, but records indicate she enrolled in Oberlin College in 1859; other sources indicate she was born in 1845, and still more in 1840. The year of her death is also lost to history. What is known about her is that she was half black, half Chippewa, and was a sculptor who trained in Boston and Rome. Her sculpture *The Death of Cleopatra* is now in the Smithsonian National Museum of American Art, and her bust of Henry Wadsworth Longfellow is in Harvard's Widener Library. Her bust of Abraham Lincoln graces the California Municipal Library in San Jose.

EDNA: from the Hebrew for pleasure or rejuvenation. Edie is used as a diminutive.

EDNA FERBER (1887–1968) was an author who won popular as well as critical acclaim. The author of more than twenty-five books, Edna started as a reporter at the age of seventeen, then began to write short stories; novels and plays followed. *So Big*, for which she won the Pulitzer Prize for fiction, *Cimarron, Showboat, Saratoga Trunk, Giant*, and *Ice Palace* were some of her novels; she collaborated with George S. Kaufman to write plays, including *Dinner at Eight* and *Stage Door*. Many of her plays and novels were made into movies.

EDNA ST. VINCENT MILLAY (1892–1950) was the first woman to receive a Pulitzer Prize for poetry, for her book *The Harp-Weaver and Other Poems*. Her first book of poetry was published when she was twenty-five; it included her poem "Renascence," the winning entry in a poetry contest that earned her a scholarship to Vassar College. After graduation she moved to Greenwich Village, where she worked to stay the execution of Sacco and Vanzetti. Her somewhat early death and the legacy of some of the best poems of the twentieth century may have been foretold in her lines "My candle burns at both ends, / It will not last the night; / But ah, my foes, and oh, my friends, / It gives a lovely light!"

EFFA: from the Greek for spoken well of. Effie is a variation; both names may be variations on Euphemia.

EFFA MANLEY (1900–1981) was called the Queen of the Negro Leagues. The owner and manager of the Newark Eagles baseball team, Effa advocated for better schedules, travel conditions, and salaries for her players. She provided them with an air-conditioned bus—the first one in the Negro Leagues—and arranged for them to play in Puerto Rico during the off-season. After the Negro National League disbanded in 1947, Effa devoted the rest of her life to preserving the history of the Negro Leagues.

ELEANOR: from the Greek for light. A variation on Helen, this name may also be spelled Elinor or Eleonore. The most common nicknames are Ellie, Ella, Nelly, and Nora.

ELEANOR RAYMOND (1888–1989) was an architect who specialized in using innovative materials and construction in residential design. She created the Plywood House in 1940 and designed the Dover Sun House, one of the first buildings to use solar heat, in 1948.

ELEANOR ROOSEVELT (1884–1962) was christened Anna Eleanor but always went by her middle name. Her philanthropy and activism began long before she was First Lady during the Great Depression. She worked for the League of Women Voters, the Women's Trade Union League, the National Consumers' League, and the New York State Democratic Committee, and was indispensable to her husband, Franklin Delano Roosevelt, after a bout of polio left his legs paralyzed. After her husband became president she advocated on behalf of working women as well as for civil rights, blacks, and tenant farmers. After her husband's death, President Harry Truman appointed her to the United Nations Commission on Human Rights.

ELIZA: a familiar form of Elizabeth, from the Hebrew for consecrated to God.

ELIZA FARNHAM (1815–1864) was a prison matron at the notorious Sing Sing Penitentiary. After she quit at age thirty-four, she became an outspoken—and outrageous—crusader for prison reform, as well as for women's rights, suffrage, and abolition. She worked as the matron of California's first insane asylum, then served with Dorothea Dix as a nurse at Gettysburg, where she contracted tuberculosis.

ELIZA McCARDLE JOHNSON (1810–1876) became First Lady when her husband succeeded Abraham Lincoln as president. She stood by him throughout the scandal that nearly led to his impeachment, and she saw him vindicated when he was elected to the Senate in 1875.

ELIZABETH: from the Hebrew for consecrated to God. A name with enduring popularity, Elizabeth and its variations seem above the whims of fashion and trends. Many variations can be traced back to this classic name: Eliza, Elise, and Alyssa have roots in Elizabeth; and the nicknames are almost endless: Liz, Liza, Lisa, Beth, Betty, Betsy, and Libby are just a few of the most common.

ELIZABETH BLACKWELL (1821–1910) was the first woman to receive a medical degree in the United States—graduating first in her class from the Geneva Medical College in Geneva, New York. Hospitals refused to allow her to practice, and even landlords refused to rent her office space. She bought a house from which to practice medicine, and opened a dispensary there, and later established the New York Infirmary for Indigent Women and Children, which still exists as the New York University Downtown Hospital.

ELIZABETH FREEMAN (1742–1829) was a slave who sued for her freedom and won. Her case, *Brom & Bett v. Ashley*, became the first in which slaves in Massachusetts were freed under the Massachusetts Constitution, and it led to Massachusetts's ban on slavery. Elizabeth worked as a nurse and midwife after she won her freedom, and was the great-grandmother of W. E. B. DuBois. Her tombstone is located in the old burial ground in the cemetery in Stockbridge, Massachusetts.

ELIZABETH SCHUYLER HAMILTON (1757–1854) was the wife of Alexander Hamilton and a Founding Mother of the United States. Her role in her husband's life would be difficult to overstate: one Hamilton biographer attests that her social standing and character were instrumental in helping Hamilton rise in the new country's government.

ELIZABETH ANNESLEY LEWIS (?–1779) was a patriot whose husband was a signer of the Declaration of Independence. Like all the signers, her husband had a price put on his head, and when the British forces occupied Long Island, they shelled the Lewises' house in Whitestone, then plundered the house and arrested her. Because of her wealth and prominence, the British made an example of her, and even though General George Washington arranged for her release in a prisoner exchange, Elizabeth never recovered from the ordeal.

ELIZABETH KORTRIGHT MONROE (1768–1830) was a celebrated beauty, but she was more than just a pretty face. She lived in Paris when her husband, James Monroe, was the ambassador to France; upon hearing that the wife of the Marquis de Lafayette, an ally to the United States during the Revolutionary War, was imprisoned after the French Revolution,

Elizabeth fought for her release. As First Lady, Elizabeth entertained on a formal scale similar to the courts of Europe.

ELIZABETH SETON (1774–1821) was the first American woman to be canonized a saint. Born an Episcopalian, she converted to Catholicism after her husband died, at a time when Catholics were looked down on. She founded the Sisters of Charity of St. Joseph, the first American order of nuns; helped to establish the Catholic school system; and established the first Catholic orphanage in the United States.

ELIZABETH CADY STANTON (1815–1902) became a feminist as a young child. Her father was a judge, and she was outraged when she heard him tell abused women that they had no legal recourse for mistreatment by their husbands and fathers. Elizabeth organized the first women's rights convention in Seneca Falls, New York, and she advocated that women should have rights to own property when married, to obtain divorces and win custody of their children, and the right to vote. With Susan B. Anthony she founded the National Woman Suffrage Association.

ELLA: from the Old German for other or foreign. Ella and its close counterpart, Ellen, may be variations on Eleanor.

ELLA JOSEPHINE BAKER (1903–1986) was a civil rights activist and political reformer whose behind-the-scenes strategizing had a profound affect on the political landscape of the twentieth century. Ella worked for the NAACP, becoming a national leader; she was the first director of the Southern Christian Leadership Conference, helped to found the Student Nonviolent Coordinating Committee and the Mississippi Freedom Democratic Committee, and worked alongside Martin Luther King, Jr.

ELLA FITZGERALD (1918–1996) was one of the greatest jazz singers of the twentieth century. She won thirteen Grammy Awards over the course of her career, as well as the National Medal of Freedom and the Kennedy Center Award. Her career began when she won an amateur-night contest at the Harlem Opera House, which led to a recording contract. Her signature sound, scat singing, was born during a jam with Dizzy Gillespie. The First Lady of Song won the *Down Beat* readers' poll each and every year from 1953 to 1970, and nearly all of her records are still available.

ELLA CARA DELORIA (1889–1971) was born on the Yankton Sioux Reservation, and it was her knowledge of the Lakota language as well as Sioux customs and traditions that formed her career. She compiled the first Sioux-English dictionary, and wrote several books on the Sioux language. Her best-known work, however, was her novel *Waterlily*.

ELLEN: English, a variation on Helen or Eleanor.

ELLEN GLASGOW (1873–1945) was an award-winning novelist who wrote about the American South. Among her best-known works are *The Descendant*, which was published anonymously, *Barren Ground*, *Vein of Iron*, and *In This Our Life*, which won the Pulitzer Prize for fiction.

ELLEN SWALLOW RICHARDS (1842–1911) founded the fields of ecology and home economics. Armed with a degree from the Massachusetts Institute of Technology, Ellen created the first consumer home testing laboratory for her theories about nutrition and increasing efficiency, where she removed lead pipes, rerouted the waste-removal system away from the well that provided drinking water, and installed plants indoors to increase fresh air. She worked to increase the education opportunities, particularly in the sciences, for girls, and was an instructor in sanitary chemistry at MIT.

EMILY: from the German for hardworking. One of the most popular names for girls for the past several years, Emily can also be spelled Emilie. Amelia is another variation, and Emmy or Emma are nicknames or diminutives.

EMILY GREENE BALCH (1867–1961) was a social reformer whose colleagues included Jacob Riis, Jane Addams, and Vida Scudder. Among her achievements: she was the chair of the economics and sociology departments at Wellesley College, a position she lost when she joined the American Union Against Militarism and the Women's Peace Party; she was a delegate to the International Congress of Women; and in 1946 she was awarded the Nobel Peace Prize.

EMILY DICKINSON (1830–1886), known as the belle of Amherst, was an incredibly prolific poet. Between 1858 and 1866 she wrote more than eleven hundred poems, though only seven were published while she was alive. The predominant themes in her work are separation and death, nature, God, and love. Her poems are noted for their unconventional rhymes and grammar, and it wasn't until the twentieth century that they were published as she had written them, eccentricities intact.

EMILY GEIGER (1763–1856) might not be as famous as Paul Revere, but she too was a patriot who made a daring ride that helped the Americans win the Revolutionary War. Emily volunteered to deliver a message between Generals Nathanael Greene and Thomas Sumter, thinking that a woman would be able to pass through the British troops stationed between the two generals. On her fifty-mile ride she was stopped, and when the soldiers went to find a matron to search her, she read the message, tore it up, and ate it. When the soldiers found no message she was released and was able to deliver the message, which helped to defeat British forces in the South.

EMILY WEST MORGAN (dates unknown) was a beautiful woman of mixed race who, according to legend, helped the Texans win their independence from Mexico. In 1836 she was taken captive by the Mexican army and caught the eye of General Antonio Lopez de Santa Anna. No record of a woman in Santa Anna's tent exists, nor would Emily have known the Texas army's plans, but she supposedly kept Santa Anna occupied while the Texas army charged the Mexican army's camp in San Jacinto. This story is immortalized in the song "The Yellow Rose of Texas."

EMILY PRICE POST (1873–1960) grew up a debutante during an era of servants, chaperones, and cotillions, and her upbringing informed her career as an arbiter of manners and mores for most of the twentieth century. Though she began her writing career penning short stories for fiction magazines, an editor at one publisher encouraged her to write a book on etiquette. That work, *Etiquette: The Blue Book of Social Usage*, was first published in 1922. It went through eighty-nine printings, led to a syndicated column and a radio show, and was second only to the Bible as the book most often stolen from libraries.

EMMA: a variation on Emily or Amy that's currently very popular, but it's a distinguished name with a strong lineage.

EMMA HAYDEN EAMES (1865–1952), called the Queen of the Grand Opera, studied in Boston and Paris before making her debut at the Paris Opera in *Roméo et Juliette*. She reprised the role at the Metropolitan Opera in New York City, where she was a leading member of the company until 1909, and where she also performed the title roles in *Tosca* and *Aida*, and as Donna Anna and Donna Elvira in *Don Giovanni*.

EMMA MILLINDA GILLETT (1852–1927) founded the first law school for women. After graduating from Howard Law School, Emma became the first female notary public in the United States, and joined the Washington bar a few years later. She joined the office of a Washington attorney as associate and then was made partner, and in 1898 she cofounded the Washington College of Law, where she served as dean until she retired in 1923.

EMMA GOLDMAN (1869–1940) was a social activist and radical whose politics landed her in jail several times and finally got her exiled. Trained as a nurse and midwife, Emma was one of the first women to advocate birth control. She founded the Free Speech League, which was the forerunner of the American Civil Liberties Union, and was the author of *Anarchism and Other Essays* and *The Social Significance of the Modern Drama*.

EMMA LAZARUS (1849–1887) lived for only thirty-eight years, but in her short life she worked on behalf of Jewish immigrants in both the United States and England, was a friend of Ralph Waldo Emerson, and wrote poetry. Her sonnet "The New Colossus" is engraved on the pedestal of the Statue of Liberty on Liberty Island in New York Harbor.

EMMA SANSOM (1848–1900) was only fifteen when she guided the Confederate army general Nathan Forrest and his troops across Alabama's Black Creek, enabling him to capture nearly fifteen hundred Union soldiers. For her bravery, she was awarded 640 acres by the Alabama state legislature, and was the subject of a poem by John Trotwood Moore.

EMMA HART WILLARD (1787–1870) wasn't content that higher education for women in her era was "finishing school"—she wanted women to be able to attend academic classes and earn degrees. She established the Middlebury Female Seminary in her home in Vermont, then opened a similar school in Waterford, New York. The school was relocated to Troy, where the Emma Willard School still exists.

ESTHER: from the Hebrew for star. Ester is common in Spain; Hester is another variation. Essie is the most common familiar form. Estelle and Stella are from the Latin for star.

ESTHER HOBART MORRIS (1814–1902) was called the Mother of Women's Suffrage, and although she isn't as well known as some suffragists, her contributions are still impressive. She and her husband moved to Wyoming when it was still a territory. Esther held a tea party for the members of the first territorial legislature and asked the candidates to introduce a bill granting women the right to vote. The bill passed and Wyoming was the first state or territory to give women full voting rights. She was appointed justice of the peace, and was a delegate to the national suffrage convention in 1895 in Cleveland.

ESTHER PARISEAU (1823–1902) is better known as Mother Joseph of the Sacred Heart. A member of the Sisters of Providence, Mother Joseph was a woman of many talents: she was a seamstress, architect, carpenter, artist, blacksmith, farmer, mechanic, watchmaker, and locksmith. She built nine schools, including Providence Academy in Vancouver, Washington; fifteen hospitals, including St. Vincent Hospital in Portland, Oregon; and a mission.

ETHEL: from the English for noble.

ETHEL BARRYMORE (1879–1959), "the First Lady of the American Stage," was the daughter of an actress and a playwright; she and her brothers, Lionel and John, were known as the Fabulous Barrymores, or the First Family of Hollywood; they starred on Broadway as well as in movies. Ethel won the Academy Award for Best Supporting Actress in 1944 for her work in *None but the Lonely Heart*, and has a Broadway theater named after her.

ETHEL BUSH BERRY (1872–1948) was called the Bride of the Klondike, and she wasn't a typical bride! After their wedding, she and her husband took their honeymoon trip with a dog team over Chilkoot Pass. After a few months of working luckless claims, they moved to Eldorado Creek, where their claim yielded more than $140,000 in gold in one season.

ETHEL MERMAN (1909–1984) got her big break at Brooklyn's Paramount Theater; her powerful voice could reach to the back of the balcony in just about any theater. She starred in *Girl Crazy*, *Annie Get Your Gun*, *Call Me Madam*, and *Gypsy* on Broadway; her movie roles include *There's No Business Like Show Business* and *Alexander's Ragtime Band*.

ETHEL WATERS (1896–1977) was an award-winning actress and singer whose roots were in the vaudeville circuit. While singing "Stormy Weather" at the Cotton Club in Harlem, she was heard by Irving Berlin, who signed her to his show; her renditions of "Summertime" and "Heat Wave" were equally sensational. She starred in a radio show that aired nationally, was nominated for a Best Supporting Actress Academy Award for her role in *Pinky*, and won the New York Drama Critics' Award the following year.

ETTA: from the German for little. Etta is also a common nickname for Harriet and Henrietta.

ETTA CONE (1870–1949) was an art collector whose keen eye helped to popularize modern art and American impressionism. Through her friend Gertrude Stein, Etta met Pablo Picasso and Henri Matisse, and over the course of forty years she and her sister, Claribel, amassed what has been called the most important collection of modern art in the world. The Cone sisters donated nearly three thousand works to the Baltimore Art Museum, and another collection to the Weatherspoon Art Museum at the Greensboro campus of the University of North Carolina.

EUDORA: from the Greek for honored gift.

EUDORA ALICE WELTY (1909–2001), a Mississippi native, was one of the premier writers of the twentieth century. She began her career as a journalist, but began publishing short stories in her late twenties, and penned several novels as well; *The Optimist's Daughter* won the Pulitzer Prize for fiction in 1972. She won the American Book Award, and was the first living writer to have her work published by the Library of America. Her memoir, *One Writer's Beginnings*, was published to critical and commercial acclaim in 1984.

★ ★ ★ ★ ★ ★ ★ ★ **F** ★ ★ ★ ★ ★ ★ ★

FANNIE, FANNY: familiar forms of Frances, from the Latin for free.

FANNIE MERRITT FARMER (1857–1915) became the director of the Boston Cooking School two years after she graduated from it, and five years later she published the *Boston Cooking School Cookbook*. Now called *The Fannie Farmer Cookbook*, it continues to be the best-selling cookbook of all time, though she considered her most important book to be *Food and Cookery for the Sick and Convalescent*. She went on to pen several other books about food, cooking, entertaining, and nutrition, and taught for a year at Harvard Medical School.

FANNIE LOU HAMER (1917–1977) faced beatings, ridicule, and bombings as an advocate for civil rights. She began picking cotton when she was six years old and continued to work on farms in poverty until she was in her forties. At age forty-six she registered to vote and became involved with the Student Nonviolent Coordinating Committee and the Mississippi Freedom Democratic Party. A televised speech about the abuses she suffered in the quest for civil rights, about the barriers blacks faced in the South, and about the murders of civil rights workers cast her into the national spotlight.

FANNY BRICE (1891–1951) sang in vaudeville, on Broadway, and for radio shows, but it was her comic touches that cemented her reputation as the original "Funny Girl." Her trademark was singing "Sadie Salome, Go Home," a song Irving Berlin wrote especially for her, in a Jewish accent; most of her successful characters came from her Jewish upbringing. She appeared in movies like *My Man* and *Sweet and Low*, and after her death Barbra Streisand portrayed her in the movie *Funny Girl*.

FLANNERY: from the Irish for redhead. Another surname used as a first name, Flannery may be too inextricably linked to the famous Southern writer who bore the name. But it's a lovely name that deserves to be used more often.

FLANNERY O'CONNOR (1925–1964) finished only two novels and two collections of stories before her death at age thirty-nine from lupus, but she is still recognized as one of the South's most important writers.

Among her best-known works are *A Good Man Is Hard to Find*, *The Violent Bear It Away*, and *Everything That Rises Must Converge*.

FLORENCE: from the Latin for blooming or flowery. Also the name of a city in Italy, Florence, or Fiorenza (the Italian), has been popular since Victorian times. Flo, Flora, Flory, Flossie, and even Fleur (from the French for flower) are used as pet forms.

FLORENCE BARNES (1901–1975), nicknamed "Pancho," was a California heiress turned barnstormer and stunt pilot who for a time held the women's air-speed record of 196.19 miles per hour.

FLORENCE BASCOM (1862–1945) was the first woman to earn a Ph.D. from Johns Hopkins University and the first to join the United States Geological Survey. Her work mapping rock formations in the Atlantic states was the basis for many studies. Florence also was a professor at Bryn Mawr, where she founded the geology department.

FLORENCE CHADWICK (1918–1995) was the greatest long-distance swimmer in history. She was the first woman to swim across the English Channel in both directions, and in 1951 she set a record for swimming from England to France. She also swam the Straits of Gibraltar, the Catalina Channel, and the Bosporus.

FLORENCE MILLS (1895–1927) started dancing—and winning dance contests—when she was a toddler. By the time she was fourteen, she and her sisters, performing as the Mills Sisters, toured as a song-and-dance act. Florence helped to spark the Harlem Renaissance in *Shuffle Along*, which was written, directed, and performed by black Americans. Her signature song was about blackbirds, and she starred in a play called *Blackbirds* as well. When her life was cut short by appendicitis, more than 150,000 mourners lined the streets of Harlem, and a flock of blackbirds was released in tribute.

FRANCES, FRANCESCA: from the Latin for free; also the feminine form of Francis, meaning from France. Fran, Franny, Fanny, and Frankie are nicknames.

MARIA FRANCESCA CABRINI (1850–1917) was born in Italy, but her role as the first canonized American saint warrants her inclusion here. Known as Mother Frances Xavier Cabrini, she opened sixty-seven schools, hospitals, and orphanages from New York to Seattle. She was beatified in 1938 and canonized in 1946; a shrine in Golden, Colorado, and the chapel at Mother Cabrini High School (her final resting place) in New York City are sites of pilgrimages.

FRANCES PERKINS (1882–1965) played crucial roles in formulating labor and retirement policy. The first woman to serve in a president's cabinet, Frances was the secretary of labor under Franklin D. Roosevelt. She helped to create Social Security, was instrumental in the Fair Labor Standards Act that set a minimum wage, and established the Labor Standards Bureau. She also helped to create FDR's New Deal.

FRANCES WILLARD (1839–1898) was a founder of the Women's Christian Temperance Union. Though abolishing the sale of alcohol was one goal of this organization, members also supported women's suffrage and prison reform, and worked to abolish prostitution. Frances was a feminist who scandalized her community by riding a bicycle—in fact, one of her books is titled *A Wheel Within a Wheel: How I Learned to Ride the Bicycle, with Some Reflections by the Way*—and was strongly in favor of women participating in the church (she was a Methodist). Her motto, not too surprisingly, was "Do everything."

★ ★ ★ ★ ★ ★ ★ ★ **G** ★ ★ ★ ★ ★ ★ ★ ★

GENEVA: from the Old French for juniper tree. Gen, Gene, and Neva are nicknames; Genevieve is a French variation that is derived from the Old German for white wave. If you like Jen but want to avoid Jennifer, try Geneva.

GENE STRATTON-PORTER (1863–1924) was born Geneva Grace Stratton. She was a naturalist whose photographs of birds and animals in their natural habitats were published in several periodicals of the time, including *Recreation* and *Outing* magazines. She landed writing assignments for the magazines, and then began to write beloved children's books, like *Freckles* and *A Girl of the Limberlost*. In her later life she lived in California and formed a movie company.

GEORGIA: the feminine form of George, from the Greek for farmer. Variations such as Georgette, Georgeann(e), and Georgina are the most common; Jordan could be considered a distant cousin.

GEORGIA O'KEEFFE (1887–1986), one of the preeminent artists of the twentieth century, studied at the Art Institute of Chicago and the Art Students League in New York City. Her work was shown to Alfred Stieglitz, the photographer and gallery owner, who mounted an exhibition of her work. He persuaded her to move to New York, and in 1922 they married. After Stieglitz's death, Georgia moved to New Mexico. The landscape had a profound affect on her art, which was full of flowers, female imagery, and the colors of the desert.

GERTRUDE: from the German for beloved warrior. Once a popular name, Gertrude is often shortened to Trudy; Gert and Gerta are other options.

GERTRUDE BONNIN (1876–1938), who was also called Zitkala-Sa, or Red Bird, was a Sioux who at age twelve was sent to a Quaker mission school for Indians. Although she taught at the Carlisle Indian Industrial School, whose purpose was to save Native Americans by teaching them a trade so they could better assimilate, she became indignant over the treatment of Indians. As Zitkala-Sa, she published *Old Indian Legends* and *American Indian Stories* as a way of preserving her culture, and wrote articles for the *Atlantic Monthly* and *Harper's*, eventually becoming the editor of *American Indian Magazine*. In later life, Gertrude moved to Washington, D.C., with her husband, where she advocated for Indian rights, including citizenship and suffrage.

GERTRUDE EDERLE (1906–2003) became, on August 6, 1926, the first woman to swim across the English Channel. Although five men had swum it already, Gertrude's time of fourteen hours and thirty-one minutes broke the men's record by nearly two hours, and stood for nearly twenty years.

GERTRUDE BELLE ELION (1918–1999) was a Nobel Prize–winning biochemist who devoted her life to finding a cure for cancer. She is named on forty-five drug patents, and her research on viruses helped in the development of drug treatments for HIV. The first woman inducted into the National Inventors Hall of Fame, Gertrude shared the 1988 Nobel Prize in Physiology or Medicine with Sir James W. Black and George Hitchings.

GERTRUDE PRIDGETT (1886–1939) changed her name after marrying William "Pa" Rainey in 1904; they met as part of a vaudeville troupe. Ma Rainey sang for decades before she made her first recording, and then recorded more than one hundred songs between 1923 and 1929; among the most popular are "C.C. Rider," "Ma Rainey's Black Bottom," and "Bo Weevil Blues." She was inducted into the Blues Foundation Hall of Fame in 1983 and the Rock and Roll Hall of Fame in 1990.

GERTRUDE STEIN (1874–1946) was a poet, literary and art critic, and art collector whose tastes left a profound mark on twentieth-century art and literature. She moved to Paris in 1903, and the salons at her home were attended by artists and writers of the Lost Generation, including Pablo Picasso, Ernest Hemingway, F. Scott Fitzgerald, Sherwood Anderson, Ford Madox Ford, Paul Bowles, and Thornton Wilder. Gertrude's writings were extremely avant-garde; in later years she jettisoned most conventional literary devices, like plot and character development, and focused on the rhythm of the words themselves.

GERTRUDE VANDERBILT WHITNEY (1875–1942) was born into one of America's richest families and married into another. A sculptor and patron of avant-garde art, Gertrude used her studio in Greenwich Village as an exhibition space for artists whose works were rejected by more conservative venues. She founded the Whitney Museum, located at 945 Madison Avenue in New York City, after the Metropolitan Museum of Art rejected her collection of contemporary works. Gertrude's sculptures include *Victory Arch* in Madison Square Park and *Peter Stuyvesant* in Stuyvesant Square in New York City, and the William F. "Buffalo Bill" Cody memorial in Yellowstone National Park.

GLADYS: Welsh, from the Latin for small sword, and the Irish for princess.

GLADYS ROWENA HENRY DICK (1881–1963) earned a medical degree from Johns Hopkins University in 1907; from 1914 to 1953 she and her husband worked at the John R. McCormick Memorial Institute for Infectious Diseases in Chicago, where they isolated the germ that causes scarlet fever. The Dicks developed a serum to combat the disease as well as a test for susceptibility, which they patented.

GRACE: from the Latin for graceful; in Greek mythology, the three Graces were goddesses of nature.

GRACE ABBOTT (1878–1939) was born into a political family: her father was the lieutenant governor of Nebraska and her mother was a suffragist and abolitionist. Grace worked with the social worker Jane Addams as the director of Hull House's Immigrants Protective League. She also established the United States Children's Bureau, enforcing child labor and maternity laws, and helped to draft the Social Security Act that guarantees aid to dependent children. The author of *The Immigrant and the Community* and *The Child and the State*, Grace was a professor of public welfare at the University of Chicago in later life.

GRACE ANNA COOLIDGE (1879–1957) was known as the First Lady of Baseball as well as the First Lady of the United States. After her husband left the Oval Office, Grace raised money to bring Jewish children from Germany to the United States and for Dutch victims of Nazis. She also lent her house to the WAVES (Women Accepted for Volunteer Emergency Service, a branch of the U.S. Navy) during and after World War II.

GRACE MURRAY HOPPER (1906–1992) was a graduate of Vassar College and earned her doctorate from Yale. A rear admiral in the navy, Grace helped to develop the programming language COBOL and the first programmable digital computer. Finding a moth in the relay of a computer that had crashed, Grace coined the phrase "computer bug." Grace served in the navy until she was seventy-nine, and the USS *Hopper* was named after her.

GRACE KELLY (1929–1982) was a Philadelphia debutante-turned-Academy Award–winning actress-turned-princess. After appearing in *High Noon*, *Dial M for Murder*, *Rear Window*, *To Catch a Thief*, *High Society*, and *The Country Girl* (for which she won the Academy Award for Best Actress), Grace met and married Prince Rainier of Monaco. She retired from Hollywood and devoted her life to rearing her three children and to philanthropy; her fairy-tale life was cut short by her death in a car accident.

GWENDOLYN: from the Welsh for white wave. Gwen and Wendy are the most common diminutives; Gwyneth and Gwynn are variations.

GWENDOLYN BROOKS (1917–2000), the daughter of a janitor and a teacher, published her first poem when she was only fourteen, and went on to become the first black woman to win the Pulitzer Prize for poetry. She was named poet laureate for the state of Illinois and was the first black woman to be Consultant in Poetry to the Library of Congress. "I wrote about what I saw and heard on the street," Gwendolyn once said, and her poetry is imbued with a distinctive rhythm and style.

HALLIE: a familiar form of Harriet.

HALLIE Q. BROWN (1850–1949) was an elocutionist who performed—twice—before Queen Victoria, a lecturer and teacher, and a social activist who worked on behalf of black women and the Women's Christian Temperance Union. Her books include *Homespun Heroines and Other Women of Distinction* and *Tales My Father Told Me*. The Hallie Q. Brown Library is located at her alma mater, Wilberforce University, in Ohio.

HANNAH: from the Hebrew for gracious. Hannah is related to Anne and Anna; it has a slightly more casual feel to it. Hanne is the German spelling.

HANNAH ADAMS (1755–1832) was a student of comparative religion who found most of the texts she consulted prejudiced toward Christianity. She wrote *An Alphabetical Compendium of the Various Sects Which Have Appeared from the Beginning of the Christian Era to the Present Day* (1784), but when her agent took all the proceeds from the sale, she lobbied for a law to protect copyright; the law passed in 1790, and Hannah went on to write several more books.

HANNAH WHITE ARNETT (1733–1823) was the impetus behind the founding of the Daughters of the American Revolution. With the British troops overwhelming the Americans, a group of revolutionaries met at the Arnett home in New Jersey to discuss accepting Britain's offer of amnesty. As the men discussed the merits of swearing allegiance to England, Hannah chastised them roundly and threatened to leave her husband should they accept the offer. More than seventy years after Hannah's death, a letter to the *Washington Post* protested the "one-sided heroism" and bias of the Sons of the American Revolution and told of Hannah Arnett's act. The DAR was an outcome of the letter.

HANNAH WHITALL SMITH (1832–1911), an evangelist, wrote some of the best-selling Christian inspirational books in American history, *The Christian's Secret of a Happy Life* and *The God of All Comfort*.

HARRIET: the feminine form of Harry, which is a diminutive of Henry, from the German for ruler of the household. Harriette and Harriot are alternate spellings; Halle, Hallie, Hattie, and Etta are often seen as diminutives.

HARRIET CHALMERS ADAMS (1875–1937) traveled more than 100,000 miles, going places no white woman had ever gone. You'd have trouble finding someone with more wanderlust than she. Fascinated by Spanish culture, she traveled the routes of Columbus and the conquistadores, visiting every country that was or had been under Spanish and Portuguese rule. She wrote for the *National Geographic* for more than twenty-eight years and helped to found the Society of Women Geographers.

HARRIET MAXWELL CONVERSE (1836–1903) was the first white woman to be named an Indian chief. Her father and grandfather were traders who had been adopted by the Senecas, and as an adult Harriet became a political advocate for the Six Nations. The Seneca Nation adopted her too, and in 1891 made her a chief, giving her the name Gaiiwanoh, or "she who watches over us."

HARRIET HARDY (1905–1993) was a world-renowned expert in occupational medicine. One of her first investigations of work-related illnesses took place shortly after she joined the Massachusetts Department of Labor. Several young women at two lightbulb factories complained of respiratory problems; Harriet discovered that beryllium, a substance used in fluorescent lights, caused an often fatal lung disease. While she was on the faculty at Harvard Medical School she reviewed a host of toxic substances for their effects on humans. As a result of her research, insurance companies, employers, and lawyers began to take responsibility for illnesses caused by toxins.

HARRIET ANN BOYD HAWES (1871–1945), the first woman to head a large archaeological dig, was also a social activist. Because she was not allowed by the American School of Classical Studies to take part in excavations, she financed her own excavations with her scholarship money; eventually she discovered the ancient town of Gournia. After World War I, Harriet Ann worked for women's suffrage and assisted factory workers on strike. Smith College, her alma mater, created a scholarship in her name.

HARRIET ANN JACOBS (1813–1897) was born a slave in North Carolina; her book, *Incidents in the Life of a Slave Girl: Written by Herself*, was published in 1861 under a pseudonym. It chronicled sexual abuse and the seven years she spent in hiding in a "living coffin" above her grandmother's porch. After she escaped, she became famous for her relief efforts and helping black refugees, and established the Jacobs Free School for their children.

HARRIET MANN MILLER (1831–1918) wrote children's books as Olive Thorne Miller. She was an avid birder and naturalist who moved frequently as a child. Harriet's early stories were about animals or lonely children; later, she wrote a series of birding books that were based on field observation, and her reports of ecosystems helped to give rise to the conservation movement.

HARRIET QUIMBY (1875–1912), the first American woman to get a pilot's license, was a journalist and photographer in love with speed. She began her career writing about cars and auto racing, and when she reported on a flight exhibition in 1910 she became fascinated by aviation. She earned her license a year later and became the first woman to fly across the English Channel. Although she died after being thrown from her plane while exhibition flying for an aviation meet, Harriet helped to tear down the stereotype that women were less able than men to fly.

HARRIET PRESCOTT SPOFFORD (1835–1921) began writing as a means to support her family after her father was paralyzed and her mother had a nervous breakdown. Her stories were featured in the *Atlantic Monthly* on a regular basis, and although she is thought to be the first American woman to write detective fiction, she is best known for her short stories. "Her Story" is a powerful account of a woman's descent into madness by her marriage.

HARRIET BEECHER STOWE (1811–1905) was, arguably, the most famous American writer of the nineteenth century. Her book *Uncle Tom's Cabin* was, according to legend, credited by Abraham Lincoln as starting the Civil War—but whether it did or not, this best-selling book made Americans aware of and unable to ignore or deny the horrors of slavery. Although Harriet wrote thirty books, including volumes of poetry, none matched the popularity of *Uncle Tom's Cabin*.

HARRIET TUBMAN (c. 1820–1913) was born a slave on Maryland's Eastern Shore. In 1849 she ran away to Philadelphia following the North Star. Harriet became involved with the Underground Railroad, a secret network that helped slaves escape, and personally conducted more than twenty missions that led more than three hundred slaves to freedom; there was soon a forty-thousand-dollar reward for her capture. After the Civil War, she founded the Harriet Tubman Home for elderly poor blacks and devoted herself to working for educational opportunities for free blacks.

HARRIOT EATON STANTON BLATCH (1856–1940), the daughter of the abolitionist Henry Brewster Stanton and the suffragist Elizabeth Cady Stanton, shared her mother's passion. Combining civil disobedience with activism, Harriot lobbied in Albany for New York women to win the vote, organized mass demonstrations at Cooper Union in New York

City, and staged annual Suffrage Day parades, one of which drew twenty thousand marchers and eighty thousand spectators. After women's suffrage passed, Harriot worked for the League of Nations.

HATTIE: a familiar form of Harriet.

HATTIE ELIZABETH ALEXANDER (1901–1968) headed the microbiology lab at the Columbia-Presbyterian Medical Center in New York City. Armed with a medical degree from Johns Hopkins University, she dedicated her life's work to fighting bacterial or influenza meningitis, an inflammation of the spinal cord and brain that was almost always fatal. The antiserum she discovered was used in a vaccine, and the death rate for this deadly disease dropped by 80 percent within two years. Hattie was the first woman to become president of the American Pediatrics Society.

HATTIE OPHELIA WYATT CARAWAY (1878–1950) was the first woman elected to the U.S. Senate. This reserved farmwife first gained a seat in the Senate when she was appointed upon her husband's death in 1931. When the term expired, Hattie did not step aside so that another man could be elected to assume her husband's seat. Instead, she joined the seven men who were running and, with the help of Huey P. Long, won the race. She also won in 1938, beating an opponent whose slogan was "Arkansas needs another man in the Senate."

HATTIE McDANIEL (1898–1952) was the first African-American woman to win an Academy Award. Her Best Supporting Actress honor came for her portrayal of Mammy in *Gone With the Wind*. Although this was her most famous role, Hattie appeared in more than three hundred films, twelve in 1936 alone. She starred opposite Shirley Temple in *The Little Colonel* and with Paul Robeson in *Show Boat*, and starred on *The Beulah Show*, a radio program.

HAZEL: from the English for commanding authority.

HAZEL MINER (1904–1920) wasn't the first to do or win anything remarkable, but her selfless courage merits remembering her. During a blizzard on the plains of North Dakota, the sleigh with Hazel and her two younger siblings tipped over. Hazel wrapped the two in a robe and lay down over them to keep the robe from blowing away, urging them not to go to sleep and to keep wiggling their feet so they wouldn't freeze; every so often she would get up to break the crust of snow that formed around them. It took twenty-five hours before the children were found; the two younger ones were still alive, sheltered by Hazel's frozen body.

HAZEL HOTCHKISS WIGHTMAN (1886–1974) dominated women's tennis for decades, winning more than forty-five national championships (including one when she was sixty-eight). For three straight years (1909–1911) she won the singles, doubles, and mixed doubles championships at Wimbledon. She founded the Wightman Cup competition and was named a Dame of the British Empire, but still referred to herself as "a little old lady in tennis shoes."

HELEN: from the Greek for light. An ancient name—Zeus's mortal daughter was Helen of Troy—Helen has myriad variations and pet forms: Helene, Halina, Helle, Ellen, Aileen, Eileen, Ilona, Ilene, Elena, Lenore, Eleanor, Ellie, Nell, and Ella are just a few.

HELEN HAYES (1900–1993) won two Academy Awards and two Tony Awards, for her roles in *The Sin of Madelon Claudet* and *Airport*, and *Happy Birthday* and *Things Remembered*, respectively. In addition to appearing in dozens of films and Broadway productions, Helen established a treatment and therapy department to help paralyzed survivors of polio. Today, the Helen Hayes MacArthur Hospital in Nyack, New York, is as renowned for its physical therapy as Helen was for her acting talent.

HELEN ELNA HOKINSON (1893–1949) drew more than seventeen hundred cartoons and covers for the *New Yorker* over a period of twenty-four years. She was known for "those Hokinson ladies," befuddled, slightly plump matrons.

HELEN HUNT JACKSON (1830–1885) was called the most brilliant woman of her time. A fierce advocate for Native American rights, Helen wrote *A Century of Dishonor* in 1881 and sent a copy to every member of Congress. When this book had little effect on the treatment of Indians, she wrote the novel *Ramona*, which enjoyed enduring popularity.

HELEN ADAMS KELLER (1880–1968), when she was eighteen months old, contracted an illness that left her blind and deaf; the few words she had learned were soon forgotten. Taught sign language by Anne Sullivan, Helen became an insatiable learner. Accepted to Radcliffe College in 1896, she graduated cum laude in 1904. She traveled the world speaking on behalf of the disabled and wrote several books, including *The Story of My Life*.

HELEN HERRON TAFT (1861–1943), called Nellie, left as her legacy the cherry trees that blossom in Washington, D.C. As a seventeen-year-old, Nellie visited the White House and made up her mind to become First Lady. Her husband served as the secretary of war under Theodore

Roosevelt, and when Roosevelt decided not to run again, Nellie urged her husband to run, campaigning so hard that Roosevelt reprimanded her. She was the first First Lady to accompany her husband in the inaugural parade, and until 1994 she was the only First Lady to be buried alongside her husband in Arlington Cemetery.

HELEN TAMIRIS (1905–1966) was a classically trained dancer who was introduced to international styles of dance while on tour in South America. When she returned to the United States, she began to choreograph dances with spontaneity and sexuality. Her most popular dances are known as the Negro Spirituals, created between 1928 and 1941. Helen also choreographed Broadway shows, such as *Annie Get Your Gun*, *Showboat*, and *Touch and Go*, for which she won the Tony Award for Best Choreography.

HELEN TAUSSIG (1898–1986) earned a medical degree from Johns Hopkins University and specialized in pediatric cardiology. Working with Alfred Blalock, she developed an operation designed to help "blue babies," those who are born with holes in their hearts. She was the first woman to become a full professor on the Johns Hopkins faculty, and the children's heart center there is named after her.

HELENA: an alternate form of Helen.

HELENA STUART DUDLEY (1858–1932) was a member of the first graduating class of Bryn Mawr College. While there, she heard of the movement to establish settlement houses for immigrants, and after she graduated she worked at ones in Philadelphia and Boston, bringing services to poor neighborhoods. She realized that social services couldn't replace decent wages and began to assist labor unions, helping to organize the National Women's Trade Union League in 1903.

HENRIETTA: the feminine form of Henry, from the German for ruler of the house. Hettie and Etta are the most common nicknames; Henriette is an alternate spelling.

HENRIETTA SWAN LEAVITT (1869–1921) was an astronomer who created a method for ranking stars' magnitude, figured out how to calculate fundamental distances in the universe, and discovered more variable stars than anyone else of her era.

HETTY: a familiar form of Henrietta.

HETTY GREEN (1834–1916) parlayed a million-dollar inheritance into an estate of more than $100 million. Investing in war bonds, railroad and other stocks, and other holdings, she became a major financier on Wall Street, where her eccentricities were the stuff of legend. Her legacy included bequests to libraries, hospitals, Wellesley College, the Girl Scouts of America, and many other organizations.

HILDA: from the German for warrior.

HILDA DOOLITTLE (1886–1961) was a mystic whose poetry was filled with imagery and emotion. Her novel *Palimpsest* chronicles the trials faced by women and artists too sensitive for a harsh world. Other works include *Helen in Egypt, Tribute to Freud*, and *End to Torment: A Memoir of Ezra Pound*, to whom she was briefly engaged.

HILLARY: from the Greek for cheerful, merry.

HILLARY RODHAM CLINTON (b. 1947) graduated from Wellesley College and Yale Law School, where she made law review. While interning with the children's advocate Marian Wright Edelman, she met William Jefferson Clinton, whom she married in 1975. As First Lady, Hillary advocated for expanding health insurance coverage and the rights of women and children. She was elected to the U.S. Senate in 2000.

HORTENSE: from the Latin for gardener.

HORTENSE POWDERMAKER (1896–1970) was an anthropologist who received her Ph.D. from the London School of Economics. Like her contemporary Margaret Mead, she went to the South Pacific and wrote a book about her observations, but unlike Mead she soon turned her attention to racial struggles in the American South and then to Hollywood. She founded the Department of Anthropology and Sociology at Queens College in New York City.

HORTENSE SPARKS WARD (1872–1944) was a firebrand who became the first female admitted to the bar in the state of Texas. Outraged that married women had no property rights, she lobbied until a law (named after her) was passed. She also fought for a system of workers' compensation and for limits to the number of hours in a workweek. She established a court for domestic relations, and fought for a law granting women the right to serve as officers of corporations.

★ ★ ★ ★ ★ ★ ★ ★   I   ★ ★ ★ ★ ★ ★ ★ ★

IDA: from the English for prosperous. A name popular 150 years ago, Ida has a rich meaning. Whether you hope your daughter grows up to be a scientist, an artist, or simply a woman of courage, you'll have several strong role models to choose from.

IDA HENRIETTA HYDE (1857–1945) was a neurophysiologist who didn't get a college degree until she was thirty-four. A brilliant student, she was urged to study in Germany, and became the first woman to earn a doctorate from Heidelberg University—despite the school's refusal to allow her to attend lectures or participate in labs. She received her medical degree at fifty-five, and during World War I was appointed by President Wilson to chair the Women's Commission on Health and Sanitation. Ida Hyde was the chair of the physiology department at the University of Kansas for many years, and established scholarships there as well as at Cornell University.

IDA REDBIRD (1892–1971) was an artist whose medium was clay, and her talents as a potter and her advocacy helped to revitalize Native American crafts, particularly pottery making, among the Maricopa and Pima. She used local clay that she gathered herself and made her own paints, and her polished red pots with delicate black designs were noted for their grace and beauty. She worked for recognition and better pay for potters—at one point, she earned a nickel for each pot—and was elected the first president of the Maricopa Pottery Makers Association. Her work today is considered priceless; it can be seen at the Gila River Indian Reservation in Arizona.

IDA MINERVA TARBELL (1857–1944) was an investigative journalist who wrote for *McClure's Magazine*. Her series of articles about Abraham Lincoln were so popular that circulation for the magazine nearly doubled during its run. From 1902 to 1904, *McClure's* published her investigation of Standard Oil and John D. Rockefeller. Ranked as the fifth most important work of journalism in the twentieth century, this series of articles was critical to the Supreme Court's decision to break up the Standard Oil trust.

"Imagination is the only key to the future. Without it none exists—with it all things are possible." —Ida Minerva Tarbell

IDA B. WELLS (1862–1931) was born a slave and became a crusading journalist who helped set the stage for the civil rights movement in the 1950s and 1960s. Seventy-some years before Rosa Parks refused to move to the back of the bus, Ida refused to move from her seat on a train. After she was removed by force she sued the railroad and won, but the decision was overturned by the Supreme Court. Ida was co-owner and editor of the *Memphis Free Speech,* but after receiving death threats she moved to Chicago. A founding member of the NAACP, Ida is quoted as saying, "One had better die fighting against injustice than die like a dog or a rat in a trap." After three friends were killed, Ida instigated a national crusade against lynching.

IMOGEN, IMOGENE: from the Latin for image or likeness; may also be from the Gaelic for maiden. Gen or Gene may be diminutives.

IMOGEN CUNNINGHAM (1883–1976) was a photographer who specialized in highly detailed, tightly focused portraits and studies of plants. She got her first camera at age twenty-three, and after receiving a degree from the University of Washington, she went to Germany to study printmaking. She joined Group f/64 (other members included Ansel Adams and Edward Weston). Some of her work is part of the permanent collection of the Museum of Modern Art. She published several books of her work; some are still in print.

INA: from the Irish for pure.

INA CLAIRE (1892–1985) is best remembered for the role taken from her life: she and silent screen star John Gilbert were the couple that *A Star Is Born* was based on. A vaudeville comedienne–turned–Ziegfeld Girl, Ina was starring on Broadway in the 1920s and appeared on the cover of *Time* magazine in September of 1929—just as her husband, the highest-paid star of 1928, lost his money in the stock market crash. The marriage fell apart, and Ina went on to star on Broadway, as well as in such films as *Ninotchka* with Greta Garbo.

INEZ: from the Spanish for pure.

INEZ MILHOLLAND BOISSEVAIN (1886–1916), a suffragist and labor advocate, captured the attention of the nation when she led a parade for women's voting rights seated upon a white horse and wearing white clothes. In 1916 she supported a strike among garment workers, and she won a reprieve for a condemned man by bringing the judge new evidence after a late-night, last-minute trip to the judge's house. She died at age thirty from pernicious anemia after collapsing on a tour to promote suffrage.

IRENE: from the Greek for peaceful. Irina is common in Eastern European countries; Rena is another variation.

IRENE MCCOY GAINES (1892–1964) began her career as a juvenile court typist in Chicago. After hearing firsthand about the problems of blacks and women, she became a social worker for Cook County. She organized a march in Washington, D.C., to protest employment discrimination in 1941, and was the first black woman to run for state office in Illinois.

ISABEL, ISABELLE, ISABELLA: Spanish and Italian variations on Elizabeth, from the Hebrew for consecrated to God. Isobel and Ysabel are somewhat less common spellings.

ISABEL BEVIER (1860–1913) started teaching school when she was only fifteen years old. She earned her doctorate and became a school principal, and then became a professor at the Pennsylvania College for Women; there, her interest in the chemistry of food took root. Isabel conducted studies in nutrition and food sanitation, and it was she who first used a thermometer for testing the doneness of meat. The University of Illinois recruited her to develop its home economics department in 1900, and in 1921 she became the chair of the home economics department at UCLA.

ISABELLA BAUMFREE (1797–1883) is much better known as Sojourner Truth. Born a slave in Ulster County, New York, she was freed when New York abolished slavery in 1827. Deeply religious yet illiterate, she memorized most of the Bible; at age forty-six she renamed herself Sojourner Truth and began preaching and lecturing on feminism and abolition. Possessed of a rich and powerful voice and standing more than six feet tall, Sojourner commanded the attention of her listeners and was respected enough to meet with Abraham Lincoln during the Civil War. The site of her "Ain't I a woman?" speech has been renamed the Sojourner Truth Building; it stands at 27 North High Street in Akron, Ohio.

ISABELLA STEWART GARDNER (1840–1924) was a patron of the arts and a collector. She and her husband, the financier John Gardner, lived in Europe for several years and traveled the globe, eventually acquiring more than twenty-five hundred works of art that are today considered priceless. Housed in the lavish Italianate villa they built in and bequeathed to the city of Boston, their collection includes Titian's *Europe*, Vermeer's *The Concert*, and several Rembrandts. Their former home is now the Isabella Stewart Gardner Museum.

ISABELLA BEECHER HOOKER (1822–1907), like her sisters, Catharine and Harriet, was an activist; her passion was suffrage. Working with Susan B. Anthony, Elizabeth Cady Stanton, Paulina Wright Davis, and others, she helped to found the New England Woman Suffrage Association. Isabella's book *Womanhood: Its Sanctities and Fidelities* was published in 1874.

ISADORA: from the Latin for gift of Isis. Dory or Dorrie are diminutives.

ISADORA DUNCAN (1878–1927) was one of the founders of modern dance; she combined classical Greek performance, folk dance, ballet, and natural movements like running, jumping, leaping, and skipping to create a wholly new art form. She and her followers wore togas and loose, flowing robes while dancing. The life of this free spirit was cut short when her scarf became tangled in the wheels of the sports car in which she was riding.

JACKIE: a familiar form of Jacqueline, a feminine form of Jack. Although Jackie is almost always a diminutive for Jacqueline, there's no reason you can't name your daughter Jackie.

JACKIE MITCHELL (1914–1987) was named Virne Beatrice at birth. She learned the basics of baseball as a toddler from her father and Dazzy Vance, a neighbor who played for the minor leagues. By age seventeen, Jackie had become the first woman to play in the minors, pitching for the Chattanooga Lookouts. When the New York Yankees stopped in Chattanooga to play an exhibition game, Jackie struck out Babe Ruth and Lou Gehrig, only to have baseball's commissioner, Kenesaw Mountain Landis, void her contract because baseball was "too strenuous" for a woman.

JACQUELINE: a feminine form of Jacques, the French for James or Jacob; from the Hebrew for he who supplants. Alternate spellings and variations are myriad, but the most common are Jacquelyn, Jaclyn, and Jacquetta; the nickname may be spelled Jacqui or Jackie.

JACQUELINE COCHRAN (1908–1980) might not be as famous an aviator as Amelia Earhart, but she was no less talented a pilot. After she earned her license she learned that women were barred from piloting commercial planes, so she joined a flying circus. She became a test pilot and flew a bomber to England to promote women pilots in World War II. Rejected by the United States military, she joined the British army—until the United States asked her to create the Women's Air Force Service Pilots. By the end of the war she was the first woman to be commissioned a lieutenant colonel in the Air Force Reserves. Jacqueline won the Bendix Cup race in 1938 and again in 1946, and after her friend Chuck Yeager introduced her to jet planes, she flew at twice the speed of sound, earning the sobriquet "the fastest woman on earth."

JACQUELINE LEE BOUVIER KENNEDY ONASSIS (1929–1994), known as Jackie, redecorated the White House with elegant and sophisticated American decorative arts, but this First Lady's sense of style was also demonstrated in her attire—whatever she wore was soon imitated by

American women all over the country. After her husband's assassination she became a symbol of strength and courage, raising her two children, lending her name and her time to several philanthropic organizations, and, from 1978 until her death, working as a book editor at Doubleday.

JANE: from the Hebrew for God is gracious. Like Jean and Joan, the name Jane was originally a feminine form of John. This classic name has a simple elegance. It's a strong first name immortalized by a powerful American woman. It's sometimes spelled Jayne, and although it isn't shortened, Janie is a common pet form.

JANE ADDAMS (1860–1935) was the first American woman to win the Nobel Peace Prize. A social reformer who graduated first in her class from Rockford Female Seminary, Jane had decided at a young age to work with the poor. She founded Hull House, a settlement house in Chicago that served as a center for immigrants; Hull House hosted a nursery, health clinic, playground, gym, cooking and sewing courses, and a boardinghouse for unmarried working women, and served more than two thousand people a week at its peak. Jane was also a leader in labor reform; she worked to improve conditions for women and children, and was a founder of the NAACP. The Jane Addams Hull-House Museum stands at 800 South Halstead Street in Chicago.

JANE ARMINDA DELANO (1862–1919) was the superintendent of the Army Nurse Corps and recruited the majority of the 21,480 nurses who served during World War I. She was also the chair of the American Red Cross Nursing Service. Though she survived epidemics of typhoid and yellow fever—not to mention Apache raids while nursing at a mining camp in Arizona—she died after an ear infection turned into mastitis while she was inspecting nursing units in Europe after the armistice. Her last words were: "I must get back to my work."

JANE WILKINSON LONG (1798–1880), called the Mother of Texas, was a pioneer who survived a winter at a fort on Bolivar Point, opposite Galveston, alone, save for a twelve-year-old servant and her six-year-old daughter. Jane later owned a hotel in Brazoria, where Stephen Austin delivered his pro-independence address in 1835.

JANE MEANS PIERCE (1806–1863) was the wife of President Franklin Pierce. Though her life was beset with tragedy—her three sons all died as children—and she fought depression during her time in the White House, Jane was an abolitionist who disagreed with her husband: Franklin believed in preserving the Constitution and the Union at all costs, but Jane supported the end of slavery, even if it meant a war that sundered the country.

JANE GREY SWISSHELM (1806–1863) published a feminist, abolitionist newspaper in Pittsburgh. Her views were often at odds with her husband's, but her editorials contributed to Pennsylvania's passing laws to protect women's property rights. Jane later moved to St. Cloud, Minnesota, and started a newspaper there, and her ardent antislavery views so offended local Democrats that they broke into her office and vandalized her press. Undaunted, she continued writing, and eventually became the first woman to sit in the press gallery of the United States Senate.

JANET: from the Hebrew for gracious or merciful. Originally a diminutive of Jane, Janet has been a given name for centuries. Janette is usually pronounced with the emphasis on the second syllable.

JANET GAYNOR (1906–1984) was the winner of the first Academy Award for Best Actress, and starred in nearly forty movies in a career that spanned both silent films and talkies. Among her best known are *Street Angel*, *A Star Is Born*, *State Fair*, and *Bernardine*.

JEAN: from the Scottish; a feminine form of John, from the Hebrew for God is gracious. Jeanne is the French spelling, from the feminine of Jean (the French spelling for John).

JEAN HARLOW (1911–1937) was Hollywood's first blond "sex goddess" in a career that was tragically cut short. Cast in Howard Hughes's film *Hell's Angels*, she became a star overnight with the line "Would you be shocked if I changed into something more comfortable?" With her platinum hair and bias-cut dresses, Jean fit the part of the vixen, but she also showed a flair for comedy; in the film *Bombshell* she spoofed her own career.

JEANNETTE: the feminine form of the French Jean, from the Hebrew for God is gracious.

JEANNETTE RIDLON PICCARD (1895–1981) said, "I'm not going to have it said there's anyplace I can't go." Among the places she went: into the stratosphere and onto the altar. Acting as the pilot for her husband, a high-altitude balloonist, Jeannette ascended 57,579 feet into the stratosphere in 1934, a record she held until a Soviet cosmonaut went into space thirty years later. When Jeannette was seventy-nine, she became the first woman to be ordained a priest in the Episcopal Church.

JEANNETTE RANKIN (1880–1973) was the first woman elected to the United States Congress. An elegantly attired suffragist, she was a media darling who dispelled the myth that women who fought for equal rights were unfeminine. In Congress she voted against entering World War I and World War II, and after the war worked for peace. She studied with Gandhi, marched on Washington with Coretta Scott King, and protested the Vietnam War. Asked what she would do if she had the chance to live her life over, she said, "This time I'd be nastier."

JEMIMA: from the Hebrew for dove.

JEMIMA WILKINSON (1752–1819) was the first woman born in the United States to start a religious movement. After a vision in which she died and was sent back to earth to preach a message of repentance to a sinful world, she called herself the Publick Universal Friend. She insisted she had been resurrected, and like the Quakers she advocated plainness in language and clothing and opposed slavery and war. Jemima dressed in flowing robes and performed faith healings, and she established the Jerusalem Township in upstate New York.

JENNIE: a familiar form of Jennifer, from the Welsh for fair one. It can also be a nickname for Virginia or Janet. Jen, Jenny, and Jenna are other forms.

JENNIE AUGUSTA BROWNSCOMBE (1850–1936) was a popular illustrator whose work appeared on calendars and in magazines for decades. A founding member of the Art Students League, she studied at Cooper Union and the National Academy of Design, then went to Paris to study with Henry Mosler. Her oil paintings were extremely well received; they captured American life with a nostalgic quality that transcended trends in art.

JENNIE COLLINS (1828–1887) worked for labor reform, and her efforts were all the more powerful because she had worked in cotton mills as a teenager in New Hampshire and had firsthand experience of the dire conditions. In 1870 she realized a dream of creating a shelter for single working women: at Boffin's Bower, needy women found food, clothing, shelter, and companionship, and Jennie also helped them to find employment.

JENNIE JEROME CHURCHILL (1854–1921) was a Brooklyn girl who married into the British aristocracy. Strikingly beautiful and more than a little outrageous (her left wrist sported a tattoo of a snake), Jennie became engaged to Lord Randolph Churchill, the younger son of the Duke of Marlborough, three days after they met. Her first son, Winston, was born after she fell from a horse. After her first husband died, Jennie turned her attention to philanthropy, travel, writing, and affairs. Several books have been written about her.

JENNIE WADE (1843–1863) was born Mary Virginia Wade, and was the only civilian killed during the Battle of Gettysburg. Throughout the days of fighting, Jennie baked bread for the Union soldiers and handed out water. When Confederate troops ordered her to leave the house, she refused. The house was bombarded with bullets and an artillery shell, but Jennie endured for three days before she was hit by a stray minié ball. The house, located at 528 Baltimore Street in Gettysburg, is now a museum, and Jennie's ghost is said to haunt it.

JERRIE: a familiar form of Geraldine, from the Old German and French for spear ruler.

JERRIE MOCK (b. 1925) was a pilot and manager of the airport in Columbus, Ohio, when her husband joked that she should fly around the world. Thirty-eight years old and the mother of three, Jerrie did just that, leaving Columbus on March 19, 1964, on a solo journey that took her more than twenty-three thousand miles before returning to Columbus on April 17. She set two official records: the first woman to fly around the world, and a new world speed record for piloting an airplane weighing less than 3,858 pounds. President Lyndon B. Johnson presented her with the Gold Medal of the FAA, and the FAI awarded her the Louis Blériot Silver Medal.

JESSIE, JESSYE: familiar forms of Jessica, from the Hebrew for he sees.

JESSIE DANIEL AMES (1883–1972) was a civil rights activist. A suffragist and businesswoman (she ran a telephone company), Jessie was instrumental in making Texas the first Southern state to ratify the Nineteenth Amendment. She then turned her efforts to racial equality. By 1924 she was the director of the Texas chapter of the Commission on Interracial Cooperation, and in 1929 she was the organization's national director. Jessie founded the Association of Southern Women for the Prevention of Lynching a year later; this group of white women strove to fight racial violence at the hands of mobs or vigilantes. Their efforts took time to pay off, but 1940 marked the first year since the end of the Civil War that there were no recorded lynchings of black Americans.

JESSIE TARBOX BEALS (1870–1942), a self-taught photographer, was the first woman to become a news photographer. After working as a staff photographer at the *Buffalo Courier* for a few years, Jessie went to St. Louis to photograph the World's Fair; her photographs appeared in magazines nationwide and her reputation as a premier photographer was established. She moved to Greenwich Village, where she spent the rest of her life photographing New York City's architecture. Collections of her work are located at the New-York Historical Society and at the Museum of the City of New York.

JESSIE BINFORD (1876–1966), known as the conscience of Chicago, wasn't as famous as her colleague Jane Addams, but her work was every bit as important. Jessie's passion was "a crusade aimed at the delinquency of adults against children," and in fighting for children's rights, she founded and was the director for thirty-six years of the Juvenile Protection Association. She also went to court to prevent the sale of Hull House to the University of Illinois, and while she lost the court battle, she was able to persuade the university to preserve the building and turn it into a museum.

JESSIE ANN BENTON FRÉMONT (1824–1902) was the daughter of Senator Thomas Hart Benton, and married the explorer John Frémont against her father's wishes. She took her husband's notes of his expeditions and rewrote them into dramatic narratives that inspired thousands of Americans to venture west. Jessie traveled through the Isthmus of Panama to join her husband in California, and wrote a book about the grueling journey. After John squandered his fortune, Jessie supported the family with her writing.

JESSYE NORMAN (b. 1945) was born in Georgia to parents with musical talent: her father was a singer, her mother a pianist. Jessye won a scholarship to Howard University, where she studied music; she made her debut at the Berlin State Opera in 1969, and sang with Italian and German opera companies; her American debut came at Lincoln Center in 1973. With her soaring soprano voice and commanding stage presence, Jessye has made her mark not only in opera, but as a singer of sacred songs and jazz.

JOANNA, JOHANNA: German variant of Joan.

JOANNA TROUTMAN (1818–1879) designed the Lone Star flag for Texas and sewed it from silk skirts. In 1835, when soldiers from Georgia marched to Texas to help the fight for independence, this Georgia native presented the flag to Colonel William Ward. Recognized as the official flag of Texas after the Battle of Goliad, Joanna's flag was the first to fly over a free Texas.

JOSEPHINE: a feminine form of Joseph, from the Hebrew for Jehovah increases. Other forms include Josepha and Josette; Josie is a pet form.

JOSEPHINE BAKER (1906–1975) was born in a ghetto in St. Louis, Missouri, but grew up to rub elbows with the rich and royal, and at one point was the highest-paid entertainer in the world. Josephine moved to Paris, where she was taken in by Ada "Bricktop" Smith, and became a sensation in a country that was fascinated by American jazz. Best known for her banana dance costume—nothing but a string of fake bananas tied around her waist—she opened her own nightclub, Chez Josephine, when she was just twenty years old. During World War II Josephine worked with the Résistance and was a nurse with the Red Cross; she was awarded the Croix de Guerre, the Légion d'Honneur, and the Rosette of the Résistance.

JOSEPHINE SOPHIA WHITE GRIFFING (1814–1872), an ardent abolitionist, made her Ohio home a station on the Underground Railroad, and throughout the 1850s worked heroically to eradicate slavery. After the Civil War she worked with the National Freedman's Relief Association in Washington, D.C., distributing food and money to former slaves and finding shelter for them. At the same time she crusaded for women's rights, working closely with Susan B. Anthony and Elizabeth Cady Stanton.

JOSEPHINE LOUISE NEWCOMB (1816–1901) turned tragedy into philanthropy. After losing her infant son and her husband, Josephine doted on her second child, a daughter named Sophie. Sophie died at age fifteen from diphtheria. Although Josephine was distraught, she came up with a plan. An astute businesswoman, Josephine increased the fortune left by her husband, and in 1886 she created the H. Sophie Newcomb Memorial College as part of Tulane University; its focus was to train and educate women artists.

JOSIE: a familiar form of Josephine.

JOSIE BASSETT MORRIS (1870–1964) lived for fifty years in a cabin at Utah's Cub Creek. Alone in the wilderness, this courageous pioneer raised cattle, pigs, chicken, and feed for her animals while raising two sons after her marriage fell apart. Tough till the end of her life, Josie won a calf-roping contest when she was in her eighties.

JOSIE PEARL (1873–1962) started prospecting when she was twelve and staked her first claim at thirteen; by fourteen she was a cook at a mining camp. Although she worked in restaurant kitchens as an adult, she found mining irresistible and would ride into Nevada's Black Rock Desert to mine at night before going into work in the morning. Although she and her husband never found a big strike, Josie was, in the words of the reporter Ernie Pyle, a true "woman of the West," and she found enough gold to afford a diamond bracelet (which she wore with old battered shoes).

JUDITH: from the Hebrew for praised. Judy and Jody are common nicknames.

JUDITH SERGANT MURRAY (1751–1820), a feminist and writer, is best remembered for her essay "On the Equality of the Sexes," where she wrote, "Yes, ye lordly, ye haughty sex, our souls are by nature *equal* to yours." Other essays, published in the *Gleanor*, were read by both John Adams and George Washington, and her play *The Medium* was the first by an American playwright to be performed at the Federal Street Theatre.

JULIA: a feminine form of Julius, from the Greek for Jove's child. Giulia is the Italian spelling; variations include Juliet, Juliette, Julianne, and Julene; Julie is the familiar form.

JULIA CHILD (1912–2004) found her calling when she was in her forties. After a childhood in Pasadena, California, and getting a degree at Smith College, Julia worked for the Office of Strategic Services during World War II. While stationed in Sri Lanka she met her husband, and after the war they settled in Paris. Julia's culinary awakening came during their time in France. She learned to cook, and collaborated with Louisette Berthold and Simone Beck to open a cooking school and to write a cookbook. *Mastering the Art of French Cooking* was published at the height of Americans' fascination with French culture in the early 1960s, and Julia's down-to-earth charm, encyclopedic knowledge, and grace made her the star of many cooking shows on television and led to several more books. Julia was the cofounder of the American Institute of Wine and Food. She received the French Legion of Honor in 1991 and the U.S. Presidential Medal of Freedom in 2003.

JULIA CAROLINE RIPLEY DORR (1825–1913) moved from her native South Carolina to Vermont at a young age, and went on to become one of her adopted state's most beloved authors and poets. The founder of the Rutland [Vermont] Free Public Library, Julia published hundreds of poems, which were collected in more than ten volumes, as well as novels whose female characters rose from poverty through education, discipline, and perseverance. Guests at her home included members of the Concord Group, such as Ralph Waldo Emerson and Oliver Wendell Holmes.

JULIA DENT GRANT (1826–1902) was a First Lady who was as sophisticated and outgoing as her husband was awkward and shy. A Southern belle who loved to entertain, Julia returned the White House to the center of Washington, D.C.'s, social life. Her parties were famous, and the Grants' daughter's wedding was elaborate, even by White House standards. Julia Grant was the first First Lady to write her memoirs.

JULIA WARD HOWE (1819–1910), a writer and social reformer, wrote the lyrics to "The Battle Hymn of the Republic," for which she was paid five dollars by the *Atlantic Monthly*. Originally a song against slavery, the anthem was later adopted by women's suffragists and later still by civil rights advocates. The author of several volumes of poetry and essays, Julia was the first woman elected to the American Academy of Arts and Letters. Her journals are in the Houghton Library at Harvard University.

JULIA CLIFFORD LATHROP (1858–1932) spent more than fifty years working to improve the lives of immigrants, women, children, and the mentally ill. An Illinois native and a graduate of Vassar College, Julia returned to Illinois and worked at Jane Addams's Hull House. After inspecting institutions like the Cook County infirmary and various asylums and almshouses in Illinois, Julia worked to create the first juvenile court system in the world, as well as the Immigrants' Protective League. President Taft appointed her to head the Children's Bureau.

JULIA BOWMAN ROBINSON (1919–1985) planned to become a teacher to please her family, but when she transferred from San Diego State College to the University of California, she found others who shared her passion for mathematics. She earned her doctorate and later was appointed a professor at Berkeley. Julia turned her mental energy to solving the Tenth Problem on David Hilbert's famous list; she created the Robinson Hypothesis, which a Russian mathematician used to find the solution in 1970. Julia's work on zero-sum games has been called the most important theorem in elementary game theory, and she was awarded a MacArthur Fellowship.

"Rather than being remembered as the first woman this or that, I would prefer to be remembered, as a mathematician should, simply for the theorems I have proved and the problems I have solved." —Julia Bowman Robinson

---

JULIA TUTWILER (1841–1916), a highly educated and well-traveled woman, was an educator and an advocate for prison reform. She started the first kindergarten in Alabama, as well as the Alabama Normal School (now the University of West Alabama), where she trained teachers. She prevailed upon the University of Alabama to admit female students—in fact, her impact on education in her home state was so pervasive that nearly every college and university has a building named after her. After seeing what Alabama's prisons were like she began a crusade to improve conditions. Among the reforms she won were separate facilities for juvenile offenders, separate facilities for men and women, and the establishment of systems for inspection, sanitation, and education.

JULIA GARDINER TYLER (1820–1889), a member of one of Long Island's oldest families, met and married President John Tyler while he was in office. Thirty years his junior, Julia hosted elaborate balls at the White House. After her husband died, Julia successfully lobbied Congress to establish pensions for presidential widows.

JULIETTE: a French variation on Julia, a feminine form of Julius, from the Greek for Jove's child.

JULIETTE GORDON LOW (1860–1927) was born into a privileged family from Savannah, Georgia. After a brief, ill-fated marriage, she met Sir Robert Baden-Powell, the founder of the Boy Scouts. Impressed by Baden-Powell's discipline and sense of honor, if not by his shortsighted refusal to consider opening scouting to girls, Juliette returned to Savannah and began the Girl Scouts of America. Teaching physical fitness, independence, and service, Juliette made it her mission to instill in girls and young women the qualities they would need to find success in any field or activity they chose. By the time of her death, there were more than 165,000 Girl Scouts in the United States.

KAREN: the Danish form of Katherine, from the Greek for pure.

KAREN DANIELSEN HORNEY (1885–1952) channeled her natural tendency to rebel and became one of the great thinkers of modern psychology. Her father was a very strict ship captain who believed that women belonged in the home; Karen rebelled by going to medical school. As a student of psychoanalysis, she rebelled against Freud's idea that women were discontented with their gender and envious of men. When Karen and her then-radical theories of neurosis and mental illness were rejected by the New York Institute, she formed the American Institute of Psychoanalysis. The Karen Horney Foundation carries out her work today.

KATERI: an Iroquois variation on Katherine, from the Greek for pure.

KATERI TEKAKWITHA (1656–1680) was the first Native American to become a saint. Orphaned, severely scarred, and nearly blinded after she contracted smallpox at age four, Kateri was reared by her uncle, the chief of the Turtle Clan, and his wife, who renamed her Tekakwitha, which means the One Who Walks by Groping Her Way. When she was eighteen she was baptized and chose the name Kateri; she resisted pressure to marry and instead dedicated herself to prayer and penitence. Rejected and persecuted, she fled to Canada. Upon her death, a priest reported that her face, disfigured in life, became so beautiful that he yelled in amazement; this miracle was witnessed by others at her funeral, and as news of it spread, her grave became a site for pilgrims (a shrine is located off exit 27 of the New York State Thruway, on Route 5S, in Auriesville). Beatified by Pope John Paul II in 1980, she is now the patron saint of Native Americans; her feast day is July 14.

KATHARINE, KATHERINE: from the Greek for pure. A name that has been popular for centuries, variations appear in dozens of languages: Katerina, Kathleen, Kaitlyn, Katrina—all of which may also be spelled with an initial C—are among the most common. Nicknames include Kate, Katie, Kathy, and Kitty.

KATE CHOPIN (1851–1904) was born in St. Louis to an Irish father and a Creole mother. She spent so much time with her family's Creole and mixed-race slaves that she became familiar with their dialects; as an adult, the speech patterns and characters of the Louisiana bayou figured prominently in her stories. Her first novel, *At Fault,* sold poorly, but her second, *The Awakening,* has become a classic. Kate's sensual prose about the sexual awakening and emotional life of a married woman shocked Victorians, but as the first writer to deem sex an acceptable topic for fiction, Kate is among the most important writers of nineteenth-century fiction.

KATE KENNEDY (1827–1890) was a teacher and labor activist. She fled Ireland during the potato famine of 1846 with her family and settled in San Francisco. Kate became a teacher, but was outraged when she learned that women were paid lower wages than men for the same jobs. Drawing on her experience of working in a sweatshop as a young girl, Kate joined the Knights of Labor and spoke publicly about workers' rights. In 1886 she was nominated by the Labor Party for the position of superintendent of public institutions. She lost, and the board of education demoted her. She fought them in court and won, and the case set tenure laws for civil service workers in California.

KATE MULLANY (1845–1906) was born in Ireland and immigrated to New York with her family. While laboring in a laundry in Troy, New York, she and her coworkers—all women—dealt with harsh chemicals and steaming-hot water and irons; they were paid two dollars a week and worked fourteen-hour days. Kate organized the Collar Laundry Union, went on strike, and demanded a twenty-five-cent raise. The laundry owners agreed to the demand within a week. The Collar Laundry Union wasn't the first labor union for women, but it was the first that lasted after a strike. In 1868, Kate became the first woman appointed to a labor union's national office.

KATE DOUGLAS WIGGIN (1856–1923) wrote many books, but her best known is the children's classic *Rebecca of Sunnybrook Farm.* She was born in Philadelphia but grew up in Hollis, Maine, which bears similarities to her beloved heroine's home, and moved to California in

1873. She started San Francisco's first free kindergarten and, with her sister, a school to train kindergarten teachers. Among her other books for children are *The Birds' Christmas Carol*, *Mother Carey's Chickens*, and *Timothy's Quest*; her autobiography is entitled *My Garden of Memory*.

KATHARINE LEE BATES (1859–1929) was born in Falmouth, Massachusetts; when she was a month old her father died. Her entire family eked out a living as best they could, and although money was extremely tight, Katharine's older brothers insisted that she receive the best education available to women. Katharine attended Wellesley College and eventually became the head of the English department there. Robert Frost, Carl Sandburg, and William Butler Yeats were among her friends. Today, Katharine is remembered as the poet who wrote "America the Beautiful."

KATHARINE DREXEL (1858–1955) was at one point declared "the richest nun in the world." The daughter of a Philadelphia banker, Katharine inherited more than $14 million and earned more than $1,000 a day from the interest. She honored her vows of poverty, however, and lived extremely frugally. She used her fortune to establish Xavier University, the first Catholic college for blacks, as well as the Sisters of the Blessed Sacrament. At the time of her death, this order's members numbered more than five hundred in fifty-one convents. Katharine was canonized on October 1, 2000, and is only the second American-born saint.

KATHERINE DUNHAM (b. 1909) founded a dance company in 1930, with the goal of bringing Native African, South American, and Caribbean dance to the American stage. Over the course of her career, Katherine had a profound affect on Broadway, jazz, and other forms of dance. Besides choreographing more than a hundred original works, including such movies as *Stormy Weather* and *Mambo*, she devised a method of teaching dance that bears her name. Katherine helped to create a performing arts training center and a dance anthropology program at Southern Illinois University.

KATHERINE ANNE PORTER (1890–1980) began writing as a child and once declared that creating stories was the unifying passion of her life. Educated at convent schools in Louisiana and Texas, Katherine published her first collection of short stories to critical praise and won a Guggenheim Fellowship. She traveled to Europe to study aboard a tramp steamer; this journey was the impetus behind *Ship of Fools*, for which she won the Texas Institute of Letters fiction award. Her *Collected Stories*, published in 1966, earned her a Pulitzer Prize and the National Book Award.

"I knew what death was, and had almost experienced it. I had what the Christians call the 'beatific vision,' and the Greeks call the 'happy day,' the happy vision just before death. Now if you have had that, and survived it, come back from it, you are no longer like other people." —Katherine Anne Porter on nearly dying during the Spanish flu epidemic in 1918

KITTY KNIGHT (1775–1855) was a heroine during the War of 1812. The men of Maryland were off to war when the British invaded the Eastern Shore; only older men, women, and children were home. Citizens fled as the British burned Fredricktown and lower Georgetown, but Kitty met the British "with head erect and flashing eyes" and announced that she would not leave: "If you burn this house, you burn me with it." She also prevailed upon the troops not to burn two other houses, one of which was occupied by a sick old lady. The British admiral Cockburn was so moved that he and the troops moved on, leaving several houses and a church untorched. One stands today as the Kitty Knight House, and operates as a restaurant and inn.

★ ★ ★ ★ ★ ★ ★ ★ ★ **L** ★ ★ ★ ★ ★ ★ ★ ★ ★

LAURA: from the Latin for laurel. Laurel, Laurine, Loretta, Lorna, and Lauren are variations; alternate spellings include Lora and Laure. Lori or Laurie, both given names in their own right, are common nicknames for Laura.

LAURA WELCH BUSH (b. 1946) is a Texas native. She taught school before earning her master's degree in library science, then worked as a public-school librarian in Austin, Texas. As First Lady, Laura has promoted educational advancement and literacy programs. Teach for America, the New Teacher Project, and Troops to Teachers are recruitment initiatives she works with, and she has partnered with the Library of Congress to launch the National Book Festival. She spearheads an effort to build a teacher-training institute for Afghani women. Laura also supports educational campaigns for breast cancer (her mother is a breast-cancer survivor) and heart disease.

LAURA SMITH HAVILAND (1808–1898) was a conductor on the Underground Railroad. While living in Michigan, she helped to organize the first antislavery society in the early 1830s, and in 1837 she and her husband founded the Raisin Institute, one of the first American schools to admit anyone regardless of race, creed, or sex. In 1845 her husband died, leaving her a widow with seven children. Laura became even more deeply involved in the Underground Railroad and, after going as far as Kentucky to escort runaway slaves to Canada, had a price on her head of three thousand dollars. After the Civil War, Laura helped to found a school in Kansas, where the city of Haviland was named in her honor.

LAURA INGALLS WILDER (1867–1957) is perhaps more beloved than any other American author. Her Little House books tell the story of her childhood on the frontier, traveling from the "Big Woods" of Wisconsin by covered wagon to the Indian Territory of Kansas, with later moves to Minnesota, Iowa, and the Dakotas. As an adult, Laura and her husband, Almonzo, lived on a farm near Mansfield, Missouri, where Laura edited the *Missouri Realist*. At her daughter Rose's urging, Laura wrote down the stories of her childhood, which have been enjoyed by millions.

LENA: from the Greek for light. Originally a diminutive for names like Angelina, Helene, and Marlena, Lena and the alternate spelling Lina have been used on their own since the early 1900s.

LENA HORNE (b. 1917), a singer, dancer, actress, and breathtaking beauty, fought to break down racial stereotypes and the color line in the entertainment industry. She was acting professionally at age fourteen, and by sixteen was singing and dancing at Harlem's famed Cotton Club, where she worked with Cab Calloway and Duke Ellington, and then later with a white swing band. By twenty-one she was working in Hollywood, and was the first black woman to sign a studio contract. Her films include *Stormy Weather* (the title song has become her signature), *Cabin in the Sky* (which is regarded as her finest performance), and *Death of a Gunfighter*. During World War II she was the premier pinup girl for thousands of soldiers. Because of her friendship with Paul Robeson she was suspected of Communist sympathies. Although she rose above being typecast as a domestic, Lena was no stranger to racism. She marched on Washington in 1963 and performed for the National Council of Negro Women.

"It was a damn fight everywhere I worked, in New York, Hollywood, all over the world." —Lena Horne, on racism

---

LENA LEVINE (1903–1965) was a pioneer in enabling women to take control of their sexual lives. A colleague of Margaret Sanger, Lena received her medical degree from Bellevue College in 1927 and specialized in obstetrics and gynecology. In 1942, tragedy struck: her husband died suddenly, and their infant son suffered brain damage after an illness. Lena devoted her life to marriage counseling and planning parenthood. She started the first group counseling program on sex and contraception in the United States, and was the medical secretary of the London-based International Planned Parenthood Federation. Free access to birth control, frank discussion about sexual techniques, and women's sexual enjoyment were the hallmarks of her groundbreaking work.

LENORE, LEONORA: from the Greek for light. Both names are variations on Eleanor; Lee is a frequent nickname.

LENORE KRASSNER (1908–1984) was always known as Lee; she changed the spelling of her last name to Krasner. Born the sixth of seven children in Brooklyn to Russian immigrants, Lee decided at age thirteen to become an artist. She attended the Women's Art School of Cooper Union and the National Academy of Design, and from 1934 to 1943 she was part of the New Deal's Federal Art Project and helped to establish abstract expressionism as a movement. She met Jackson Pollock in 1942; until his death eleven years later they lived and worked in East Hampton, New York, each artist influenced by the other. Lee's talent and work were often in her larger-than-life husband's shadow, but in the 1960s and 1970s she was the subject of two large exhibits and her work was rediscovered. It is now part of the permanent collections of many of the world's major art museums.

LEONORA O'REILLY (1870–1927) grew up in dire poverty on New York City's Lower East Side; her mother worked long hours in a factory and did piecework at night, and Leonora went to work in a collar factory at age eleven. When she was only sixteen she formed the Working Women's Society, and later became involved with Lillian Weld's Henry Street Settlement House. Leonora helped to found the National Women's Trade Union League and led the investigation of the Triangle Shirtwaist Factory fire. She led the International Ladies' Garment Workers' Union strike in 1909, which went on for five months before winning wage increases for thousands of workers. That same year she helped to found the NAACP.

LEONTYNE: a feminine form of Leon, from the Greek for lion.

LEONTYNE PRICE (b. 1927) is the first African-American to ascend to the pinnacle of opera stardom. She won a scholarship to study voice at Central State University in Ohio, then attended the Juilliard School. One of her first roles was Bess in *Porgy and Bess*. She soon moved beyond traditional black roles to sing the lead in NBC's production of *Tosca* and Verdi's *Aida*, which became her signature role. Leontyne's 1961 debut in Verdi's *Il Trovatore* at the Metropolitan Opera garnered a forty-two-minute ovation, one of the longest in the Met's history. Several of her recordings are available on CD.

LETA: from the Latin for gladly. Lita, an alternate spelling, is often used as a nickname for Carmelita, Angelita, or Letitia.

LETA STETTER HOLLINGSWORTH (1886–1939) was born in a sod dugout on the Nebraska frontier. A brilliant student, she attended the University of Nebraska and then earned her Ph.D. from Columbia University. Her field was clinical psychology, and she focused her attention on the psychology of women. Leta's early research compared the mental and motor skills of women during and outside of menstruation, and her discovery that there was no difference in women's perfor-mances helped to change the perception of women in the workplace and led to laws against sexist hiring practices. Other research demon-strated that men are not intellectually superior to women because of bi-ology, but that any differences are due to socialization. Leta's later research focused on mentally challenged and gifted children.

LETITIA: from the Latin for joy. Common nicknames include Lettie and Tish.

LETITIA PATE WHITEHEAD EVANS (1872–1953) was the first woman to shatter the glass ceiling. In 1899, this Virginia native and a business associ-ate approached the Coca-Cola Company with the idea of bottling the beverage. They negotiated the exclusive contract to bottle and sell Coke across the United States. When her husband died, Lettie assumed the roles of chairman of the Whitehead Holding Company and president of Whitehead Realty Company, and during this time she oversaw the growth of the bottling operation. She was appointed to the board of di-rectors of the Coca-Cola Company in 1934, the first woman to serve in such a capacity for a major corporation. Her business acumen was matched by her generosity: Lettie donated millions of dollars to more than 130 religious and educational institutions, and during World War II she was awarded the Wings of Britain for her donations to the Queen's Fund.

LETITIA CHRISTIAN TYLER (1790–1842) was the first wife of President John Tyler. For most of their marriage he was in public office; during this time she devoted herself to tending their home and nine children (seven of whom survived infancy). She suffered a stroke in 1839 and was confined to bed, and while her husband was president she only ap-peared at one White House function, which was their daughter's wed-ding in early 1842. She suffered a fatal stroke the following September.

LIBBIE: familiar form of Elizabeth, from the Hebrew for con-secrated to God.

LIBBIE HENRIETTA HYMAN (1888–1969) parlayed a passion for animals into a career as a zoologist. She was the youngest in her high school class yet was valedictorian, but worked in a factory until a former teacher encouraged her to go to college—something she had never considered. She earned her Ph.D. in zoology from the University of Chicago, and after she graduated wrote two very successful lab manuals. An advanced text followed, and soon Libbie was earning enough from her royalties that she was able to quit her job. Fascinated by sea creatures like jellyfish and coral, she joined the staff of the American Museum of Natural History as an unpaid researcher; in exchange, she was given a free office for life. While there she wrote *The Invertebrates*, a six-volume text that even today remains the primary reference.

LILLIAN: from the Latin for lily. Alternate forms are Lila, Lilian, Liliana, and Lillianna. Common nicknames include Lillie and Lily.

LILLIAN EVELYN MOLLER GILBRETH (1878–1972) was the real-life person behind the book (and movie) *Cheaper by the Dozen*. Not only was she the mother of twelve; she was also an engineer with a degree from the University of California. Working with her husband, she was a pioneer in motion study and industrial efficiency, and she proved that the behavior and efficiency of individual workers was directly tied to the quality and effectiveness of the workplace. Lillian also applied her ideas to household efficiency, designing equipment and adapting kitchens to meet the needs of the disabled.

LILLIAN GISH (1893–1993), born Lillian de Guiche in Springfield, Ohio, was "the first lady of the silent screen," but she made the transition to talkies successfully. She and her sister Dorothy began acting as young children to help the family make ends meet; Lillian was six years old when she first appeared onstage, and nineteen when she made her film debut. Despite her frail appearance, her performances were notable for their emotional power. Her most famous movies include *Broken Blossoms*, *Intolerance*, *One Romantic Night*, and *Scarlet Letter*.

LILLIAN HELLMAN (1906–1984) was arguably America's greatest female playwright, as well as an outspoken social radical. Born to Jewish parents in New Orleans, Lillian attended New York University and Columbia University. Her plays often address controversial themes: *The Children's Hour* was based on the true story of a child in Scotland accusing two teachers of lesbianism; *The Little Foxes* depicts a family rife with greed and malice; *Toys in the Attic* deals with obsession. Although she was blacklisted by the House Un-American Activities Committee, she was fearless in her condemnation of Joseph McCarthy. She won several awards, including two New York Drama Critics' Circle Awards, and a National Book Award for *An Unfinished Woman*.

"I cannot and will not cut my conscience to fit this year's fashions." —Lillian Hellman in a letter to the House Un-American Activities Committee

---

LIZETTE: an American variation on Elizabeth, from the Hebrew for consecrated to God.

LIZETTE WOODWORTH REESE (1856–1935) was arguably as talented a poet as Emily Dickinson, but her body of work has been quietly admired and largely forgotten. She worked as a schoolteacher, which left her little time for the writing she so loved. Her best-known poem, "Tears," was published in 1899 in *Scribner's Magazine*, but most of her accolades came late in her life. She was awarded an honorary Doctor of Letters from Goucher College and the Mary P. L. Keats Memorial Prize, and ten years after her death her work was included in Louis Untermeyer's *Modern American Poetry*.

"*The long day sped / A roof, a bed / No years, / No tears.*" —Verse on the gravestone of Lizette Woodworth Reese

---

LIZZIE: an American diminutive of Elizabeth, from the Hebrew for consecrated to God.

LIZZIE PLUMMER BLISS (1864–1931) was a cofounder of the Museum of Modern Art. Her father was the secretary of the interior under President McKinley; Lillie (as she was called) acted as his hostess and became a fixture in New York's cultural circles. Her passion for modern art began in 1907, when she purchased a painting by Arthur B. Davies, who in turn showed her the works of such artists as Matisse, Modigliani, Picasso, Cezanne, Renoir, Degas, and Seurat. Her mother disapproved of the paintings, so Lillie hid them in her attic, but when she and her friends Abby Aldrich Rockefeller and Mary Quinn Sullivan conceived of and opened the Museum of Modern Art, her collection formed its core.

LOLA: familiar form of Dolores, from the Spanish for sorrowful.

LOLA MONTEZ (1818–1861) was christened Marie Dolores Eliza Rosanna Gilbert when she was born in Limerick, Ireland, but she reinvented herself as a Spanish dancer. Her infamous Spider Dance, in which she imitated a woman fighting off a spider under her petticoats, gained her notoriety in Europe. She was married twice and counted a number of rich and famous men among her lovers before she moved to America. Lola settled in California, where forty-niners flush with gold relished her flamboyant performances. Lola eventually settled in Grass Valley, where she hosted European-style salons and kept a grizzly bear in her yard, and where she quietly gave food and medicine to the sick and injured.

LORRAINE: French place name, meaning from Lorraine; it may also be derived from Laura, from the Latin for laurel.

LORRAINE VIVIAN HANSBERRY (1930–1965) was the first black American woman to write a play that appeared on Broadway. Lorraine grew up in a middle-class home in Chicago. In college, she was deeply influenced by feminists and political radicals; she counted Paul Robeson among her friends, and met her husband while protesting the executions of Julius and Ethel Rosenberg. During this time she began to write her most famous play, *A Raisin in the Sun*; she took its title from a poem by Langston Hughes. It opened on March 11, 1959. A television drama aired after her death of cancer at thirty-four.

LOUISA: variation on Louise, from the Old German for renowned warrior.

LOUISA CATHERINE ADAMS (1775–1852), the wife of John Quincy Adams, was born in France while her father served as a commercial agent for the state of Maryland; she met her husband when she was living in London. They were married in 1797, and Louisa saw her first glimpse of American soil in 1801. She followed her husband to Russia when he was appointed American minister, and then to Washington when he served as secretary of state under James Monroe. Though Americans didn't entirely warm up to the foreign-born First Lady, she opened her home on Tuesday evenings for parties and later strove to make the White House welcoming.

LOUISA MAY ALCOTT (1832–1888) wrote several best-selling books of the nineteenth century, and their popularity continues today. Part of a community of New England intellectuals that included Ralph Waldo Emerson, Henry David Thoreau, and her father, the famous transcendentalist Bronson Alcott, Louisa grew up in genteel poverty. She worked a variety of jobs to help the family make ends meet, and drew on her experiences when she later turned to writing. *Hospital Sketches* was based on her tenure as an army nurse; *Little Women* includes characters from her family. Its printing of thirteen thousand copies sold out in two weeks. Louisa was incredibly prolific: she wrote more than 250 books, including *Little Men*, *Jo's Boys*, *An Old Fashioned Girl*, and *Eight Cousins*.

"I'd rather be a free spinster and paddle my own canoe." —Louisa May Alcott, on why she never married

LOUISE: from the Old German for renowned warrior.

LOUISE NEVELSON (1900–1988) was born in Kiev but came with her family to Maine as a child. She moved to New York when she was twenty, but it wasn't until she was in her fifties that she began creating the sculptures that became her signature: collages or reliefs of wood or metal, painted a flat black and mounted in shallow boxes. Her 1958 show, *Moon Garden +*, established Louise as a major American talent, and other one-woman shows at the world's important museums and galleries followed. Several of her works are on public display: the Louise Nevelson Plaza is located in lower Manhattan, and *Night Presence IV* stands at East Ninety-Second Street and Park Avenue in New York City. Princeton University commissioned an outdoor sculpture.

LUCIA: an Italian variation on Lucy, from the Latin for light.

LUCIA FAIRCHILD FULLER (1870–1924) was a painter of miniatures. The daughter of a wealthy Boston investor, Lucia counted such artists as John Singer Sargent as family friends. She attended art school in New York and Boston, and became renowned for her lavishly detailed diminutive paintings; her colorations were compared to stained glass. Lucia's clients included J. P. Morgan and his family. She was a founding member of the American Society of Miniature Painters and the National Academy of Design. Her *Portrait of a Child* is on display at the Metropolitan Museum of Art.

LUCRETIA: from the Latin for succeed. Tia may be a nickname.

LUCRETIA COFFIN MOTT (1793–1880) was one of the most influential women in American history. Raised by women (her father was a sea captain who was away for extended periods), Lucretia learned early that "women's rights . . . was the most important question of my life." A birthright Quaker, she embraced the more radical branch known as Hicksite. She was a passionate abolitionist and refused to use any product of slavery, including cotton fabric and sugar, and was a founder of the Philadelphia Female Anti-Slavery Society. She faced down angry mobs who threatened to burn her home and who tarred and feathered a companion. In 1840 Lucretia allied herself with Elizabeth Cady Stanton and Abby Kelley Foster and sowed the seeds of the women's movement in America. Believing that education was critical for success, she helped to found both Swarthmore College and the first women's medical college in the country.

LUCY: familiar form of Lucia, from the Latin for light.

LUCY BURNS (1879–1966) was an ardent suffragist and holds the distinction of spending more time in jail than any of her compatriots. Educated at Vassar, Yale, and Oxford, Lucy abandoned her studies and a promising career in linguistics for political activism. In 1912, she and Alice Paul began the fight for a constitutional amendment guaranteeing American women the right to vote, and together they founded the Congressional Union of Women Suffrage. She edited the *Suffragist*, organized the Woman Suffrage March in Washington, D.C., and was arrested six times.

LUCY WARE WEBB HAYES (1831–1889) was both a formidable lady and a staunch abolitionist. The first female student at Ohio Wesleyan University, Lucy met her husband, Rutherford B. Hayes, when she was sixteen; he thought her a child then, but when they were reintroduced five years later, he fell in love. During the Civil War, he served as an officer while she tended the wounded; during his tenure as governor of Ohio she helped to establish the Ohio Soldiers' and Sailors' Orphans' Home. A longtime temperance advocate, Lucy is perhaps best remembered for banning liquor at the White House; her opponents dubbed her "Lemonade Lucy."

LUCY CRAFT LANEY (1854–1933) believed fervently in the power of education. Her father was a freedman who was ordained as a Presbyterian minister after the Civil War and went on to found the first all-black synod in the country. Lucy herself was well educated; when the first black college opened in Atlanta, she was among its first students. She went on to teach, and in 1886 she opened a school for black children that eventually became the Haines Normal and Industrial Institute. Because so many schools didn't admit blacks, Lucy founded schools for black students, including a kindergarten, a nurses' training school, and a program that blended arts and sciences with vocational training.

"The educated Negro woman, the woman of character and culture, is needed in the schoolroom, not only in the kindergarten and primary school, but in the high school and the college." —Lucy C. Laney

---

LUELLA: a combination of Louise, from the Old German for renowned fighter, and Ella, from the Old German for other or foreign. May also be spelled Louella.

LUELLA AGNES OWEN (1852–1932) was a geologist whose specialty was loess soil. She was the first person to identify, study, and publish papers about the loess in northwestern Missouri, and she traveled to the Loess Plateau of central China and the loess hills of Germany. When skeletons were found buried under the loess in Kansas, Luella, who hailed from nearby Missouri, guided visiting geologists on the expeditions.

LUTIE: an alternate form of Lucy.

LUTIE A. LYTLE (1871–?) was one of the first black women to earn a law degree. She was appointed assistant enrolling clerk for the Kansas legislature and worked at a newspaper, but she dreamed of being a lawyer. In 1897 she attained her goal: Lutie graduated from law school and was admitted to the criminal court in Memphis. She became the first black woman to be licensed to practice law in Tennessee and the third in the entire United States; shortly after that she was admitted to the Kansas bar, and in 1913 she became the first woman to join the Negro Bar Association.

LYDA, LYDIA: from the Greek for from the land of Lydia. Lydie is the French spelling.

LYDA BURTON CONLEY (1874–1946) was the first Native American lawyer and the first to argue a case before the U.S. Supreme Court. She is best known for her impassioned defense of the Huron cemetery in Kansas City, Missouri. The federal government had entered into a treaty with the Wyandot Indians promising that the burial ground would not be sold; when the government put the land up for sale, Lyda got an injunction against the sale and argued the case all the way to the Supreme Court. She lost the case, but she garnered so much support that the Huron cemetery was not sold.

"I will go to Washington and personally defend it. . . . If I do not then there is no cemetery in this land safe from sale, at the will of the government." —Lyda Burton Conley

LYDIA MARIA CHILD (1802–1880) wrote the poem that begins "Over the river and through the woods." Although this endures as her most famous work, she became a celebrity after the publication of her first novel, *Hobomok: A Tale of Early Times*. *The Frugal Housewife* was another extremely popular book, filled with ingenious ideas for making do with little. Lydia became active in the abolitionist movement, and her 1833 book *Appeal in Favor of that Class of Americans Called Africans* was one of the first to call for emancipation. Her ideas were too radical for her times, though, and publishers rejected her subsequent book ideas.

LYDIA ESTES PINKHAM (1819–1883) was born the tenth of twelve children to Quaker parents. She married Isaac Pinkham at twenty-four, and soon the couple had six children. Business reversals created financial problems, but when neighbors offered to purchase the herbal medicine Lydia usually gave away, an empire was born. Lydia E. Pinkham's Vegetable Compound, advertised as "A medicine for women. Invented by a woman. Prepared by a woman," was touted as a cure for women's ailments. Lydia's image was used in advertising and merchandizing, and such items are now popular collectibles.

★ ★ ★ ★ ★ ★ ★ ★ **M** ★ ★ ★ ★ ★ ★ ★

MADELINE: from the Hebrew for woman from Magdala. The French variation, Madeleine, is also popular. Common nicknames include Lena (or Lina), Maddie (or Maddy), and Madge.

MADELINE CHEEK HUNTER (1916–1994) was an educator who developed a philosophy of teaching that gained widespread acceptance by the end of the twentieth century. Its predominant theme is that people respond better to positive reinforcement. Building children up rather than tearing them down, she believed, would help prevent problems later in life. Her ideas have stood the test of time, and Madeline was named one of the one hundred most influential women of the twentieth century and one of the ten most influential in the field of education by the Sierra Research Institute and the National Women's Hall of Fame.

MAE: from the English for the fifth month, and from the Roman goddess of the earth, Maia.

MAE WEST (1893–1980) was as famous for her racy sense of humor and double entendres as she was for her curvaceous figure. She started acting in vaudeville at age six, and by the time she was fourteen she was known as the Baby Vamp. She wrote, produced, directed, and starred in the Broadway show *Sex*, for which she was arrested for obscenity, but went on to star in other Broadway shows and in movies. Her first starring role was in *She Done Him Wrong*, which broke box-office records; a string of hits followed. Despite her bawdy, tough-broad image, Mae neither smoked nor drank, and her witty quips were often directed at herself.

"Too much of a good thing is wonderful." —Mae West

MAGGIE: a familiar form of Margaret, from the Greek for pearl.

MAGGIE LENA WALKER (1867–1934) was the first woman in America to charter a bank. Born in Richmond to former slaves, Maggie helped her mother to support the family after her father died. As a teenager she joined the Independent Order of St. Luke, an organization that does community service, and eventually became its leader. In 1902 she founded a newspaper, the *St. Luke Herald*, and the following year established the St. Luke Penny Savings Bank. Later she merged her bank with two other local banks; the Consolidated Bank and Trust Company is the oldest continually run African-American-operated bank in the country.

"I was not born with a silver spoon in my mouth, but with a laundry basket practically on my head." —Maggie Lena Walker

---

MAHALIA: from the Hebrew for tender one.

MAHALIA JACKSON (1911–1972) began singing as a child and was known as the little girl with the big voice. Born in New Orleans, she moved to Chicago at sixteen and joined a gospel quintet. At one point she considered singing secular music; around this time her grandfather had a stroke. Mahalia prayed that if her grandfather recovered she would only sing gospel. He recovered, and she went on to become "the Gospel Queen." Her signature song, "Move On Up a Little Higher," sold 100,000 copies overnight, and soon she was selling out Carnegie Hall. She sang for presidents Dwight D. Eisenhower and John F. Kennedy, and before Martin Luther King, Jr., gave his "I Have a Dream" speech at the March on Washington, Mahalia sang "I Been 'Buked and I Been Scorned." Several of her recordings are available on CD.

MAMIE: a familiar form of Margaret or Mary.

MAMIE GENEVA DOUD EISENHOWER (1896–1979) was married to President Dwight D. "Ike" Eisenhower, who was a career military officer; at one point, Mamie guessed the family had moved nearly thirty times in thirty-seven years. By the end of World War II Ike was a national hero; he ran for president in 1952, and although Mamie considered herself a homebody, she was active in helping her husband campaign. As First Lady, she worked to reclaim authentic presidential antiques and memorabilia for the White House.

MARGARET: from the Greek for pearl. Margarita is the Spanish spelling; Marguerite is French, and Margherita is Italian. Greta, Gretchen, Madge, Maggie, Meg, Peg, and Rita are variations or nicknames.

MARGARET BOURKE-WHITE (1904–1971) was one of the original staff photographers at both *Fortune* and *Life*, and she photographed several major advertising campaigns. During the height of the Depression she earned more than $35,000 a year, but while on assignment in the plains she saw firsthand the suffering and economic trials most Americans were facing and decided to use her art to inform the public. *You Have Seen Their Faces*, on which she collaborated with her husband, the writer Erskine Caldwell, chronicled the social conditions in the South. During World War II she covered the war in Europe and was with General Patton when his troops liberated Buchenwald; her photographs captured the horrors of the Holocaust.

"Work is something you can count on, a trusted, lifelong friend who never deserts you." —Margaret Bourke-White

---

MARGARET MEAD (1901–1978) changed the way people view indigenous cultures—as valid civilizations with different customs rather than as "savages." The daughter of a professor at the Wharton School and a sociologist, Margaret attended Barnard College, where she met the famous anthropologist Franz Boas. She studied with him at Columbia University, then set off to spend a year in Samoa. The product of her research, *Coming of Age in Samoa*, caused a sensation. Though she later traveled to New Guinea and Bali to do field research, and worked as a curator at the American Museum of Natural History, her focus was on how culture affects people. After her death she was awarded the Presidential Medal of Freedom.

MARGARET MITCHELL (1900–1949) wrote but one book in her life, and it happens to be the most popular novel ever. As a child in Atlanta, Margaret grew up hearing stories of the Civil War from relatives who had lived through it. Her first marriage lasted only two years; her second husband encouraged her to write a novel. It took her ten years to complete *Gone With the Wind*. An acquisitions editor found the manuscript compulsively readable, and the book was published in 1936. The following year, Margaret won the National Book Award and the Pulitzer Prize for fiction. By 1949 the book had sold 8 million copies; the movie version won ten Academy Awards, and for twenty years was the highest-grossing picture ever.

MARGARET LOUISE HIGGINS SANGER (1879–1966) changed the lives of generations of women. As a midwife, she saw the horrors of amateur abortions and infant mortality, as well as the desperation of women pregnant against their will and of parents with too many unwanted or unplanned children. Shocked that women could not find accurate information or effective means of preventing unwanted pregnancies, she coined the term "birth control" and set about providing it. She was indicted and arrested, and her birth control clinic (the nation's first) was raided—but Margaret believed that women had the right to control their bodies and, like men, were entitled to fulfilling sexual lives. Planned Parenthood grew out of Margaret Sanger's work.

MARGERY: a French variation on Marguerite; the English spelling is Marjorie. Maggie and Marge are common diminutives.

MARGERY WILLIAMS BIANCO (1881–1944) was born in London but moved to the United States as a child. Although she wrote novels for adults and more than thirty books for children, she is most famous for a book based on the toys she loved as a child: *The Velveteen Rabbit.*

---

*"Real isn't how you are made. . . . It's a thing that happens to you. When a child loves you for a long, long time, not just to play with, REALLY loves you, then you become real." —*Margery Williams, in *The Velveteen Rabbit*

MARGUERITE: the French form of Margaret, from the Greek for pearl. Marguerite is also the French word for daisy.

MARGUERITE HIGGINS (1920–1966) reported on the Korean War from the front lines. Born in Hong Kong, she moved to California at age three. In 1941 she graduated from the University of California at Berkeley, and began her journalism career writing for the *New York Herald Tribune.* Her first war reports were eyewitness accounts of the liberation of concentration camps. In Korea, she won the respect of soldiers and male reporters for enduring difficult and dangerous conditions, and she won the Pulitzer for international reportage. She later covered the civil war in the Congo, the Vietnam War, and everyday life in the Soviet Union. She was honored for her service as a war correspondent with burial in Arlington National Cemetery.

MARIA: from the Latin form of Mary, from the Hebrew for bitterness. The name is popular worldwide, but perhaps more common in Spain, Italy, and Germany than other forms of Mary are.

MARIA MITCHELL (1818–1889) founded the astronomy department at Vassar College. Her father was an amateur astronomer, and as a twelve-year-old she helped him record the time of an eclipse. By age seventeen she had started a school for girls to teach them the sciences, including mathematics. She spent her evenings in her father's observatory, and on October 1, 1847, sighted a comet using a telescope—the first person in America to do so. Thirteen years later she was invited by Matthew Vassar to become a professor at his newly formed school. In addition to receiving an honorary degree from Columbia University, Maria has a crater on the moon named for her.

MARIA TALLCHIEF (b. 1925) was born in Oklahoma of Irish, Scottish, and Indian ancestry, and was the first American to dance at the Paris Opera. She started taking dance lessons at age four, and by age twelve was studying with Madam Bronislava Nijinska, the sister of the famous dancer. She joined the Ballets Russes de Monte Carlo and married the choreographer George Balanchine. She became prima ballerina at the New York City Ballet, where she danced what is considered her greatest role: Firebird. After retiring from the New York City Ballet she moved to Chicago, where she was artistic director at the Chicago Lyric Opera Ballet and then founded the Chicago City Ballet.

MARIAN, MARIANNE: a combination of Mary and Ann(e); from the French (Marion is the English spelling).

MARIAN ANDERSON (1902–1993) had, in the words of the conductor Arturo Toscanini, "a voice heard but once in a century." This contralto was the first black singer to perform at the White House, Carnegie Hall, and the Metropolitan Opera in New York. In 1939 she was not allowed into Washington, D.C.'s, Constitution Hall, however, because of her race, so Eleanor Roosevelt invited her to sing at the Lincoln Memorial on the morning of Easter Sunday. Her audience numbered more than seventy-five thousand. After she retired from performing, she was a delegate to the United Nations, and later was awarded the Presidential Medal of Freedom and the Congressional Gold Medal of Honor.

MARIAN WRIGHT EDELMAN (b. 1939) was born in South Carolina; she attended Atlanta's Spelman College and Yale University's law school. She moved to Jackson, Mississippi, where she was the director of the local office of the NAACP's Legal Defense and Education Fund, and in 1968 she was the first black woman admitted to the Mississippi bar. By 1973 Marian had moved to Washington, D.C., and had founded the Children's Defense Fund, a lobby that works to obtain health care and government funding for educational programs for poor children. The author of several books, Marian has also won many honors and awards, including the Albert Schweitzer Humanitarian Prize, the MacArthur Foundation Fellowship, and the Presidential Medal of Freedom.

MARIANNE MOORE (1887–1972) was a poet whose best-known work was called "Poetry." In it, she describes her art form as "imaginary gardens with real toads in them." She graduated from Bryn Mawr College in 1909, and moved to Europe in the 1920s; there, she edited a literary journal and met such poets as Wallace Stevens, William Carlos Williams, T. S. Eliot, and Ezra Pound. In 1951, her *Collected Poems* earned her the Pulitzer Prize, the National Book Award, and the Bollingen Prize. A fan of boxing and baseball, Marianne threw out the first pitch of the 1968 season at Yankee Stadium.

MARIE: the French form of Mary, from the Hebrew for bitterness. Marie is often used as a middle name.

MARIE THERESE COINCOIN (1742–1816) was born a slave but went on to found a business empire. She and her owner fell in love and had ten children; he gave them their freedom and, when they parted, sixty-eight acres and an annuity. Marie went on to build a fortune in cattle and tobacco, and her house, Melrose Plantation, became an artists' colony.

MARITA: a familiar form of Mary, from the Hebrew for bitterness.

MARITA ODETTE BONNER (1899–1971) was a writer during the Harlem Renaissance. A graduate of Radcliffe College, Marita moved to Washington, D.C., to teach school; there, she became a regular at Georgia Douglas Johnson's salons. She began writing essays—her most famous is "On Being Young—A Woman—and Colored"—and short stories. She stopped writing in 1941, but in 1987 a collection of her work was published and has been rediscovered by a new generation of readers.

MARTHA: from the Aramaic for lady or mistress of the house. Marta and Marthe are less common spellings; Marty is the diminutive form.

MARTHA CANARY (1852–1903) is better known as Calamity Jane. As a child she learned to drive a team and snap thirty-foot bullwhips; as an adult she dressed in men's clothes and worked as a mule skinner, bullwhacker, and scout. She met Wild Bill Hickok in 1875 and rode into Deadwood, South Dakota, as part of his entourage. Calamity Jane was rumored to have had a daughter with Wild Bill, even though she married a

Californian named E. M. Burke. Flamboyant and unconventional, she began to earn fame and eventually joined expositions and traveling shows as a Western attraction. She returned to Deadwood for her final days and is buried next to Wild Bill.

"The law ain't given me a square deal—it never gives a woman a square deal, nohow." —Calamity Jane, when a judge awarded her worthless husband custody of their children

---

MARTHA GRAHAM (1894–1991) helped to popularize dance as an art form. She enrolled in Ruth St. Denis and Ted Shawn's Denishawn Studio in 1914, and after touring with Shawn's company began choreographing on her own. Unlike most choreographers, Martha first developed the movement, and then commissioned music to fit it. She established the Dance Repertory Theater in 1930, and later founded the Martha Graham School of Contemporary Dance.

"I wanted to begin not with characters or ideas but with movement . . . I did not want it to be beautiful or fluid. I wanted it to be fraught with inner meaning, with excitement and surge." —Martha Graham

---

MARTHA WAYLES SKELTON JEFFERSON (1748–1782) died before her husband was elected president. Her first husband died two years after they were married, and she and Thomas Jefferson married in 1772. They lived in Monticello, though the house remained unfinished during her life there. Martha gave birth to six children in ten years and died shortly after the youngest was born. Her grief-stricken husband threw himself back into politics; their daughter Patsy served as First Lady.

MARTHA DANDRIDGE CUSTIS WASHINGTON (1731–1802) was the country's first First Lady. A Southern belle, she camped with her husband at his winter quarters in upstate New York and other cold climes during the American Revolution, and they settled at his home, Mount Vernon, after the war. When George Washington became president in 1788 they moved to the temporary capitals in New York and Philadelphia. Their style of entertaining was formal (they wished the new government to be perceived as the equal of established European ones), but Martha's gracious hospitality was welcoming to all guests.

"I think I am more like a state prisoner than anything else, there is certain bounds set for me which I must not depart from. . . ." —Martha Washington, in a letter

---

MARY: from the Hebrew for bitterness.

MARY MCLEOD BETHUNE (1875–1955) was an educator, advisor to presidents, and civil rights advocate. The fifteenth of seventeen children born to former slaves, she started her first school in Daytona Beach, Florida. In 1923, the Daytona Literary and Industrial School for Training Negro Girls merged with the Cookman Institute to become Bethune-Cookman College; Mary served as its president until 1942. She was also the founder and president of the National Council of Negro Women, and served on the National Child Welfare Commission; presidents Calvin Coolidge and Herbert Hoover each appointed her to this post. In the Roosevelt administration she was a special advisor on minority affairs and was the National Youth Administration's director of African-American affairs.

MARY CASSATT (1845–1926) painted in the impressionist style; she is best known for a series of mother-and-child paintings. After studying at the Pennsylvania Academy of Fine Arts in Philadelphia, Mary traveled through Europe. She settled in Paris and began studying with Edgar Degas. Her first American exhibit was in 1879, and she is credited with introducing impressionism to the United States. Her paintings are part of the permanent collections of many museums.

MARY BAKER EDDY (1821–1910) founded the Christian Science Church. Her belief in the connection between religion and health is described in her book *Science and Health*, whose principles she based on her own life. She was a sickly child and an invalid, but in 1862 she met Dr. Phineas P. Quimby and began following his methods; by 1866 she was cured, and four years later she was teaching what she called Christian science, working with practitioners who effected the actual healing. In 1879 the Church of Christ, Scientist was chartered. It emphasizes the complex relationship among the mind, body, and spirit, as well as Mary's conviction that the will, intellect, faith, and psychology all play a role in healing.

MARY FIELDS (1832–1914) was known as Stagecoach Mary. Born a slave, she grew up an orphan and ended up in the frontier town of Cascade, Montana. Six feet tall and armed with a pair of six-shooters and a shotgun, Mary was reputed to have broken more noses than any other central Montanan. She began to drive a U.S. Mail coach in 1895—hence her nickname—and never missed a day in eight years' work.

MARY HARRIS JONES (1830–1930) is remembered today as Mother Jones. She moved from Ireland to the United States at age five, and as an adult taught school and worked as a dressmaker before marrying a member of the Iron Molders' Union. Tragedy struck when she was in her late thirties: her husband and children died in a yellow fever epidemic, and after she moved to Chicago she lost everything in the Great Chicago Fire. Mother Jones became a labor activist and helped to form both the Social Democratic Party and the Industrial Workers of the World. Arrested at the age of eighty-four while helping coal miners organize in West Virginia, she was convicted of conspiring to commit murder and was sentenced to twenty years in prison. She was freed by the governor, but was still working to help striking coal miners nine years later.

"I'm not a humanitarian. I'm a hell-raiser." —Mother Jones

MARY TODD LINCOLN (1818–1882) lived a life marked by tragedy. Her well-to-do family frowned on her marriage to the poor, debt-ridden Abraham Lincoln. Of their four children, one died before he was four, a second died in 1862, and a third in 1871. Although she had eagerly anticipated arriving at and living in the White House, her time there wasn't easy. Because she was a Southerner, Northerners suspected her of being a spy during the Civil War; fellow Southerners considered her a traitor. When her husband was fatally shot, he was holding her hand.

". . . Look at him: Doesn't he look as if he would make a magnificent President?" —Mary Todd Lincoln, speaking somewhat facetiously about her husband

MARY LYON (1797–1849) founded the first women's college in the United States. She opened a girls' secondary school in 1824, and watched and participated in establishing several other schools, including Wheaton College. Mary was determined to enable women to receive the type and quality of education previously available only to men. Her college, the Mount Holyoke Female Seminary, opened in 1837 with eighty students.

"Do what nobody else wants to do; go where nobody else wants to go." —Mary Lyon

MARY PICKFORD (1892–1979) was America's Sweetheart; she won fame as an actress by playing lovable young girls and ingénues. A savvy businesswoman, she was one of the first in Hollywood to control her career, and she founded a production company called United Artists with Charlie Chaplin, D. W. Griffith, and Douglas Fairbanks, whom she married in 1920. She became the first millionaire actress, and she worked to win insurance coverage and retirement benefits for actors and actresses.

MARY EDWARDS WALKER (1832–1919) was the first and only woman to receive the Medal of Honor. She became a doctor in 1853, and after the Civil War broke out she sought a commission to serve as a surgeon in the United States Army. Her request was refused, so she volunteered her services as a nurse. In 1864 she was appointed assistant army surgeon and given a lieutenant's rank—the first woman to hold such a distinction. She was captured and held in Richmond, Virginia, for four months before she was released.

"Let the generations know that women in uniform also guaranteed their freedom." —Dr. Mary Edwards Walker

---

MATHILDA: from the German for mighty in battle. Also spelled Mathilde, Matilda. Common nicknames include Mat or Mattie, Tilda, Tildie, and Tilly.

MATHILDA TAYLOR BEASLEY (1832–1903) was born a slave in New Orleans, but little else is known of her life until 1859. By then, she was running a clandestine school for black children in Savannah—in the days before the Civil War, this was a criminal offense punishable by fine and whipping. She later worked in a restaurant and married the owner; when he died, she went to England and became a nun. She returned to Savannah and donated her husband's estate to the Sacred Heart Catholic Church to set up an orphanage, and in 1889 she founded the first order for black nuns in Georgia, the Third Order of St. Francis.

MAUD: a French variation on Mathilda, from the German for mighty in battle. Sometimes spelled Maude.

MAUD CAROLINE SLYE (1879–1954) was called America's Marie Curie for her single-minded devotion to and passion for scientific research. She studied at the University of Chicago and at Brown University, and in 1908 received a grant to do postgraduate research. Her chosen field was the hereditary nature of disease, particularly with cancers. She became the director of the University of Chicago's cancer laboratory in 1919 and a professor in 1922. She made many important discoveries, but two were that cancer was not contagious—a popular belief at the time—and that its causes were far more complicated than the presence of one gene.

MAUREEN: an Irish variation on Mary, from the Hebrew for bitterness.

MAUREEN CONNOLLY (1934–1969), known as Little Mo, stood only five feet three but was one of the greatest tennis players in history. By the time she was ten she knew she wanted to play tennis; she'd won fifty championships by age fifteen and was ranked tenth among women singles players. In 1953 she won the Grand Slam—the U.S. Nationals, Wimbledon, the Australian Championship, and the French Open. She was given a horse in recognition for this feat; two years later, the horse spooked and she was thrown, shattering her leg. Maureen announced her retirement from her beloved sport before she turned twenty-one.

MAY: English for the fifth month, from the Roman goddess of the earth, Maia.

MAY SARTON (1912–1995) was born in Belgium but came to America when she was two; her family settled in Cambridge, Massachusetts. When May was ten she joined the Unitarian Church. A sermon with the message "Go to the inner chamber of your soul—and shut the door" went on to inform her writing. May penned more than fifty books, and is best known for her contemplations on solitude. Her memoirs and poems have touched a chord in generations of readers; most of her books are still in print.

"One must believe that private dilemmas are, if deeply examined, universal, and so, if expressed, have a human value beyond the private. . . . I am willing to give myself away and take the consequences, whatever they are."
—May Sarton, in *Journal of a Solitude*

MILDRED: from the Old English for gentle strength. Often shortened to Millie or Milly.

MILDRED AUGUSTINE BENSON (1905–2002) is known to millions of readers as Carolyn Keene, the author of more than 130 books, including the Nancy Drew mysteries. Millie sold her first story when she was fourteen, and while earning a master's degree in journalism from the

University of Iowa she supported herself writing stories and articles. One story was submitted to a syndicate and became her first series; Nancy Drew was her second. Besides writing many of the books in the series, Millie worked as a reporter and columnist for two Ohio newspapers; when she died at age ninety-six, she was still writing a monthly column. The typewriter she used for the Nancy Drew books is part of the Smithsonian's collection.

MILDRED "BABE" DIDRIKSON ZAHARIAS (1914–1956) was arguably the best woman athlete of all time: she won three medals in the 1932 Olympics and held American, Olympic, or world records in five track-and-field events. Adored by the media, she refused to conform to standards of ladylike behavior and dress, and played baseball, basketball, tennis, and billiards, as well as dived and boxed. She took up golf and played well enough to qualify for the Los Angeles Open. When asked if there was anything she didn't play, she answered, "Yeah, dolls." The Babe Didrikson Zaharias Memorial Museum is in Beaumont, Texas.

MIRIAM: from the Hebrew, perhaps a variation on Mary. Other spellings include Miryam, Meriam, and Mariam. Nicknames include Mimi and Mitzi.

SISTER MIRIAM THERESA (1886–1962) was named Caroline Gleason at birth. As an adult, she conducted a study for the Oregon Consumer's League that has come to affect every laborer in the United States. Her research consisted of thousands of interviews, as well as working in a factory herself under grueling and horrible conditions, earning fifty-two cents for a ten-hour day. When the results of her study were made public, Oregon passed the Wage-Hour Act, the first such law to protect women and children; the Fair Labor Standards Act was based on the Oregon law. Sister Miriam taught social sciences at Oregon's Maryl-hurst College, urging her students to work to improve society through service, volunteering, and good works.

MOINA: from the Irish for noble. Mona and Myrna are variants.

MOINA BELL MICHAEL (1869–1944) started the tradition of wearing red poppies in memory of soldiers who died in service to their countries. She was in Europe when World War I broke out; the idea for the Flanders Fields Memorial Poppy came to her two days before the armistice was declared. She was reading a poem by Dr. John McCrae called "In Flanders Fields" and was struck by the lines "To you from failing hands we throw the Torch; be yours to hold it high. If ye break faith with us who die, we shall not sleep, though poppies grow in Flanders Fields." She vowed to "keep the faith," and her persistence and a poem entitled "We Shall Keep the Faith" saw her idea spread to more than fifty countries. The poppies are made by disabled veterans, and the proceeds go to them and their dependents. By the time Moina died, her cause had raised more than $200 million.

MOLLIE, MOLLY: Irish; a familiar form of Mary.

"THE UNSINKABLE" MOLLY BROWN (1867–1932) was born Margaret Tobin. A survivor of the *Titanic*, she grew up in Missouri and went to Leadville, Colorado, in her late teens. Her husband invented a way to mine gold more efficiently and the two became rich. Molly went to the Carnegie Institute to study language and literature, and had been traveling in Egypt before she sailed home on the *Titanic*. Her heroic rescue efforts earned her the French Legion of Honor medal, and she later gave financial assistance to other survivors who had lost everything. Molly was not allowed to testify before Congress about the sinking because of her gender, so she wrote a newspaper account of the events.

MOLLY PITCHER (1753–1832) was a heroine of the Revolutionary War. Named Mary Ludwig at birth, she married William Hays, and, when he enlisted in the artillery, she joined him at Valley Forge. She earned her nickname carrying water to exhausted and thirsty soldiers at the Battle of Monmouth. Molly Pitcher also tended wounded soldiers, and even acted as a gunner in the face of heavy fire. General George Washington issued her a warrant as a noncommissioned officer, and in 1822 the state of Pennsylvania awarded her a pension for her service.

MURIEL: from the Irish for sparkling, shining sea.

MURIEL SIEBERT (b. 1932) is the first woman to own a seat on the New York Stock Exchange. A college dropout, Muriel was hired as a trainee research analyst by a Wall Street firm in the 1950s, and in 1967 she started her own company, which did research for other institutions. Ten years later she was superintendent of banks for the state of New York; during her tenure, no New York banks failed. In 1990 she created the Siebert Philanthropic Program, which shares half of her company's profits from new securities with charities chosen by the securities' issuers.

★ ★ ★ ★ ★ ★ ★ ★ N ★ ★ ★ ★ ★ ★ ★ ★

NANCY: a variation on Ann, from the Hebrew for gracious. Alternate forms include Nan and Nanette.

NANCY ASTOR (1879–1964), called Nannie, was the daughter of a railroad tycoon in Danville, Virginia. She moved to England, where she married Waldorf Astor. He was a member of the House of Commons; when he inherited a title, he had to resign. Nancy ran for his seat and won, becoming the first woman to sit in the British Parliament. She was a supporter of Winston Churchill and a passionate advocate for women's rights and temperance.

NANCY BATSON CREWS (1920–2001) was a World War II pilot. She learned to fly through the Civilian Pilot Training Program in Alabama, received her private and commercial licenses in 1940, and became an instructor in 1942. That same year, she was one of only twenty-eight women admitted to the Women's Auxiliary Ferrying Squadron. After the war she continued to fly, teach flying, and compete in air shows. She flew her last flight shortly after her eightieth birthday.

NANCY ELIZABETH PROPHET (1890–1960) was born in Providence, Rhode Island. The only mixed-race student at the Rhode Island School of Design (she was part black, part Narragansett Indian), Nancy paid her tuition by working as a domestic. Her talent as a sculptor caught the attention of Gertrude Vanderbilt Whitney, who provided funds for Nancy to study in Paris. She became known for her life-size marble sculptures. In 1932 she returned to the United States and taught for a time at Spelman College in Atlanta. Unhappy in the South, she returned to Rhode Island, and was largely forgotten at the time of her death.

NANCY DAVIS REAGAN (b. 1921) was an actress long before she became First Lady of California and the United States. Born in New York City and reared in Chicago, Nancy graduated from Smith College before beginning her acting career. She appeared in eleven movies, but she quit after marrying Ronald Reagan so she "could be the wife I wanted to be," and her devotion to her husband is legendary. While First Lady, she concentrated her charitable efforts on the fight against drug and alcohol use among young people, and on promoting the arts.

NANCY WARD (1738–1822) was one of the most powerful women in the Cherokee Nation. Her Indian name, Nanye-Hi, means one who goes about, and in later life she earned honorific names. Admired and revered by settlers as well as Cherokee, Nancy was known for her courage. Her husband was killed in battle by the Creeks; she rallied the forces to a decisive victory and earned the name Beloved Woman for her valor. She ruled over the Council of Women and had a voting seat in the Council of Chiefs, and she helped to negotiate the Treaty of Hopewell.

NATALIE: from the Latin for birthday; it often refers to the birth of Christ. Alternate forms include Nathalie (French) and Natalia (Italian); nicknames include Nat, Nettie, Tallie, Talia, and Tasha.

NATALIE CURTIS BURLIN (1875–1921) made preserving Native American and African music her life's work. Born in New York City, Natalie was a pianist who studied in Berlin, Paris, Bonn, and Bayreuth. While visiting Arizona in 1900, she was so struck by the music that she gave up her career as a concert pianist. Armed with a phonograph—or simply a pencil and paper—she went from village to village, recording the songs and poetry of the Zuni, Hopi, and other tribes of the Southwest. She appealed to President Roosevelt to repeal a ban on the performance of Native American music and won. By 1911, she was also working to preserve music of African-American culture. She was a founder of the Music School Settlement for Colored People in New York City, and she was the author of a four-volume book entitled *Hampton Series Negro Folk-Songs*.

NELLIE: it may be a familiar form of Cornelia, Eleanor, or Helena. Variations include Nell, Nella, and Nelly.

NELLIE BLY (1864–1922) was born Elizabeth Jane Cochrane Seaman. The most famous American journalist of the nineteenth century, Nellie made a name for herself with her exposé of the horrific conditions at an insane asylum in New York; she feigned insanity and was committed for ten days to get the inside story. Other subjects she reported on were equally controversial for a "lady" of her time: divorce, slums, and factory conditions. Capitalizing on the popularity of Jules Verne's book *Around the World in 80 Days*, Nellie set off on a trip to travel the globe in less time—and she did, in seventy-two days. Her reports from her trek made her a household name, and she became the inspiration for a board game, doll, and trading card. She retired from journalism when she married, but was in Europe when World War I erupted, and came out of retirement to cover the war from the eastern front.

NELLIE CASHMAN (1845?–1925) was called the Angel of Tombstone and the Angel of the Cassiars. Feisty and fearless, Nellie lived the life of a miner in towns and settlements from Arizona to the Klondike. She ran boardinghouses and restaurants, built churches and hospitals, and risked her life on several rescue missions. One of her most famous missions: traveling for seventy-seven days through a bitter winter with six men and pack animals laden with supplies to rescue one hundred desperately ill miners.

NELLIE TAYLOE ROSS (1876–1977) never set out to be in politics, but she was the first American woman to become a governor. Nominated to replace her husband (who died suddenly), she won the race and served as governor of Wyoming for two years, working for legislation to protect miners as well as women and children. She lost her bid for reelection but was named vice chairman of the Democratic National Committee, then campaigned for Franklin D. Roosevelt. After his inauguration he appointed her director of the United States Mint.

NETTIE: it may be a familiar form of Annette, Antoinette, Henrietta, Nanette, and Natalie.

NETTIE MARIA STEVENS (1861–1912) was a brilliant student who didn't pursue her passion for the sciences until she was in her thirties. A native of Vermont, she went to Stanford University at age thirty-five and earned a master's degree in biology, then received a Ph.D. from Bryn Mawr. Nettie went on to work with the Nobel Prize winner Thomas Hunt Morgan at the Carnegie Institute, studying sex determination in insects and worms. She found that the X and Y chromosomes were responsible for gender—and announced her findings—before Edmund Wilson did, though he received most of the credit.

NORA: a feminine form of Norman; also an alternate form of Eleanor and Lenore.

NORA FONTAINE MAURY (1836–1929) was the principal of a girls' school; in 1864, she took her students to decorate the graves of Confederate soldiers who died in the battle of Petersburg, Virginia. The wife of General John Logan saw the graves, decorated with flowers and flags, and told her husband. He issued an order for the graves of all soldiers who died for their country to be so honored—and thus was born National Decoration Day, which is now called Memorial Day.

NORMA: from the Latin for standard, norm. (Norma is not the feminine of Norman, which means man from the north.)

NORMA TALMADGE (1893–1957) was a silent movie star who became one of the richest women in Hollywood. She started acting in 1910, and by 1916 she had married and then formed a film corporation with her husband. She made fifty-one films, but only two of them were talkies; her most famous movies are *Camille* and *Woman Disputed*. Her footsteps were the first to be immortalized at Mann's Chinese Theater in Hollywood.

★ ★ ★ ★ ★ ★ ★ ★ O ★ ★ ★ ★ ★ ★ ★ ★

OLIVE: from the Latin for olive tree. Olivia, Olivette, and Olivine are alternate forms; Liv is a common nickname.

OLIVE HIGGINS PROUTY (1882–1974) dreamed of becoming a writer. After she graduated from Smith College, she returned home, and although she feared that marriage would be the end of her dream, she began to be courted by Lewis Prouty. He encouraged her to take writing courses and introduced her to an editor. The two married, and by 1920 Olive had published four books. To protect her husband's image as the breadwinner, she described her writing as a hobby. In 1923 disaster struck: her one-year-old daughter died of encephalitis; two years later she suffered a nervous breakdown. After her daughter's death, as part of her therapy, she continued to write; *Stella Dallas*, *Conflict*, and *Now, Voyager* are three of her books that draw upon these events.

OLIVE RUSH (1873–1966) was an artist and illustrator best known for her renderings of women and children. Born to Quaker parents in Fairmont, Indiana, Olive studied at the Corcoran School of Art and the Art Students League in New York. Her work appeared in such magazines as *St. Nicholas* and *Woman's Home Companion*. She later studied in Wilmington, Delaware, with Howard Pyle, and then in England, France, and at the Boston Museum School. When she moved to Santa Fe in 1920, her home became a mecca for artists.

OLIVE RYTHER (1849–1934) was called Ollie; later she was known as Mother Ryther. Ollie devoted her life to caring for orphans. She and her husband settled in Seattle, and she found her calling when she promised a dying neighbor that she would adopt the woman's four children. At the time there was no orphanage in Seattle, so she established one. Ollie vowed that she would never turn an orphan away. One story tells of her marching into a shoe store with twenty-five children; she announced to the proprietor: "These children are staying here until you fit them all with shoes—that will be your contribution to the Ryther Home." In 1954, the Ryther Child Center moved to a ten-acre campus in north Seattle; its focus today is caring for moderately to severely disturbed children.

OLYMPIA: from the Greek for Mount Olympus.

OLYMPIA BROWN (1835–1926) was the first woman in the United States to be a fully ordained minister. She attended Mount Holyoke and Antioch Colleges, then decided to go to theological school. Because the school didn't admit women, she went to the Universalist Divinity School at St. Lawrence University; her first parish was in Weymouth Landing, Massachusetts. Olympia worked with Susan B. Anthony and Lucy Stone, and her church gave her a leave of absence to campaign for the vote in Kansas. When she was fifty-three she devoted herself to fighting for women's rights, and she often used militant tactics. When the Nineteenth Amendment finally passed, Olympia was one of the few original suffragists still alive to savor the victory, and she cast her first vote in a presidential election when she was eighty-five years old.

OSA: from the Norwegian for fate; also from the Spanish for bear.

OSA JOHNSON (1894–1953) and her husband, Martin, went to places most people only dream about. As writers, photographers, explorers, and naturalists, Osa and her husband traveled to Kenya, the Congo, the Solomon Islands, New Hebrides, and British North Borneo, and brought back information about cultures and wildlife. Their research has become an important source of ethnological and zoological material; the films they created document tribal cultures and a wilderness that have long since ceased to exist.

OVETA: from a Native American word for forget. Oveta became popular in the South in the late 1800s, and may have come from a novel.

OVETA CULP HOBBY (1905–1995) was the first director of the Women's Army Auxiliary Corps (WACs), the first woman to be awarded the Distinguished Service Medal, and the first woman to serve as the secretary of health, education, and welfare in a presidential cabinet. Her political career began as a parliamentarian in the Texas House of Representatives. She then worked as a reporter for the *Houston Post*— and married the paper's president—and eventually took over the paper and a radio station in Houston. World War II saw her back in government working with the WACs, and in 1953 she joined President Eisenhower's cabinet, where she fought for national health care and for widespread distribution of Jonas Salk's polio vaccine. She returned to her media empire when she left the political arena.

PAMELA: British, from the Greek for honey. Samuel Richardson's 1740 novel *Pamela: or, Virtue Rewarded* popularized the name. The most common nickname is Pam.

PAMELA DIGBY HARRIMAN (1920–1997) led an extraordinary life. Born in England, she made her debut before King George VI and married Randolph Churchill, the son of the prime minister, two weeks after they met. The marriage soon fell apart, but Pamela worked with Sir Winston throughout World War II to foster Anglo-American relations. She later married the Hollywood producer Leland Hayward, and after his death married the diplomat and statesman Averell Harriman, whom she had met during the war years. Through Averell, Pamela became active in the Democratic Party, raising funds and helping such candidates as Bill Clinton win elections. In the 1990s she was appointed United States ambassador to France.

PATIENCE: an Early American name for one of the Christian virtues.

PATIENCE LOVELL WRIGHT (1725–1786) was one of the first professional sculptors in Colonial America. The daughter of a strict Quaker who made his seven children dress in white, Patience grew up to love color. Using wax as her medium, she began to sculpt portraits of people and created a traveling exhibit. Most of her pieces were destroyed in a fire, but one of William Pitt survives in Westminster Abbey.

PATRICIA: the feminine form of Patrick, from the Latin for noble or patrician. Familiar forms include Pat, Patty, Patsy, Trish, and Tricia.

PAT RYAN NIXON (1912–1993) was christened Thelma Catherine, but because she was born the day before St. Patrick's Day, her Irish father nicknamed her Pat. While acting in a play with a theater group in California, Pat fell in love with another actor, a lawyer named Richard Nixon. The two married in 1940, and in 1950 Richard was elected a senator; two years later he became vice president under Dwight D. Eisenhower. Nixon was elected president in 1968. Pat was the first First

Lady to promote volunteerism; literacy and the "Right to Read" program were her passions, and she worked to establish recreation areas in and around cities for those who were unable to travel to national parks.

PATSY CLINE (1932–1963), a beloved country singer with fan clubs still active more than forty years after her death, was born Virginia Patterson Hensley in Virginia. Gifted with an unforgettable voice, she started entertaining neighbors when she was only three. Dressed in her trademark attire of cowgirl skirt and boots, she was a regular at the Grand Ole Opry. Her biggest hits include "Walkin' After Midnight," "Crazy," "I Fall to Pieces," and "Sweet Dreams." Patsy died in a plane crash at age thirty. A postage stamp was issued in her honor in 1993, and in 1995 she was posthumously awarded a Grammy Lifetime Achievement Award.

PATSY TAKEMOTO MINK (1927–2002), the first woman of Asian descent in Congress, served twelve terms and wrote the Women's Educational Equity Act. Born in Hawaii, Patsy wanted to become a doctor, but the schools she wanted didn't accept women. Instead she attended the University of Chicago's law school as a "foreign" student, and was elected to Hawaii's House of Representatives in 1956. Nine years later she was elected to the U.S. House of Representatives. Throughout her career she introduced legislation that would improve the welfare of women and children, and her impact was so profound that Norman Mineta called her "An American hero . . . who made an irreplaceable mark in the fabric of our country."

PATTY SMITH HILL (1868–1946) was a pioneer in introducing kindergarten to the United States. One of six children, Patty and her siblings were encouraged to think independently and play creatively. As an adult, Patty was the principal of the Louisville Kindergarten Training School, and when the kindergarten movement swept America, Patty incorporated some of the ideas espoused by its founder, Friedrich Fröbel. She also studied with Luther Gulick, a proponent of the playground movement in the United States, and became a founding member of the International Kindergarten Union. Her ideas of free play, creativity, and social living were embraced by the Horace Mann School at Teachers College, part of Columbia University. But perhaps the thing Patty Hill is best remembered for is that she and her sister Mildred composed the song "Happy Birthday to You."

PAULINA, PAULINE: the feminine form of Paul, from the Latin for small. Other forms include Paula and Paulette; nicknames include Polly.

PAULINA KELLOGG WRIGHT DAVIS (1813–1876) was orphaned at age seven and reared by a cruel aunt, and grew up to be a great suffragist, abolitionist, and feminist. Her first marriage was to Francis Wright, a wealthy merchant; after she was widowed, Paulina lectured to women about their anatomy and physiology using a human model—an extremely controversial thing to do at the time. Paulina created a petition to support the New York Married Woman's Property Rights Bill, and during her second marriage, to Congressman Thomas Davis, she used her money to publish the suffrage journal *Una*, one of the first devoted to women's rights. Paulina supported Susan B. Anthony and Elizabeth Cady Stanton, and in 1868 she cofounded the New England Woman Suffrage Association and the Rhode Island Woman Suffrage Association.

PAULINE FREDERICK (1883–1938) was regarded as one of the greatest actresses to grace films. From the time she was a child she wanted to be in show business, and she started making a name for herself on Broadway before starring in films in her thirties. She specialized in playing commanding, authoritative women—her greatest role was in *Madame X*—and her best-remembered roles were as sacrificing mothers, angry matriarchs, and women having a last fling at youth and romance. Pauline was a stunning beauty, and her looks didn't fade as she aged.

PEARL: from the Latin for the jewel. The Greek variation, Margaret, has historically been more popular, but Pearl became common in the Victorian era.

PEARL S. BUCK (1892–1973) won the Nobel Prize in Literature and the Pulitzer Prize for her book *The Good Earth*, which sold 1.8 million copies in its first year. She was born in China, where her parents were missionaries; with the exception of her time at Randolph-Macon Women's College and Cornell University, she lived there until 1934. Pearl was a crusader for women's rights; as a young woman she worked at a shelter for Chinese slave girls and prostitutes. She began to write when she was in her twenties and published eighty works, including novels, plays, short stories, poems, children's books, and biographies. *The Child Who Never Grew* was about her mentally challenged daughter.

PEGGY: a familiar form of Margaret, from the Greek for pearl.

PEGGY GUGGENHEIM (1898–1979) used her considerable wealth and connections to support twentieth-century artists and writers. She became part of the bohemian art community while working in an avant-garde bookstore, and moved to Paris in 1920, where she became friendly with James Joyce, Ernest Hemingway, Man Ray, Constantin Brancusi, and Marcel Duchamp. After her marriage to the sculptor Lawrence Vail she opened a gallery featuring the abstract and surrealist art that she collected, including works by Pablo Picasso, Joan Miró, Rene Magritte, Man Ray, Salvador Dali, Paul Klee, Marc Chagall, and Max Ernst, whom she married after her divorce from Vail. After World War II, Peggy moved to Venice, where the Peggy Guggenheim Collection became the most important gallery of American art in Europe.

PEGGY WARNE (1751–1840) was one of the most skilled doctors in the colonies. Known as Aunt Peggy, she cared for her own nine children as well as the newborns of Washington, New Jersey, while all the male doctors tended the troops fighting the Revolutionary War. Her specialty was obstetrics, and she practiced medicine until her death. The stone building where she stored her herbs and medicines still stands in the village of Broadway, on New Jersey's Route 57.

PENELOPE: from the Greek for weaver, after the clever and loyal wife of Odysseus. Nicknames include Nell and Penny.

PENELOPE BARKER (1728–1796) was a housewife from North Carolina who decided she wanted to do something for the American cause in the months before the Revolution. Despite her husband's disapproval, Penelope invited more than fifty women to a "tea party," where she encouraged each lady to take a pledge to "abstain from the pernicious custom of taking tea" and to boycott all British goods, especially cloth. More than forty women signed. By persisting with her plan, Penelope organized the first women's political movement in the United States.

PENINA: from the Hebrew for pearl.

PENINA MOÏSE (1797–1880) was a Jewish poet and hymnist whose legacy still endures today. She was born in Charleston, South Carolina, to a family that encouraged learning and literary efforts. The dramatist and editor Isaac Harby was Penina's intellectual and religious mentor, and encouraged her writing. For more than six decades, her stories, poems, and essays appeared in local newspapers from New Orleans to New York, as well as in such national publications as *Godey's Lady's Book*. Her hymns were collected into the first Jewish work of its kind, and are still used today in Reform congregations. Her last words were "Lay no flowers on my grave. They are for those who live in the sun, and I have always lived in the shadow."

PHOEBE: from the Greek for shining.

PHOEBE CARY (1824–1871) was a writer whose prolific career began at age fourteen, when her first poem was published in a Boston paper. Her poems attracted the attention of John Greenleaf Whittier, Edgar Allan Poe, Horace Greeley, and Rufus W. Griswold, who included poems by Phoebe and her sister Alice in his 1849 collection *The Female Poets of America*. Phoebe and Alice bought a house on East Twentieth Street in Manhattan, and for more than fifteen years hosted salons every Sunday. They were passionate abolitionists and supported women's rights—Phoebe was an assistant editor at Susan B. Anthony's newspaper *Revolution*. Her hymn, "Nearer Home," was often sung at funerals, including her own.

PHOEBE WILSON COUZINS (1839?–1913) was the first female U.S. marshal. From her father, who was a U.S. marshal in Missouri, and her mother, a pacifist who cared for injured soldiers on the battlefields of Wilson Creek, Shiloh, and Vicksburg (and was herself wounded at Vicksburg), Phoebe learned of commitment. With her mother she organized the Western Sanitary Commission, which cared for thousands of wounded during the Civil War. During this time she became an avowed pacifist and proponent of women's rights. She graduated from St. Louis Law School at Washington University and was the first woman to practice law in Arkansas, Utah, Kansas, and Dakota Territory. President Chester A. Arthur considered her for a position on the Utah Territory Commission, but Grover Cleveland appointed her a U.S. marshal, a position she took over from her father.

PHOEBE FAIRGRAVE OMLIE (1902–1975) was the first woman to receive a federal pilot's license and the first aircraft mechanic license. The day before she graduated from high school, Phoebe saw her first air show. She fell in love with aviation, and later with her flight instructor, whom she married. She and Vernon Omlie flew mercy missions during forest fires and floods, and were the first to demonstrate that planes had value outside of the military. Phoebe did the stunt flying in the *Perils of Pauline* movies, and was Franklin Delano Roosevelt's pilot during his 1932 presidential campaign.

PHILLIS, PHYLLIS: from the Greek for leafy bough.

PHILLIS WHEATLEY (1753?–1784), the first black American woman to become a writer, was born in Gambia but was captured as a small child and sold to John and Susanna Wheatley of Boston in 1761; her first name came from the ship that carried her to the United States. Phillis's first poem, "On Messrs. Hussey and Coffin," was published when she was twelve, but her elegy of George Whitefield, a popular Methodist minister, brought her instant success. Phillis's elegiac style of writing may have been influenced by the tradition of oration used by women in her African tribe. Phillis was freed on October 18, 1773. That same year she traveled to England, where she met the Countess of Huntingdon, who financed Phillis's book *Poems on Various Subjects, Religious and Moral*.

POLLY: a familiar form of Paula or Pauline.

POLLY BEMIS (1853–1933) became the most famous Chinese-American pioneer in the Old West. She was born in China, sold by her father to bandits, and shipped to the United States, where she was again sold, this time as a concubine. Her life took a turn for the better when Charles Bemis fell in love with her and won her freedom; they married in 1894, after Idaho changed its law against marriages of mixed race. The Bemises moved to the Salmon River, where Charles staked a mining claim and Polly became a successful entrepreneur with the creation of a ranch named Polly's Place. Her story was made famous by RuthAnne Lum McConn's biographical novel *Thousand Pieces of Gold*.

POLLY SLOCUMB (1760–1836) was a legend of the American Revolution. Born Mary Hooks, Polly married a young soldier named Ezekiel Slocumb when they were both eighteen. One night, the story goes, she dreamed Ezekiel had been wounded in battle. In her dream she saw a body wrapped in her husband's cloak, covered in blood, and surrounded by other dead and wounded. She got out of bed and rode to the battlefield sixty miles away, arriving at daybreak. There, she saw the wounded just as in her dream. She spent the day tending the injured soldiers, and in the afternoon she heard her husband's voice—he was bloody and mud-soaked, but alive. Polly's daring ride and bravery was an inspiration to the troops.

PRISCILLA: from the Latin for venerable; it is common among Quakers and Puritans.

PRISCILLA ALDEN (1604–1680) was born in Surrey, England, and sailed to America on the *Mayflower*. Her parents and younger brother died during the first, brutal winter at Plymouth. Priscilla and her courtship with Miles Standish were immortalized by Henry Wadsworth Longfellow, who based his account on a story found in a book by one of her descendants. Supposedly Miles Standish sent John Alden to ask Priscilla for her hand in marriage, and Priscilla replied, "Why don't you speak for yourself, John?" Whatever happened, Priscilla married John Alden in 1623 and had eleven children; she is the only woman of Plymouth Colony who is remembered by name.

PRUDENCE: from the English for thoughtful or sensible; it is common among Quakers and Puritans.

PRUDENCE CRANDALL (1803–1890) was an educator and abolitionist who went to jail for enrolling black girls in her school. Born to a Quaker family in Rhode Island and reared in Connecticut, Prudence ran the Canterbury Female Boarding School. When Sarah Harris, the daughter of a free black farmer, applied for admission to the school so she could teach other blacks, she was accepted. Townspeople were outraged and pressured Prudence to rescind Sarah's acceptance. Instead, she made her school into a school for black girls: the white students were dismissed, and a few months later twenty African-American girls had been admitted. The Connecticut legislature immediately passed a law prohibiting such a school; Prudence was arrested, but the case was dismissed.

RACHEL: from the Hebrew for sheep.

RACHEL LOUISE CARSON (1907–1964) could be called the mother of the modern environmental movement. A biologist who raised the alarm about the use of pesticides in America with her landmark book *Silent Spring*, Rachel worked for the United States Bureau of Fisheries. She supplemented her income first by writing articles that appeared in the *Baltimore Sun*, and later won fame as a naturalist and science writer with three books about the ocean. *Silent Spring*, published in 1962, warned of dire threats to humanity, wildlife, and nature from the use of chemical pesticides and herbicides. Rachel's testimony before Congress led the United States to ban DDT. Sadly, Rachel died at age fifty-one of cancer, perhaps the result of exposure to toxic substances.

"The 'control of nature' is a phrase conceived in arrogance, born of the Neanderthal age of biology and philosophy, when it was supposed that Nature exists for the convenience of man." —Rachel Carson, in *Silent Spring*

RACHEL DONELSON JACKSON (1797–1828), the wife of America's seventh president, was an unpretentious and unfailingly kind woman whose first husband was obsessively jealous. She left him and believed herself to be divorced when she met and married Andrew Jackson in 1791. To their dismay, the couple discovered that her divorce had not been finalized, and they were remarried in 1793. Rachel supported her husband as he won fame fighting Indians and after he was elected governor of Florida, but she was reluctant to move into the White House after he was elected president. She suffered a fatal heart attack as she was preparing to move.

REBECCA: from the Hebrew for bind. Sometimes spelled Rebekah; common nicknames include Reba, Becky, and Becca.

REBECCA LATIMER FELTON (1835–1930) was the first woman to become a United States senator. She taught school after graduating first in her class from Madison Female College, but when she married Dr. William Felton, a congressman, she became his secretary. Rebecca began writing a column for the *Atlanta Journal* in 1899 and wrote two books; she also prevailed upon the University of Georgia to admit women. When Rebecca was eighty-seven, the governor of Georgia appointed her to fill a vacancy when the incumbent U.S. senator from Georgia died, but it was mainly symbolic because the appointment came while the Senate was in recess. She was senator for only a day, but her appointment acknowledged her decades of advocacy and activism.

"Mr. President, the women of this country are going to come and sit here. There may not be very many the next few years, but in time they will come. When they do I pledge that this body will get ability, integrity and unstinted usefulness." —Rebecca Felton, minutes after being sworn in as the first woman U.S. senator

---

REBECCA COX JACKSON (1795–1871) was a religious visionary and the founder of a religious commune in Philadelphia. Born to free black parents, Rebecca had a religious epiphany during a thunderstorm in 1830. Illiterate before, she found she could read the Bible afterward. She was guided only by her inner voice, and aroused controversy by preaching that celibacy was necessary for holiness. She joined the Shaker community in Watervliet, New York, and lived there for four years, but left to form an "outfamily" of predominantly black women. The writer Alice Walker called Rebecca's spiritual autobiography "an extraordinary document."

REBECCA PENNOCK LUKENS (1794–1854) learned the iron business from her father; as an adult, she owned a steel mill on the banks of the Brandywine River that is still in operation. Rebecca married a doctor, who gave up his practice to join what was then his father-in-law's business. In 1818, the Lukenses' steel mill became the first to roll iron boilerplate. After her husband died, Rebecca ran the business on her own. She pulled the company out of debt and solicited orders from railways to build locomotives, increasing her company's profits and creating a thriving industry.

REBECCA BREWTON MOTTE (1738–1815) lived in Charleston, South Carolina. Her home was commandeered by the British during the American Revolution, and after her husband's death she and her daughters were allowed to move to her plantation in Calhoun County. In 1781, the same British commanders took over, exiling Rebecca and her children to a nearby farmhouse. Two American patriots told Rebecca the only way to expel the British from "Fort Motte" would be to burn the house, so this spunky widow offered bow and arrows to accomplish the task.

RHETA, RITA: short forms of Margherita or Margarita, from the Greek for pearl.

RHETA CHILD DORR (1866–1948) was christened Reta but added the *h* later because she liked it. This influential suffragist and born rebel became a feminist after seeing a tombstone that read "Also Harriet, wife of the above." She became a muckraking journalist whose first book, *What Eight Million Women Want*, sold more than 500,000 copies. She went to Russia to observe the revolution, but when she tried to leave the country her notes were confiscated. Her book *Inside the Russian Revolution* was written from memory. During World War I, Rheta became a war correspondent. Her son was stationed in France and she tried to get a press pass, but the French government refused to grant her press credentials. Ever resourceful, she became a lecturer with the YMCA and went to France that way; her book *A Soldier's Mother in France* came out in 1918.

RITA HAYWORTH (1918–1987) was born Margarita Carmen Cansino in Brooklyn, New York, to a Spanish father and Irish-American mother. A dancer so talented that Fred Astaire called her his favorite partner, Rita began dancing professionally with her father when she was twelve and landed her first film role at sixteen. Shy and retiring in person, she projected sensuality and charisma on-screen—so much, in fact, that Hollywood publicists dubbed her the "love goddess." Her first big movie was *The Strawberry Blonde* in 1941; in *You'll Never Get Rich* she danced her way to stardom with Fred Astaire, and in *Gilda* she was at the top of her career. In later life Rita developed Alzheimer's disease and was cared for by her daughter Yasmin.

RHODA: from the Greek island of Rhodes, which was named for its roses.

RHODA SMITH FARRAND (1747–1839) was a patriot who was immortalized in a poem. In 1777, her husband was stationed at Jockey Hollow in Morris County, New Jersey; he wrote his wife about his fellow soldiers: "a sorry sight. . . . No socks or shoes. By dropping blood you can trace their tracks." Rhoda started knitting, and she persuaded women from neighboring farms and settlements to knit, too. Stockings flooded into the New Jersey camp "in a perfect shower," and Rhoda's great-granddaughter, Eleanor A. Hunter, wrote "An Ode to Rhoda" so none would forget.

RHONDA: from the Greek island of Rhodes, which was named for its roses.

RHONDA FLEMING (b. 1923) starred in more than forty movies, but her most spectacular role has been offscreen as a philanthropist. She is a founding member of Stop Cancer with Dr. Armand Hammer and a member of the advisory board of Olive Crest Treatment Centers for Abused Children. In addition, she created the Rhonda Fleming Mann Research Fellowship to research treatments for women's cancers, and established the Rhonda Fleming Clinic for Women's Comprehensive Care at the UCLA Medical Center. While she was on the board of P.A.T.H. (People Assisting the Homeless) she set up the Rhonda Fleming Family Center, a shelter for homeless women and children.

ROBERTA: the feminine form of Robert, from the Old English and Old German for shining with fame. Nicknames include Bobbie, Berta, and Robin.

ROBERTA CAMPBELL LAWSON (1878–1940) was born in Oklahoma, the great-granddaughter of the first Delaware Indian to convert to Christianity. Roberta's lawyer husband started a bank and acquired holdings in oil fields, and Roberta used her money to improve the lives of local women. She organized the town of Nowata's first women's club, as well as a park and public library. When the family moved to Tulsa she helped to start the Oklahoma College for Women. The collection of books, paintings, and Indian artifacts that she and her husband acquired can be seen at the Philbrook Museum of Art in Tulsa.

ROSA: from the Latin for rose. Rosa may also be short for Rosamond, Rosalie, Rosalind, or even Rosanne.

ROSA PARKS (1913–2005) was working as a seamstress in Montgomery, Alabama, when she entered the history books. In 1955, she was riding a bus home from work and refused the bus driver's order to give her seat to a white man. She had long been active in the civil rights movement, but her refusal and subsequent arrest prompted the Montgomery Bus Boycott, which set off a chain reaction of protests against segregation and unfair treatment. Called the mother of the American civil rights movement, Rosa at the end of her life received many awards, including the Presidential Medal of Freedom and the Congressional Gold Medal; *Time* magazine called her one of the twenty most influential people of the twentieth century. Rosa was the first woman and the first American who was not an elected official to lie in state in the U.S. Capitol Rotunda.

"My resisting being mistreated on the bus did not begin with that particular arrest. . . . I did a lot of walking in Montgomery." —Rosa Parks

---

ROSALYNN: from the Spanish for fair rose.

ROSALYNN SMITH CARTER (b. 1927), like her husband, Jimmy Carter, has devoted her life to humanitarian efforts and public service. She was an important member of his campaign team during the 1962 election, when Jimmy won a seat in the Georgia senate, and her efforts helped him win the election for governor of that state eight years later. Rosalynn traveled throughout the United States, independently of her husband, during his presidential campaigns. Once he was elected to the Oval Office she attended cabinet meetings and served as an emissary to Latin America. A supporter of the arts, she also served on the President's Commission for Mental Health, and later became vice chair of the Carter Center in Atlanta, focusing on mental illness and mental health care. She also has joined her husband in Habitat for Humanity.

ROSE: from the English for the flower. Rose may also be used as a diminutive for Roseanne, Rosemary, Rosalie, Rosamond, and Rosalind.

ROSE PHILIPPINE DUCHESNE (1769–1852), the founder of the Society of the Sacred Heart, was born in Grenoble, France, and became a nun against the wishes of her father. In 1818 she fulfilled a childhood dream of going to America to work as a missionary in "the faraway land of the Indians." She and four companions took seventy days to cross the Atlantic, then another forty days to travel up the Missouri River to St. Charles. She opened a convent for the daughters of Louisiana planters as well as an orphanage and a parish school, and later she was allowed to open a mission for the Pottawatomie Indians in Kansas. She was canonized as St. Philippine Duchesne by Pope John Paul II; her feast day is November 18.

ROSE O'NEAL GREENHOW (1815–1864) was called Wild Rose as a child, and she grew up to be one of the most famous spies in the Civil War. Operating a spy ring from her home in Washington, D.C., Rose sent General P. G. T. Beauregard a secret message that helped him to win the Battle of Bull Run (First Manassas), and was credited by Jefferson Davis as being instrumental to the Confederate army's victory. She was caught by the detective Allan Pinkerton, but during her imprisonment still managed to get messages to the Confederates. After her parole, Davis sent Rose to Europe to plead the Confederacy's cause, and in 1864 she returned home on a British blockade-runner called the *Condor*. The ship ran aground near Wilmington, North Carolina, and although Rose escaped in a rowboat, it capsized as well and she drowned. Rose was buried with full military honors.

ROSE HUM LEE (1904–1964), a renowned sociologist, was the first Asian-American woman to chair a department at an American university. The daughter of Chinese immigrants, Rose was born in Butte, Montana, and overcame discrimination. She put herself through college and earned her doctorate at the University of Chicago, then specialized in the experience of Chinese immigrants in the United States. She became the chair of Roosevelt University's sociology department in 1956.

ROSE SCHNEIDERMAN (1882–1972) was a labor organizer and social reformer. Born in Poland to an Orthodox Jewish family, Rose emigrated to New York when she was eight years old and settled with her family on New York's Lower East Side. After her father died, Rose dropped out of school to work as a sales clerk and then, despite her mother's objections, quit for a more dangerous—and more remunerative—job in the garment industry. By 1903 she had organized her first union shop, the Jewish Socialist United Cloth Hat and Cap Makers' Union, and by 1907 was devoting most of her energies to the Women's Trade Union League. In the aftermath of the Triangle Shirtwaist fire, Rose helped to found the International Ladies Garment Workers Union and led its 1913 strike, and later in life became the secretary of the New York State Department of Labor.

"I would be a traitor to those poor burned bodies if I came here to talk good fellowship. . . . Every year thousands of us are maimed. The life of men and women is so cheap and property is so sacred." —Rose Schneiderman, speaking to workers after the Triangle Shirtwaist fire

---

RUBY: from the English for red gemstone.

RUBY PICKENS TARTT (1880–1974) was a folklorist who collected African-American folk songs, field calls, and other forms of folklore. During her childhood in rural Alabama, she had been fascinated by the stories and songs of blacks and became a lifelong student of their culture and their contributions to American culture. She published a book of folklore entitled *Toting the Lead Row*, and she helped Carl Carmer to write his *Stars Fell on Alabama*. She also assisted others: Ruby first gained recognition through the help she provided to John Allan Lomax and Harold Courlander, and later she received royalties for recordings based on her findings by the Kingston Trio and Harry Belafonte. Ruby worked as a librarian in Sumter County, Alabama, from 1940 to 1964, at a time when blacks were not allowed to enter. Nevertheless, she made sure that black children had access to books, and she often kept her library open after hours for black adults.

RUTH: from the Hebrew for friend or companion.

RUTH FULTON BENEDICT (1887–1948) was one of the premier anthropologists of the twentieth century. Her childhood was unhappy—her father died when she was a toddler, she suffered hearing loss brought on by measles, and she was emotionally scarred by her mother's "cult of grief." Ruth married in 1914 and in 1919 began to study anthropology at Columbia University with Franz Boas; she received her Ph.D. in 1923. She went on to write several books, including *Patterns of Culture*, *Race: Science and Politics*, and *The Chrysanthemum and the Sword: Patterns of Japanese Culture*. She became a full professor of anthropology at Columbia in 1948.

RUTH BADER GINSBURG (b. 1933) was named Joan Ruth at birth. She received her bachelor's degree at Cornell and studied at Harvard Law School before transferring to Columbia Law School; she made law review at both schools and graduated with the highest grades in the Columbia Law School's history. Despite her stellar record, she had trouble finding work because of her gender. After clerking for a judge of the U.S. District Court in New York, she eventually became a professor of law, wrote a law book on gender equality law, and was the chief litigator for the American Civil Liberties Union. She was appointed to the U.S. Court of Appeals in 1980, and in 1993 she became the second female associate justice on the United States Supreme Court.

RUTH ST. DENIS (1877–1968), one of the founders of modern dance, was born Ruth Dennis in Newark, New Jersey. She started dancing at age ten and, after seeing an advertisement for Egyptian Deities cigarettes, decided to create a dance with an Egyptian theme. While researching Egyptian dances she discovered the dances of India, and from 1906 to 1909 she toured Europe with her Oriental dances, focusing more on the expressive movement than the steps. She and her husband and dancing partner, Ted Shawn, established the first serious dance school in America, and later she formed the Church of the Divine Dance, where she conducted dance rituals.

SADIE: a familiar form of Sarah, from the Hebrew for princess.

SADIE KNELLER MILLER (1867–1920) was a pioneer in the field of photojournalism. She began writing for a local paper in Westminster, Maryland, then moved to Baltimore in the late 1800s and became the first woman in the country to report about baseball. Using the byline SKM to disguise her gender, she covered the Orioles, and she eventually learned to use a camera, becoming one of the first female journalists to photograph her stories. She didn't just cover sports, though: among her scoops were photographs of the Baltimore fire of 1904, famous portraits of Teddy Roosevelt and Susan B. Anthony, as well as the Taft inauguration and, most notably, the sinking of the *Maine* in 1912. Sadie was the only female war correspondent of her time.

SADIE CREEK ORCHARD (1860–1943) liked to say she was from London, but she was an Iowa girl. She moved to a mining town in New Mexico in 1885, ultimately settling in Kingston. She ran a brothel there, but she soon left "the business" and operated a stagecoach line and a hotel with her husband. Sadie herself drove four and six horses every day over primitive roads, braving bandits and Apaches. When she discovered her husband was running bootleg whiskey she sent him packing—after filling him with buckshot. Sadie also raised fifteen hundred dollars to build the first church in Kingston, and adopted a blind, mentally retarded boy. During a flu epidemic she closed her hotel to tend the sick and took in orphans, then cut up her silk gowns to line the coffins of children.

"I'm a product of the 'Old West' and you know in those days we didn't have much chance to practice the refinements and niceties of high society."
—Sadie Creek Orchard

SALLY: a familiar form of Sarah, from the Hebrew for princess.

SALLY LOUISA TOMPKINS (1833–1916) was the only woman to be commissioned an officer in the Confederate army. Born into a wealthy family in Mathews County, Virginia, Sally opened a private hospital when the Confederate army asked the public to help care for its soldiers wounded in the First Battle of Bull Run. At the time, however, all hospitals were required to be run by military personnel. To skirt the rule, President Jefferson Davis appointed Sally a captain in the cavalry on September 9, 1861. Funded with Sally's inheritance, the hospital treated more than thirteen hundred soldiers in forty-five months of operation. Sally continued to do charity work after the war, and her generosity eventually exhausted her fortune. Four chapters of the United Daughters of the Confederacy are named in Sally's honor.

SALLY SAYWARD BARRELL KEATING WOOD (1759–1854), known as Madam Wood after her second marriage, was the eldest of eleven children and grew up in York, Maine, in her grandfather's mansion. Her first husband died in 1783, leaving her with three young children. Sally remained a widow for twenty-one years, finally marrying a man named Abiel Wood when she was forty-five. She began to write Gothic novels as a widow; her best-known book is *Tales of the Night*.

SANDRA: a shortened form of Alexandra, from the Greek for defender of mankind; the Italian is Alessandra. Sandra may also be short for Cassandra. Sandy is the most common diminutive.

SANDRA DAY O'CONNOR (b. 1930) was born in El Paso, and was educated at Stanford University, finishing law school in two years and graduating near the top of her class. After graduation she was offered a job as a legal secretary, so she turned to public service and worked in various capacities, eventually becoming assistant attorney general of Arizona. In 1981, Sandra became the first woman to serve on the United States Supreme Court following her nomination as associate justice by President Ronald Reagan. In 2004, she was called the fourth most powerful woman in the United States and the sixth most powerful woman in the world by *Forbes* magazine. She announced her retirement in 2005.

SARA, SARAH: from the Hebrew for princess.

SARAH FRANKLIN BACHE (1743–1808) was the daughter of Benjamin Franklin and a patriot in her own right. The mother of eight children, Sarah organized Philadelphia women to raise funds to support the Revolutionary army. General George Washington asked that the money be used for clothing, and the women decided to make the shirts for the army themselves to make the money go further. Much of the work was done in Sarah's home, and on December 26, 1780, she delivered more than two thousand handmade linen shirts to the army. Sarah's portrait, painted by John Hoppner, hangs in the Metropolitan Museum of Art in New York City.

SARAH BREEDLOVE (1867–1919), better known as Madame C. J. Walker, was born on a cotton plantation in Delta, Louisiana, and was orphaned by age seven. Married at age fourteen and widowed two years later, Sarah needed to support her daughter but was barely making a living doing laundry, so she started selling hair-care products. In July 1905, with $1.50 to her name, she moved to Colorado, and five months later married a newspaper sales agent named C. J. Walker. He became her business partner, and she began to advertise her hair products, selling them door-to-door and by mail order. As her fortune grew, so did her philanthropy: Sarah gave money to the Tuskegee Institute, Bethune-Cookman College, and many other institutions and organizations. When she died at fifty-one she was the first black female millionaire in America.

"I got myself a start by giving myself a start." —Madame C. J. Walker

---

SARAH EMMA EDMONDS (1841–1898), also known as Frank Thompson, spent two years as a Civil War soldier disguised as a man (as many as four hundred women did so, for both sides). Born in New Brunswick, Canada, Sarah ran away as a teenager to escape her abusive father. She dressed as a boy, renamed herself Franklin Thompson, and sold Bibles to make a living. Sarah enlisted in Flint, Michigan, and joined the infantry. She fought in battles at Blackburn's Ford and the First Battle of Bull Run, and she volunteered to spy behind Confederate lines, once "disguised" as a woman. Sarah deserted in 1863, perhaps to avoid having her gender discovered, and became a nurse. Her true identity was revealed in 1882 when she applied for a veteran's pension.

SARAH GRIMKÉ (1792–1873) was the daughter of a South Carolina judge whose abolitionist spirit was awakened when, at the age of four, she saw a slave whipped on the family plantation. In 1819, she moved to Philadelphia and joined the Quakers, and with her sister Angelina became one of the first women to lecture on behalf of the Anti-Slavery Society. Sarah wrote many pamphlets, including *Letters on the Equality of the Sexes and the Condition of Women*. These pamphlets were burned in public by officials in her home state, and she was warned if she ever returned she would face arrest. After the Civil War, Sarah turned her efforts to supporting women's rights.

"I ask no favors for my sex. . . . All I ask of our brethren is that they will take their feet from our necks." —Sarah Grimké, in Letters on the Equality of the Sexes and the Condition of Women

SARAH JOSEPHA HALE (1788–1879) edited the most influential women's magazine in the United States for nearly fifty years. She started writing for local newspapers as a young married woman, and when her husband died, leaving her with five children to support, she turned to writing as a career. Sarah became the editor of a new magazine called the *Ladies Magazine*, and when Louis A. Godey bought the publication and changed its name to *Godey's Lady's Book*, Sarah remained the editor, making the magazine the premier tastemaker for American women, before retiring at age ninety. Among her other claims to fame: Sarah wrote the poem "Mary Had a Little Lamb," which was first published in her book *Poems for Our Children* in 1830.

SARAH ORNE JEWETT (1849–1909) was a Maine native whose home state featured prominently in her writing. Because she suffered from arthritis, Sarah did not attend school on a regular basis; instead, her education came from accompanying her obstetrician father on his rounds and studying in their home library. It was with her father—talking with him and his patients, touring the countryside of Maine—that she found the basis of her fiction. She published her first story when she was nineteen, and the following year published one in the *Atlantic Monthly*. At the suggestion of William Dean Howells she pulled her stories and sketches into a novel. Her best work, *The Country of the Pointed Firs*, was published in 1896; the realistic depiction of the end of the era of the clipper ship, the abandoned shipyards and wharves, and the people left behind was widely regarded as a masterpiece.

SARAH KEMBLE KNIGHT (1666–1727) kept a diary, and her account of life in Colonial America is widely regarded as the most complete portrayal of that era. Sarah was a schoolteacher, a shopkeeper, and a recorder of public documents who left Boston in October of 1704 on a five-month, 271-mile journey for New York City via New Haven, Connecticut. Her witty observations of inns and rickety bridges, local color and speech patterns, and sardonic accounts of her hardships rendered in heroic verse were lost for more than one hundred years. Her diary was published in 1825 as a *Private Journal of a Journey from Boston to New York in the Year 1704* and has become a classic.

SARAH CHILDRESS POLK (1803–1891) was the wife of James K. Polk, the eleventh president. She was born into a wealthy family on the Tennessee frontier and was educated at the best girls' school in the South, but when her father died and his estate was squandered through mismanagement, her privileged life ended. She met her husband while he was a clerk in the state senate, and after their marriage she devoted her life to his career. As he rose through the state and national Congress, finally becoming Speaker of the House, James relied on Sarah: she advised him politically and helped to write his speeches. When she became First Lady, Sarah, a staunch Presbyterian, banned dancing in the White House and insisted that the Sabbath be observed.

SARAH WINNEMUCCA (1844–1891), known also as Tocmetone ("Shell Flower"), was a Paiute princess born into a family of great leaders (her grandfather led Captain John Frémont on one of his expeditions). Sarah acted as an army interpreter during the Bannock War of 1878, and traveled to Washington, D.C., in 1880 to have her people released from the Yakima Reservation. She wrote her autobiography in 1883, and founded a school for Native American children. The city of Winnemucca, Nevada, was named after her family.

SELMA: from the German for divine protector.

SELMA HORTENSE BURKE (1900–1995) was a black sculptor who immortalized some of America's greatest leaders, including Mary McLeod Bethune, Booker T. Washington, Martin Luther King, Jr., and Colonel William Hayward and the 369th Regiment. Her most famous commission was the profile of Franklin Delano Roosevelt that appears on the dime. Selma was born one of ten children in Mooresville, North Carolina. Although she always wanted to be an artist, she began her career as a nurse. After the stock market crash in 1929, she worked for "a charmingly crazy white woman"—a Cooper of Cooperstown, New York—who bequeathed to Selma a nest egg and some powerful acquaintances. Sarah went to New York City to study art at Columbia University. Her works are part of the collections of many art museums.

"I shaped my destiny early with the clay of North Carolina Rivers."
—Selma Hortense Burke

SELENA: from the Greek for moon.

SELENA SLOAN BUTLER (1872?–1964), the daughter of a white man and a woman who was of African and Indian heritage, devoted her life to fighting for racial harmony and education for all. Selena graduated from the Spelman Seminary in Atlanta at age sixteen and worked for a while as an English teacher. After she married a prominent black physician they moved to Boston, where he studied medicine at Harvard and she studied oratory at Emerson School. They returned to Atlanta, and, when their child approached school age, Selena looked for a school for him. She found none, so she started a kindergarten in her home, then established the first black Parent Teacher Association in the United States. Today she is considered a founder of the PTA movement.

SEPTIMA: from the Latin for seventh.

SEPTIMA POINSETTE CLARK (1898–1987) is known as the queen mother of the civil rights movement. Born in Charleston, South Carolina, Septima earned a teaching certificate, even though blacks were not allowed to teach in her home city. She moved to St. John's Island, where the dire poverty and dismal living conditions awakened the social reformer in her. She was fired from her teaching job in 1956 for refusing to renounce her membership in the NAACP, so she moved to Tennessee, where she became the Director of Workshops at the Highlander Folk School; one of her students was Rosa Parks. She later worked with Martin Luther King, Jr., and when Dr. King won the Nobel Peace Prize in 1965, he insisted that Septima accompany him, saying that she deserved as much credit for the achievements of the civil rights movement as he did. The same government that once fired her later bestowed upon her its highest civilian award, the Order of the Palmetto.

SHERWOOD: from the Old English for luminous wood; often a maiden name given to children as a middle name.

KATHERINE SHERWOOD BONNER (1849–1883) was born on a plantation in Mississippi and was known throughout her life by her middle name. A writer who rebelled against convention and the constraints of marriage, Sherwood sold her first story when she was fifteen. Her marriage to Edward McDowell failed after two years, and she left her daughter in the care of relatives and left for Boston. She became a protégée of Henry Wadsworth Longfellow, and her "Gran'mammy" tales were among the first to use black dialect. Sherwood died of breast cancer when she was only thirty-four.

SHIRLEY: from the Old English for bright meadow.

SHIRLEY ANITA ST. HILL CHISHOLM (1924–2005) was the first black woman to be elected to Congress. This Brooklyn native earned a master's degree from Columbia University and started as a nursery school teacher, but became active in politics soon after. She was elected to the New York assembly in 1964 and to the U.S. House of Representatives in 1969, where she served six terms. In 1972 she became the first African-American woman to make a serious bid for the presidency, and she was instrumental in changing the way many Americans perceived women and blacks. Throughout her career she was a passionate advocate for women, children, and minorities.

SOPHIA, SOPHIE: from the Greek for wisdom. Sophie is the French spelling; Sofia is common in Spain, Italy, and Scandinavian countries.

SOPHIA AMELIA PEABODY HAWTHORNE (1809–1871) was an artist and writer who, with her sisters, Elizabeth Palmer Peabody and Mary Tyler Peabody Mann, was a leader in education, the arts, and social reform. While her sisters opened a school for girls in Boston, Sophia focused her attentions on drawing and painting. In 1837 she met Nathaniel Hawthorne, and after a lengthy and secret engagement, they married in 1842. Sophia encouraged her husband's writing, acting as an editor on some of his work and illustrating some of his books.

SOPHIA SMITH (1796–1870) founded Smith College. She never married—in fact, after she went deaf at age forty, she was a recluse on her family's farm near Hatfield, Massachusetts. At age sixty-five, Sophia inherited her family's fortune. Reverend John Morton Greene, the pastor of the Hatfield Congregational Church, advised her to contribute the money to Amherst College or the Mount Holyoke Female Seminary (the schools were his and his wife's alma maters). Sophia rejected the suggestions and opted to start a women's college instead. With the help of Reverend Greene and two professors from Amherst, Smith College had a curriculum that was comparable to a men's college. Smith College was chartered in 1871 and opened in 1875; it has become one of America's premier institutions of higher learning.

SOPHIE TUCKER (1884–1966), "the Last of the Red-Hot Mamas," grew up in Connecticut. She played the piano while her sister performed, but her antics stole the show and she became an audience favorite. With a larger-than-life bosom and a personality to match, Sophie sang songs like "I Don't Want to Be Thin" and "Nobody Loves a Fat Girl, But Oh How a Fat Girl Can Love." She hired black singers to give her voice lessons and black composers to write songs for her act. She also helped to organize the American Federation of Actors, becoming the union's president in 1938. Sophie endowed a theater arts chair at

Brandeis University and started the Sophie Tucker Foundation. Her autobiography, *Some of These Days*, takes its name from her trademark song.

"I've been rich and I've been poor. Believe me, honey, rich is better."
—Sophie Tucker

SOPHONISBA: from the Greek or Hebrew for wise, sensible.

SOPHONISBA PRESTON BRECKINRIDGE (1866–1948) was born into a prominent family in Lexington, Kentucky, and made her father's words direct her life's work: "[Our] family name has been connected with good intellectual work for . . . over a century; you must preserve the connection for the next generation." Sophonisba became the first woman to pass the Kentucky bar exam, and in 1901 earned her doctorate in political science from the University of Chicago—making her the first woman to receive a Ph.D. from the school. Sophonisba lived at Hull House from 1907 to 1920 while she helped to create the Graduate School of Social Service Administration at the University of Chicago. She was among the first to insist that the government, not private charities, bore the ultimate responsibility for programs of social welfare.

SUSAN, SUSANNAH, SUZANNE, SUZETTE: from the Hebrew for lily. Susan is a short form of Susannah; it was first used in the eighteenth century. Suzanne and Suzette are French variations. Sue, Susie, Suzy, and Sukey are common nicknames.

SUSAN B[ROWNELL] ANTHONY (1820–1906) is perhaps the most famous suffragist and women's rights activist in American history. Brought up to believe in the equality of men and women, Susan was part of the abolitionist movement as well as the women's rights movement. After the Civil War, she formed the National Woman's Suffrage Association with Matilda Joslyn Gage and Elizabeth Cady Stanton, and organized a series of women's rights conventions. Susan was the target of ridicule, perhaps because men (and some women) sensed what a force she was. In the 1872 presidential election she was arrested and fined for casting a ballot; the judge directed the jury to find her guilty.

SUSAN LA FLESCHE PICOTTE (1865–1915) was born in Nebraska and was the first Native American woman to earn a medical degree; she graduated at the top of her class from the Women's Medical College of Pennsylvania in 1889. She returned to Nebraska as a government physician and rode from one reservation to another treating the sick; after she married she settled in Bancroft, Nebraska, and opened a practice where whites and Native Americans were her patients. Eventually she founded a hospital in the town of Walthill, Nebraska; the Susan La Flesche Picotte Center still stands there.

SUSANNAH SMITH ELLIOTT (1750?–?) was born in South Carolina and orphaned while very young. She married Barnard Elliott, a colonel in the Revolutionary army. After the Battle of Fort Moultrie on Sullivan's Island, she presented two flags to Colonel Moultrie's regiment; Susannah had embroidered the flags herself. At Elliott plantation she hid two American officers in a secret apartment while the British army searched the house. The British didn't find them, or the silver either—it had been buried in a nearby marsh and was dug up after the war—but a British soldier defaced Susannah's portrait by running a small sword through an eye.

SUSETTE LA FLESCHE TIBBLES (1854–1903), like her younger sister, Susan, was born on the Omaha Indian reservation. Educated at the Elizabeth Institute, a Presbyterian seminary for women in New Jersey, Susette accompanied Thomas Henry Tibbles on a lecture tour to publicize the wrongs committed against the Ponca Indians. Senator Henry Dawes was among those affected by the lectures, and he introduced legislation to grant citizenship rights to Native Americans (which passed as the Dawes Act). She married Tibbles and continued to lecture and to write and illustrate books. Known as Bright Eyes, Susette met Henry Wadsworth Longfellow, who compared her to Minnehaha, the heroine of his poem "Hiawatha."

SUZANNE FARRELL (b. 1945) has been called "simply the greatest dancer of our century . . . and the most important one who ever lived," and a "choreographer's ideal," and in fact she became the muse of the legendary choreographer George Balanchine. She was just fifteen when she first auditioned for him, and he was sufficiently impressed that Suzanne was awarded a full scholarship to the New York City Ballet's preparatory program. Within a year she joined the company, and at age nineteen she became the youngest principal dancer to perform a solo while a member of the corps de ballet. In a career that spanned almost thirty years, Suzanne performed seventy-five roles in seventy ballets, dancing her last performance at age forty-four.

SYBIL: from the Greek for prophetess or oracle. Sybil is an alternate spelling of Sibyl; other spellings include Cybele and Cybill. The Turkish spelling, Sibel, means powerful queen.

SYBIL LUDINGTON (1761–1839), like Paul Revere, made a daring ride to warn that the British were coming. The oldest of twelve children,

Sybil was babysitting her younger siblings when she heard that the British were burning Danbury, Connecticut, a town twenty-five miles away. Her father, a colonel in the local militia, needed to tell his men, and Sybil convinced him that she should ride to alert them to assemble. On the night of April 26, 1777, Sybil rode alone over forty miles—twice the distance of Paul Revere's ride—on dark, unmarked roads, spreading the alarm. The men helped to drive the British back to their ships in Long Island Sound.

SYLVIA: from the Latin for forest.

SYLVIA PLATH (1932–1963) was one of the most influential writers of the mid-twentieth century, capturing the angst and thoughts of a generation of women. A brilliant and talented poet, Sylvia went to Smith College; after graduation she won a Fulbright scholarship and earned another degree at Cambridge University, where she met Ted Hughes. Sylvia suffered from depression, and after her first suicide attempt was hospitalized; electroshock treatments were part of her therapy. Her first book of poems, *Colossus*, was published in 1960, but her novel *The Bell Jar* cemented her reputation. Increasingly plagued with depression, Sylvia suffered hallucinations, and killed herself by putting her head in the oven and turning on the gas. Her last book of poems, *Ariel*, was published after her death.

★ ★ ★ ★ ★ ★ ★ ★ **T** ★ ★ ★ ★ ★ ★ ★ ★

TABITHA: from the Aramaic for gazelle.

TABITHA MOFFAT BROWN (1780–1858) moved from Massachusetts to Oregon at age sixty-six, traveling in a wagon pulled by oxen. In the course of her nightmare journey, everything except her horse was stolen, killed, or lost, including her wagon and oxen. Nevertheless, she said that she did not once cry or lose faith that she would reach her destination. She arrived in Oregon with six cents to her name. She used the money to buy leather, with which she made gloves that she sold to support herself. The year after she arrived she opened a home and school for children who had been orphaned on the Oregon Trail, and became known as Grandma Brown. The children of local settlers attended her school, which was established as Tualatin Academy in 1848; it later became Pacific University.

TABITHA GILMAN TENNEY (1762–1837) was a best-selling author who demonstrated that American writers were every bit as capable as the British when it came to novels. Her first book was a selection of classic poetry marketed for young ladies, but her bombshell, *Female Quixotism: Exhibited in the Romantic Opinions and Extravagant Adventures of Dorcasina Sheldon*, was a wildly amusing romp about a woman's life and the limited choices available in a country where all *men* were created equal. She never published another book, but her reputation was established.

TALLULAH: from the Choctaw for leaping water.

TALLULAH BANKHEAD (1902–1968) came from one of Alabama's most political families—her father was the Speaker of the House, an uncle was a senator, and an aunt was the first woman to be director of a state agency—to be a major Hollywood star. Educated in several convents, Tallulah left her home state for New York after she won a photo contest in a magazine. An indomitable will, flamboyant antics, and outrageous wit combined with a deep voice won her attention and helped to redefine the popular notion of Southern womanhood. Tallulah was known as the ultimate professional, dedicated to fellow actors and her craft. She won the New York Drama Critics' Award for her role in *The Skin of Our Teeth* and the New York Screen Critics' Award for her role in Alfred Hitchcock's *Lifeboat*.

"If I had to live my life again, I'd make the same mistakes, only sooner."
—Tallulah Bankhead

TENLEY: English surname used as a first name.

TENLEY EMMA ALBRIGHT (b. 1935) was the first American woman to win the Women's World Figure Skating Championship and an Olympic gold medal. The daughter of a prominent Boston surgeon, she was born in Massachusetts and began skating at age eight, but when she was eleven she contracted polio. Bedridden and unable to walk, Tenley didn't give up. Four months after she began skating again she won the Eastern United States Junior Ladies Figure Skating competition, and by age thirteen she had won her first national title. In 1952 she won the silver medal at the Winter Olympics in Oslo. While preparing for the 1956 Olympics in Italy, she fell and her skate slashed through an artery to her ankle bone. Her father operated, and two weeks later she won the gold. She became a sports surgeon, and in 1988 was inducted into the U.S. Olympic Hall of Fame.

"If you don't fall down, you aren't trying hard enough." —Tenley Albright

THEA: from the Greek for goddess; sometimes a diminutive for Althea or Dorothea.

THEA FOSS (1857–1927) was the model for "Tugboat Annie." Based in Tacoma, Washington, she and her husband bought a used rowboat, which they fixed up and sold for a profit. They continued to buy and sell rowboats, keeping a few to rent to customers looking for recreational diversions. The business grew to include tugboats and powerboats used to deliver supplies and ferry customers, and eventually became the Foss Maritime Company. A World War II patrol boat was christened the *Thea Foss*, and her name was given to downtown Tacoma's Thea Foss Waterway.

THEODORA: the feminine form of Theodore, from the Greek for gift of God. Theo is a short form.

THEO ALICE RUGGLES KITSON (1876–1932) was one of the most prolific sculptors in America. She was born in Brookline, Massachusetts, and studied art in Paris and in New York with Henry Hudson Kitson, whom she married in 1893. In 1899 Theo won honorable mention for her bronze sculptures at the Salon des Artistes Français, and five years later she won a bronze medal at the World's Fair in St. Louis. Theo specialized in war memorials; the Vicksburg Civil War Memorial alone has nearly seventy of her bronzes. Her bronze *The Hiker* is in Waltham Town Common in Waltham, Massachusetts, and her sculpture of Thaddeus Kosciuszko is located in the Boston Public Gardens.

TILLY: a familiar form of Matilda, from the Old German for mighty in battle.

TILLY EDINGER (1897–1967) was a pioneer in the field of paleoneurology, a discipline that studies the brain through fossil remains. The daughter of a prominent scientist, Johanna Gabrielle Otellie Edinger was born in Frankfurt, Germany, and studied at several universities. She wrote her first book about fossil brains in 1929, and she pioneered the method of using plaster casts of the fossilized remains of skulls and cranial cavities. She fled Germany in 1939 and joined the Harvard Museum of Comparative Zoology. Her second book, *The Evolution of the Horse Brain*, was groundbreaking; in it, she asserted that evolution happened as a branching of species, not as a linear progression. In 1963 she was elected president of the Society of Vertebrate Paleontology.

TRIXIE: a familiar form of Beatrice, from the Latin for voyager, blessed.

TRIXIE FRIGANZA (1870–1955), who was born Delia O'Callahan in Grenola, Kansas, became a vaudeville legend and character actress. A favorite at New York's Palace Theatre, Trixie started out singing in the chorus, then devised an act that combined comedy and music. She made fun of her size—she once described herself as "a perfect 46." Her movie roles include *Gentlemen Prefer Blondes*, and she starred in *Free and Easy* with Buster Keaton.

★ ★ ★ ★ ★ ★ ★ ★ V ★ ★ ★ ★ ★ ★ ★ ★

VARINA: a variation on Barbara, from the Latin for foreign woman; may also be a place name, after the city in Virginia.

VARINA ANNE HOWELL DAVIS (1826–1905) was the wife of the president of the Confederacy, Jefferson Davis. Varina Anne grew up in Natchez, Mississippi. (The Briers, her home, is now a bed-and-breakfast.) Her parents opposed her marriage—her husband was eighteen years older than she—but she was a devoted wife. Varina wrote her husband's speeches, and when he was seized by the cavalry after fleeing Richmond, she sent their children to live with her mother and worked for two years to have Jefferson released from prison. After his release they lived in Canada, England, and Memphis, before a childhood friend bequeathed his Mississippi estate to them. When Jefferson died, Varina signed the estate over to the state of Mississippi as a veterans' home, and she moved to New York and wrote for the *Sunday World* until her death.

VERA: from the Latin for true.

VERA CHARLOTTE SCOTT CUSHMAN (1876–1946) was born into a very religious family. After graduating from Smith College, she joined with others to form a national Young Women's Christian Association (YWCA) and became one of the organization's leading fund-raisers. In 1913 she raised $4 million in just fourteen days, and during World War I, as the chair of the YWCA's War Work Council, she raised $170 million to finance 140 Hostess Houses in nine countries. (These provided safe lodging and recreation for nurses and women involved in war work.) Vera was one of six women to be awarded the Distinguished Service Medal in 1919.

VICTORIA: the feminine form of Victor, from the Latin for victory.

VICTORIA WOODHULL (1838–1927) was the first woman to run for president of the United States. One of nine children, she married a patent medicine salesman, who used her as a model for his "Elixir of Life." She divorced him and married twice more, and went from rags to riches twice in her life, too, first as a spiritualist and then as the first woman to work on Wall Street as a stockbroker. Victoria and her sister,

Tennessee Celeste Clafin, started a weekly newspaper that advocated short skirts for women, free love, and world government. The *Woodhull & Clafin Weekly* also published the *Communist Manifesto*, and in 1870 Victoria made history by declaring herself a candidate for president. Her views were too shocking even for Elizabeth Cady Stanton and Susan B. Anthony; they backed Horace Greeley instead.

VIDA: from the Spanish for life; also a feminine form of David, from the Hebrew for beloved.

VIDA DUTTON SCUDDER (1861–1954) was reared by a devoted mother and doting relatives after her father, a Congregationalist missionary, died shortly after her birth. She led a life of privilege, but decided to use her good fortune to serve others. She joined Helena Dudley to open the Denison Settlement House in Boston and taught at Wellesley College. Vida joined the Socialist Party in 1912, and her support of striking textile workers drew criticism of her and Wellesley, but the college defended her actions. Vida taught for nearly fifty years; after retiring from the classroom she became an expert on Franciscan and Christian ethics.

"Creation is a better means of self-expression than possession; it is through creating, not possessing, that life is revealed." —Vida D. Scudder

VIÑITA: from the Spanish for wine, vineyard.

VIÑITA REAM (1847–1914), called Vinnie, sculpted the statue of Abraham Lincoln in the U.S. Capitol Rotunda. She grew up in Washington, D.C., and showed remarkable talent for art. She studied with the sculptor Clark Mills, who had a studio in a wing of the Capitol, and soon was making busts of congressmen and notable visitors, including General George A. Custer. When she was only seventeen she was commissioned to do a bust of Lincoln. The president granted her daily sittings over the five months before he was assassinated. Vinnie transformed her clay model of the president into white Carrara marble, and the bust was unveiled in January 1871.

VIOLET: from the Latin for purple.

VIOLET OAKLEY (1874–1961) was born into a family of painters in Bergen Heights, New Jersey. She studied at the Art Students League in New York City, the Pennsylvania Academy of Fine Arts, and the Academie

Montparnasse in Paris. When Edwin Austin Abbey died in 1911, Violet assumed his commission for the murals in Pennsylvania's state capitol. These murals, which are in the governor's office, senate chamber, and state supreme court building, are among the largest ever created. Violet's other commissions include painting the first delegates of the League of Nations, and she illustrated several books.

VIRGINIA: from the Latin for maiden. Nicknames include Ginnie, Ginny, Ginger, Gigi, and Ginette.

VIRGINIA APGAR (1909–1974) created an observational method of assessing the health of newborns. She received her medical degree from Columbia University, specializing in anesthesiology. She became a professor of anesthesiology, and later became the first woman to chair the department at New York Columbia-Presbyterian Medical Center. While studying anesthesiology and childbirth, she realized that when newborns were transferred directly to the nursery, serious problems might not be noticed for several hours or even days. She devised the Apgar Score, which medical personnel use to evaluate a newborn's health; this simple test can be performed without medical equipment and has saved the lives of countless babies worldwide. Virginia earned a master's degree in public health at age forty-nine, and lectured on birth defects for the March of Dimes.

VIRGINIA DARE (1587–?) was the first white child born in North America. Her parents were part of Sir Walter Raleigh's expedition of settlers who left England in May 1587 and settled on what is now Roanoke Island, part of North Carolina's Outer Banks. Her grandfather, Governor John White, sailed back to England nine days after Virginia was born; when he returned three years later he found no trace of the settlers—only the word "croatoan" carved on a tree. Some historians believe that the survivors of this "Lost Colony" became members of the Croatan Indian tribe; others believe the colonists moved to another island.

VIRGINIA ESTELLE RANDOLPH (1874–1958), the daughter of former slaves, realized early on that she wanted an education to avoid the life of a domestic. She was an excellent student and received a teaching certificate at age sixteen; two years later she was hired by the Mountain Road School in Henrico County, Virginia. Determined to expand vocational education for black students, Virginia also saw the need for training more teachers, as well as for improved hygiene, health care, and nutrition among her students. She usually had a dozen or more of her students living in her home, and owned a bus to transport them all to school. The Virginia E. Randolph Museum is located in Glen Allen, a suburb of Richmond.

VIVIA: from the Latin for life.

VIVIA THOMAS (?–1870) and her story are a legend in Oklahoma, but she was a real woman. Born in Boston, she met and became engaged to a dashing army officer at a party after the Civil War. Shortly before their wedding he left her. Vivia discovered he was stationed at Fort Gibson in Indian Territory. She cut off her hair and dressed as a boy, then traveled to Fort Gibson and enlisted in the army. Her fiancé had begun an affair with an Indian woman. Enraged, Vivia killed him; everyone assumed he had been ambushed by Indians. After his death Vivia felt remorse and would go to his grave every night, weeping and praying for forgiveness. She collapsed on his grave one night and contracted pneumonia, confessing her crime just before she died. Because of her valor on the frontier she was buried in the Circle of Honor at Fort Gibson's cemetery; some say her ghost walks through the graveyard, weeping.

★ ★ ★ ★ ★ ★ ★ ★ ★ **W** ★ ★ ★ ★ ★ ★ ★ ★ ★

WANDA: from the German for wanderer.

WANDA GÀG (1893–1946) was a Newbery Award–winning author and illustrator of children's books. The oldest of seven children, Wanda had to support her family after her father died and her mother contracted tuberculosis; she drew and painted postcards, greeting cards, and valentines that she sold, and gave art lessons to children. She managed to finish school and saw to it that her siblings did as well, then won scholarships to art school, including the Art Students League in New York City. Her best-known book, *Millions of Cats*, was published in 1928; it won the Newbery Honor Book Award in 1929 and has sold more than a million copies.

WILLA: a feminine form of William or a short form of Wilhemina, from the German for resolute protector.

WILLA CATHER (1873–1947) was a great American writer known for her portrayals of life on the prairie. She grew up in Red Cloud, Nebraska, and attended the University of Nebraska, Lincoln before moving to New York City and joining the editorial staff of *McClure's Magazine*. Sarah Orne Jewett encouraged her to write about her home state. *O Pioneers!*, *My Ántonia*, *A Lost Lady*, and *Death Comes for the Archbishop* are her most famous novels. Willa won the Pulitzer Prize in 1923 for *One of Ours*.

WILMA: a feminine form of William or a short form of Wilhemina, from the German for resolute protector.

WILMA MANKILLER (b. 1945) was the first woman to become chief of a major Native American nation. Born in Tahlequah, Oklahoma, of Cherokee, Dutch, and Irish descent, Wilma grew up on Mankiller Flats, the farm granted to her grandfather as part of a settlement after his tribe had been forced to relocate. The farm failed and her family moved to California, but Wilma returned to reclaim Mankiller Flats in the mid-1970s. In 1983 she was elected deputy principal Cherokee chief, and when the principal chief became the head of the Bureau of Indian Affairs in 1985, Wilma assumed the title and responsibilities of principal. Among her legacies: she created the Institute for Cherokee Literacy, whose purpose is to retain Cherokee traditions.

WILMA GLODEAN RUDOLPH (1940–1994) was a track-and-field star and the first American woman to win three gold medals in one Olympics. The twentieth of twenty-two children, Wilma was born prematurely and was in frail health as a child. She suffered bouts of measles, mumps, scarlet fever, chicken pox, double pneumonia, and polio, the last of which left her left leg deformed; a doctor told her mother that Wilma would never walk. With her family helping her with physical therapy, Wilma proved the doctor wrong and was walking without a brace by the time she was twelve, and at age sixteen she won a bronze medal in the 1956 Olympics. Four years later she won gold in the 100-meter dash, 200-meter dash, and 400-meter relay. Her heroic story earned her a level of fame that helped to win women the respect in track-and-field events that had previously been the provenance of men.

WINIFRED: Welsh, from the Old English for holy, or joy and peace.

WINIFRED SWEET BLACK (1863–1936) was a journalist who wrote under the byline of Annie Laurie. Part of the era of sensational journalism made popular by Joseph Pulitzer, she went to work for William Randolph Hearst's *San Francisco Examiner* and complied with his instructions to write for "the gripman on the cable car." Winifred considered Hearst a mentor and friend, and while working with him she went undercover and pulled off daring stunts to get her scoops. By "fainting" on a street she was able to write an exposé of San Francisco's receiving hospital; and she hid under a table in President Benjamin Harrison's railcar to get an exclusive interview with him. Her biggest scoop came after Galveston, Texas's, devastating hurricane in 1900; Winifred disguised herself as a boy and crossed police lines. Ever fearless, she rushed to San Francisco after the 1906 earthquake when she received Hearst's telegram that read simply, "GO."

"The ideal newspaper woman has the keen zest for life of a child, the cool courage of a man and the subtlety of a woman." —Winifred Sweet Black

---

WINNIE: American; often a familiar form of Guinevere, Gwyneth, Winifred, or Winona.

WINNIE DAVIS (1864–1898) was born Varina Anne Davis while her father, Jefferson Davis, was president of the Confederate States of America. The youngest of six children, Winnie was dubbed "the

Daughter of the Confederacy," a name picked up for a philanthropic organization that did work with Confederate veterans and their families. Winnie became a symbol of the "lost cause," and was such a favorite among veterans that she reputedly broke off an engagement to a New Yorker because of a public outcry. She died of malarial gastritis and was buried with full military honors in Richmond, Virginia's, Hollywood Cemetery.

★ ★ ★ ★ ★ ★ ★ ★ Y ★ ★ ★ ★ ★ ★ ★ ★

YNÉS: a Spanish variation on Agnes, from the Greek for pure. Inez and Inès are alternate spellings.

YNÉS ENRIQUETTA JULIETTA MEXÍA (1870–1938) was born in Washington, D.C., and as an infant moved to Limestone, Texas, where her family owned an eleven-league grant that became the present-day town of Mexía. She enrolled at the University of California's Berkeley campus when she was fifty-two and began collecting plants. She accompanied the Stanford University botanist Roxanna Ferris on a collecting trip to Mexico; despite falling down a cliff, Ynés still managed to bring back five hundred plants. Over the next dozen years she organized expeditions to Mexico, Mount McKinley National Park in Alaska, and South America. She often traveled to the most inaccessible areas of Central and South America, and throughout her career collected roughly 145,000 specimens, including hundreds that were previously undiscovered. Her collections can be viewed at the Academy of Natural Sciences in Philadelphia.

★ ★ ★ ★ ★ ★ ★ ★ ★ **Z** ★ ★ ★ ★ ★ ★ ★ ★

ZELDA: a short form of Griselda, from the German for dark battle. The Yiddish name Zelde means happiness.

ZELDA SAYRE FITZGERALD (1900–1948) was a talented author, painter, and dancer in her own right, but she is best known as the wife of F. Scott Fitzgerald. The daughter of a supreme court justice in Alabama, Zelda was considered the prettiest and smartest girl in Montgomery when she met her husband. They married, and by the time their daughter Scottie was born, Zelda's stories were appearing in the *New Yorker* and other magazines. The Fitzgeralds moved to Paris, where Zelda began to study ballet and began to paint; her works were exhibited in New York in 1934. (The Museum of Fine Arts did a retrospective in 1974.) Their marriage grew increasingly tempestuous, with problems exacerbated by too much alcohol and Zelda's mental instability. In 1934 she was hospitalized in a catatonic state and never fully recovered; she spent the rest of her life in and out of hospitals and at her mother's house.

ZÉLIE: from the Spanish for sunshine.

ZÉLIE DE LUSSAN (1861–1949), a famous mezzo-soprano, was one of the first American opera singers to challenge European dominance. She first appeared onstage at age nine, but made her official debut in 1884 in *The Bohemian Girl* in Boston. In 1888 she sang the title role of *Carmen*; she went on to play it more than one thousand times, and made her debut at the Metropolitan Opera singing this part in 1894. Her other famous role was Zerlia in *Don Giovanni*. Zélie gave three command performances before Queen Victoria, and retired upon her marriage at age forty-three.

ZELMA: from the Old German for helmet of God.

ZELMA WATSON GEORGE (1903–1994) was an African-American diplomat, social worker, college administrator, musicologist, and opera singer. The daughter of a Baptist minister, Zelma was enrolled at the University of Chicago but was told she couldn't live in the dormitory with white women. She studied organ at Northwestern University and voice at the American Conservatory of Music, then earned her Ph.D. from New York University. She served as women's dean at Tennessee State University, then began singing in light opera; her roles included the lead in Gian Carlo Menotti's *The Medium* and in Kurt Weill's *The Three Penny Opera*. Her political career began in the 1950s, when she became an advisor to Dwight D. Eisenhower's administration. She served on the executive council of the American Society for African Culture from 1959 to 1971, and was part of the United States delegation to the United Nations in 1960. Zelma was awarded the Dag Hammarskjöld Award in 1961, the Dahlberg Peace Award in 1969, and the Mary Bethune Gold Medallion in 1973.

ZONA: from the Latin for sash.

ZONA GALE (1874–1938) won the Pulitzer Prize in 1921. She earned her degree at the University of Wisconsin before working as a journalist in Milwaukee and New York City; she wrote fiction but wasn't able to sell it. On a visit back to her home state of Wisconsin, she got the idea to write about everyday life in a Midwestern town. Her two most famous novels were *Papa La Fleur* and *Miss Lulu Bett*; the latter became a best seller, and her adaptation of the novel for the stage won her the Pulitzer. After she became involved with trade unions and women's rights, her novels became somewhat dark and more serious. Her novel *A Daughter of the Morning* addressed the working conditions most women faced.

ZORA: from the Slavic name for Aurora, or dawn.

ZORA NEALE HURSTON (1891–1960) was an integral part of the Harlem Renaissance. Born in Eatonville, Florida, she drew on her hometown for inspiration for many of her novels. Zora studied at Morgan Academy, Howard University, and Barnard College, where she became a protégée of Franz Boas. In 1936 she was awarded a Guggenheim Fellowship and traveled throughout Haiti and the British West Indies collecting folklore. She expressed her genius by combining her notes from her travels with personal experience and songs from the rural South to create some of the most inventive yet authentic literature of contemporary America. Her most notable novels were *Their Eyes Were Watching God* and *Dust Tracks on the Road*. Part of a writers' circle that included Langston Hughes, Zora found a wealthy patron who supported her while she wrote. Eventually she had a falling-out with both her patron and with Hughes. She returned to Florida and was largely forgotten until Alice Walker rediscovered her work in the latter part of the twentieth century.

★ ★ ★ ★ **BOYS** ★ ★ ★ ★

$$\star \star \star \star \star \star \star \star \quad A \quad \star \star \star \star \star \star \star \star$$

AARON: from the Hebrew for enlightened. Eron is a Spanish spelling; Aron is common in Scandinavian and Slavic countries. Ron and Ari are short forms.

AARON COPLAND (1900–1990) was a champion of American music. A gifted pianist, he decided at age fifteen to become a composer. He studied in France at the American Conservatory with Nadia Boulanger; when he returned to the United States in 1924 he began to incorporate indigenous American music, such as jazz motifs, into his compositions. By the mid-1930s, Aaron was employing folk melodies to devise a sound that was uniquely American. Among his best-known works are the ballets *Billy the Kid*, *Rodeo*, and *Appalachian Spring*, for which he won the Pulitzer Prize, as well as film scores for *Of Mice and Men*, *Our Town*, *The Red Pony*, and *The Heiress*.

AARON DOUGLAS (1899–1979) was one of the foremost artists of the Harlem Renaissance. After earning a degree in art at the University of Nebraska, he went to Paris to further his studies. In 1928 he returned to the United States and became the president of the newly formed Harlem Artists Guild. Aaron's use of African design elements and subject matter won him attention from black leaders like W. E. B. DuBois, as well as editorial and art directors. His illustrations appeared in *Vanity Fair*, *The Crisis*, and *Opportunity* magazines, and in James Weldon Johnson's book *God's Trombones* and Alain Locke's *The New Negro*. Aaron was a member of the faculty at Fisk University from 1937 until his retirement in 1966.

ABNER: from the Hebrew for father of light. It's fallen out of favor in recent decades, but Abner and its variations, Avner and Ebner, have an air of strength and masculinity. Abe is occasionally used as a nickname.

ABNER DOUBLEDAY (1819–1893) may or may not have invented baseball, but his achievements were many and varied nonetheless. A West Point graduate and civil engineer, he served in the Mexican and Seminole Indian Wars, and was at Fort Sumter when the Civil War began. Abner fought at Shenandoah Valley, the Second Battle of Bull Run, Antietam, Fredericksburg, Chancellorsville, and was at Gettysburg on

July 1, 1863; a statue in his honor stands there. After he retired from the military in 1873, Abner moved to San Francisco, where he invented the cable car.

ABRAHAM: from the Hebrew for father of many nations, after the first Hebrew patriarch. Abram, Avram, and Ibrahim are alternate spellings. Bram and Abe are short forms (though Bram is a Gaelic name meaning raven or bramble as well).

ABRAHAM BALDWIN (1754–1807) was a delegate to the Continental Congress and a signer of the United States Constitution. A graduate of Yale, Abraham served as a chaplain in the Continental army for six years, then studied law. He moved from Connecticut to Georgia, where he was approved to practice law. In addition, he drew up the charter for the University of Georgia, which he modeled after his alma mater. Abraham endowed the school with forty thousand acres of land and served as its president. Later, he was elected to the United States Congress, where he served for eighteen years.

ABRAHAM CLARK (1726–1794) was a Founding Father. A surveyor who offered legal advice on the side, Abraham held several offices during Britain's rule of the colonies, but eventually became a patriot. He was a member of New Jersey's first committee for the Continental Congress, signed the Declaration of Independence, and was active in the general assembly and Constitutional Convention. He was elected to the first U.S. Congress and served until 1794. Clark Township in Union County, New Jersey, was named after him.

ABRAHAM LINCOLN (1809–1865) was the sixteenth president of the United States. His childhood was difficult—his mother died when he was nine; he walked two miles to school and studied by lantern—but as an adult his life changed. The family moved to Illinois, where Abraham ran for the state legislature. He lost his first bid, but was elected in 1834 and served four terms, studying law and passing the bar exam at the same time. He met his beloved wife, Mary Todd, in Springfield, Illinois. When he was elected president, seven Southern states seceded from the Union in reaction. His tenure was defined by the Civil War; Abraham issued the Emancipation Proclamation after the Battle of Antietam, and his brief but compelling Gettysburg Address makes the case that the United States was a nation "conceived in liberty, and dedicated to the proposition that all men are created equal." Lincoln was assassinated while at the theater; he died on April 14, 1865, shortly after the Civil War ended.

ABRAM: from the Hebrew for exalted father.

ABRAM STEVENS HEWITT (1822–1903) was a philanthropist, educator, and humanitarian. Shipwrecked shortly after he finished college, Abram and his friend Edward Cooper drifted in rough seas in a lifeboat. During those hours, Abram vowed that he'd devote his life to serving people if he were rescued. The young men were found, and Edward Cooper's father, the industrialist Peter Cooper, founded Cooper Union as a school to educate the poor; Abram ran the college for nearly forty years and contributed nearly $1 million to it. He later served five terms in the U.S. Congress and beat Theodore Roosevelt in a bid for mayor of New York City in 1886. He also served as the first chairman of the Carnegie Foundation.

ADAM: from the Hebrew for man, or earth.

ADAM CLAYTON POWELL, SR. (1865–1953), the son of a slave owner and a woman of African and Cherokee descent, was a troubled teenager who carried a gun and brass knuckles and was, by his own admission, "a bum, a drunkard, a gambler, and a juvenile delinquent." That changed when he stumbled into a Baptist church one Sunday morning. Adam converted, studied at Yale Divinity School, and became pastor of churches in St. Paul, Philadelphia, and New Haven before helping to found the Abyssinian Baptist Church in Harlem, where he also established a community recreation center and a program for religious education. By the mid-1930s, the church was one of the largest congregations in the country, with more than fourteen thousand members. Adam helped to found the National Urban League and was a leader of the NAACP.

ADIN: from the Hebrew for pleasant. Different spellings of this name have different meanings. Aden is Gaelic and means flame; Aidin is from the Irish for fiery; Adan is the Spanish spelling.

ADIN BALLOU (1803–1890) was a pacifist whose influence endures today. As a child, Adin and his family were converted at a Christian Connexion revival. He later became a Universalist and was disowned by his father and kicked out of the Christian Connexion church, but even after becoming a minister he was spiritually unsatisfied. He embraced the tenets of social reform, specifically temperance and pacifism, and went on to form the Hopedale Community, which he hoped would be a new civilization. Adin corresponded with Leo Tolstoy, who used some of his ideas of nonviolence, which were later embraced by such twentieth-century leaders as Mahatma Gandhi and Martin Luther King, Jr.

"We cannot employ carnal weapons nor any physical violence whatsoever, not even for the preservation of our lives. We cannot render evil for evil . . . nor do otherwise than 'love our enemies.'" —Adin Ballou

---

ADLAI: from the Hebrew for my ornament.

ADLAI STEVENSON (1900–1965) ran for president twice but lost both times. Considered one of the premier political orators of the twentieth century, Adlai inherited his political inclination from his grandfather (who was Grover Cleveland's vice president) and great-grandfather (who suggested to Lincoln that he run for president). Adlai entered politics during Franklin Roosevelt's administration, working as chief of the United States delegation to the United Nations, and during Harry Truman's presidency he was a delegate to the General Assembly. In 1948 he was elected governor of Illinois by the largest plurality in the state's history, and although he lost two presidential elections to Dwight D. Eisenhower, he had more popular votes than any losing presidential candidate until Al Gore in the 2000 election. In later life he returned to the United Nations; John F. Kennedy appointed Adlai ambassador to the UN in 1961.

ADOLPH, ADOLPHUS: from the German for noble wolf. Although it has declined in popularity since World War II, Adolph is an old Germanic name with a rich history.

ADOLPH COORS (1847–1929) Americanized his name when he emigrated from Germany in 1868; he had been born Adolph Herrman Kohrs. Penniless when he arrived, he set as his goal to brew the finest beer in the world. He worked for a while at a brewery in Illinois, then moved to Denver. He chanced upon a spring of crystal-pure water, and at age twenty-six he and a partner built a brewery. During Prohibition, Coors turned the brewery into a cement plant and porcelain manufacturer; when Prohibition was repealed, Coors went back to making beer.

ADOLPHUS WASHINGTON GREELY (1844–1935) was an army officer and Arctic explorer. He joined the army as a seventeen-year-old and rose through the ranks to become a brevet major during the Civil War.

In 1881 he was the commander of twenty-five men sent to establish a meteorological station in the Arctic. He and his team went farther north than anyone previously had ventured, and supply and relief ships sent in 1882 and 1883 failed to reach his expedition. Adolphus and his men broke camp in August of 1883 and spent ten months traveling to Cape Sabine; by the time they landed, all but seven had died. Adolphus was awarded the Congressional Medal of Honor, the fourth man ever to be honored for bravery during peacetime, and was a founder of the National Geographic Society.

ALAN: from the Old German for precious or handsome. Alain is the French spelling; Allen is Gaelic; Allan is Irish, and Alun is Welsh. Alon is from the Hebrew for oak tree. Al is the most common nickname.

ALAIN LEROY LOCKE (1885–1954) was one of the forces behind the Harlem Renaissance. A brilliant student, Alain received a degree from Harvard University in just three years; he was the first black American to become a Rhodes scholar, and studied at Oxford University as well as the University of Berlin before returning to Harvard to earn his Ph.D. in philosophy. As a professor at Howard University, Alain urged black writers and artists to look to their heritage for inspiration. He edited *The New Negro*, which anthologized plays, poetry, fiction, and essays by black writers.

ALLAN PINKERTON (1819–1884) was born in Scotland; when he emigrated to the United States he settled near Chicago, where he became an ardent abolitionist and conductor on the Underground Railroad. The son of a police sergeant, Allan discovered and rounded up a gang of counterfeiters, then formed the Pinkerton Detective Agency. Its motto ("We Never Sleep") and logo (the All-Seeing Eye) inspired the term "private eye." After his agents foiled an assassination attempt on President Lincoln, Allan became the head of the Secret Service, and he later led the hunt for Frank and Jesse James.

"A friend to honesty / and a foe to crime." —from Allan Pinkerton's tombstone

---

ALLEN GINSBERG (1926–1997) was a poet who defined an era and a generation, and was originally part of the Beat movement that included Jack Kerouac. Allen was born in Newark, New Jersey; he moved first to New York, where he became a fixture in the Greenwich Village scene and where he wrote his most famous poem, "Howl." An active advocate for social justice and protester of the Vietnam War, as well as of the material values of the Establishment, he later moved to San Francisco, and then to Colorado, where he embraced Eastern spiritualism.

ALLEN TATE (1899–1979) was born John Orley Allen Tate. Part of the Southern Renaissance literary movement and a poet laureate, Allen attended Vanderbilt University, taught at Kenyon College, and then moved to New York City. He won a Guggenheim Fellowship in 1928. That same year he published his most famous poem, "Ode to the Confederate Dead," as well as a biography of General Thomas "Stonewall" Jackson; his biography of Jefferson Davis came out the following year. In 1942 Allen became Princeton University's poet in residence and began editing the *Swanee Review*, the nation's oldest literary journal.

ALBERT: from the Old German or French for noble and bright. Albert is used in Spain and Italy; Delbert and Elbert are variations. Albert is usually shortened to Al or Bert.

ALBERT RYDER (1847–1917) was known alternately as the Painter of Dreams and the Saint of Greenwich Village. A largely self-taught artist who moved to New York City at the age of twenty, Albert was a recluse who devoted his life to his paintings. His preferred medium was oil, and he experimented constantly, painting over and over his canvases without allowing the layers to dry. He only produced 160 works, and most have a grandeur that belies their small size. The Brooklyn Museum, the Metropolitan Museum of Art, the National Gallery, and the Phillips Gallery have sizable collections of his work.

ALBERT GOODWILL SPALDING (1850–1915) was one of baseball's earliest stars. He began his career at twenty-one pitching for the Boston Red Stockings, but in 1876 he joined what was then the Chicago White Stockings (which later became the Cubs), and in the same year founded a sporting goods company, A. G. Spalding & Brothers. He led the White Stockings to the National League Championship, then was team president from 1882 to 1891. Al was one of the very first inductees into the Baseball Hall of Fame, where his plaque proclaims him the "organizational genius of baseball's pioneer days."

―――――――――

"Everything is possible to him who dares." —A. G. Spalding's motto

―――――――――

ALEXANDER: from the Greek for defender of mankind, or warrior. A name that dates to the days of ancient Greece, Alexander has many variations and short forms: Alejandro (Spanish), Alessandro (Italian), Alexandre or Alixandre

(French), Alexis, Alistair, Alexi, Alex, Alec, Lex, Sandy, Sasha, and Al are only a few.

ALEXANDER GRAHAM BELL (1847–1922) was born in Scotland but came to Boston in 1871 to teach at a school for the deaf; Helen Keller was one of his students. Alexander also was an inventor of the telephone: he had the idea, and a colleague named Thomas Watson created the device. The first transmission was in June of 1875, and Bell received the patent in March of 1876. It is the most valuable single patent ever issued.

ALEXANDER HAMILTON (1755–1804) led a true rags-to-riches life. An illegitimate orphan working as a clerk in the Virgin Islands, Alexander was brilliant and found a sponsor to send him to college, first to Princeton and then to Kings College (which later became Columbia University). He met and married Elizabeth Schuyler, the daughter of a rich and powerful New Yorker, and was named a delegate to the Constitutional Convention. He collaborated with John Jay and James Madison on the *Federalist Papers*, a series of documents espousing a strong central government, then served as the first secretary of the treasury in George Washington's administration.

ALFRED: from the Old English for elf, or supernatural counselor. Avery is a French form of the name; Al, Alf, and Fred are common diminutives.

ALFRED BLALOCK (1899–1964) was a surgeon who received his medical degree at Johns Hopkins University. Alfred discovered that surgical shock was the result of blood loss, and he pioneered the use of plasma and blood transfusions. As director of surgery at Johns Hopkins, he and Helen Taussig collaborated on a surgical procedure to save "blue babies." He was awarded the Rene Leriche Prize of the International Society of Surgery and helped to found a center for children's medicine and surgery.

ALFRED STIEGLITZ (1864–1946) was an artist and champion of other artists. His medium was photography, and he was instrumental in its acceptance as a legitimate art form. He and another photographer, Edward Steichen, opened a gallery in 1905 that showed the works of a variety of artists and photographers. Georgia O'Keeffe, whom he later married, was one. His work is part of the collections of the Metropolitan Museum of Art, the Museum of Fine Arts, and the Getty Center.

ALVIN: from the Old English for elf, or friend. Elwin, Elvin, and Alwin are variations; Al is the most common nickname.

ALVIN AILEY, JR. (1931–1989) was a choreographer and founder of a dance company. Born in Texas, Alvin moved to Los Angeles when he was eleven. After moving to New York in 1954 he studied dance and acting with Martha Graham and Stella Adler. He formed his own company, the Alvin Ailey American Dance Theater, in 1958; most of the dancers were black, and Alvin's choreography was inspired by traditional African dances and rhythms. *Revelations*, the company's signature ballet, was set to Negro spirituals; *The River* was set to music by Duke Ellington. Alvin choreographed works for the American Ballet Theater, the Joffrey Ballet, the Paris Opera Ballet, and La Scala Opera Ballet.

ALVIN C. YORK (1887–1964) was one of the most decorated soldiers of World War I. A marksman from the hills of Tennessee, Alvin could shoot accurately at ranges of up to five hundred yards, but he refused to shoot at human silhouettes because he believed that killing was wrong—and had filed for conscientious objector status four times before being conscripted. On October 8, 1918, Alvin led a patrol to eliminate machine-gun fire, when he found himself, alone, facing a German machine-gun unit. Armed with a rifle and pistol, Alvin killed more than twenty Germans and captured one hundred and thirty-two soldiers, including four officers. He was awarded twelve medals, including the Congressional Medal of Honor and the French Croix de Guerre. A statue of him stands on the grounds of Tennessee's capitol. Gary Cooper played him in the movie *Sergeant York*.

AMBROSE: from the Greek for immortal.

AMBROSE GWINNETT BIERCE (1842–1914?) was a writer famed for his satire and wit. He was born in Ohio, grew up in Indiana, and moved to California as a young man, where he wrote for the *San Francisco Examiner;* later he was a correspondent for Hearst newspapers, based out of Washington, D.C. He won renown as a writer of short stories and verse, but his book *The Devil's Dictionary* is considered his best. In June of 1913, Ambrose wrote to a friend, "Pretty soon I am going . . . very far away. I have in mind a little valley in the heart of the Andes, just wide enough for one. . . . Do you think I shall find my Vale of Peace?" He went to Mexico the following year and was never heard from again.

"Acquaintance, n.: A person whom we know well enough to borrow from, but not well enough to lend to." —Ambrose Bierce, from *The Devil's Dictionary*

AMOS: from the Hebrew for borne by God.

AMOS B. EATON (1776–1842) started his schooling to become a lawyer, but he was framed on charges of forgery and served five years in jail. When he was released he decided to pursue his love of the natural sciences and went to Yale University. He moved to Troy, New York, in 1818, and conducted several geological surveys in the area. Working with Stephen Van Rensselaer, Amos cofounded the Rensselaer School (now Rensselaer Polytechnic Institute) to implement his ideas about geology; he was a senior professor at the school until his death.

ANDREW: from the Greek for manly, warrior. Andrew is the English variation on the Greek name Andreas; André is French; Anders and Andrik are Scandinavian, and Andres is Spanish. Andy and Drew are the most common short forms.

ANDREW CARNEGIE (1835–1919) personified the American dream: a poor immigrant who became the second-richest man in the world in his day. Andrew and his family left Scotland in 1848; he got a job in a cotton mill, then a few years later became a telegraph clerk. A vice president in the Pennsylvania Railroad took notice of him, and Andrew began to work his way up in the company. He bought some oil fields in Pennsylvania for $40,000; in one year they brought in more than $1 million. When he was thirty, he moved into steel, manufacturing rails for railroads. He built locomotives and owned newspapers as well. A Social Darwinist, Andrew believed that the rich should use their money to improve society, not give to the poor, and in his later life he became known for his philanthropy. Andrew gave away more than $350 million during his lifetime. He established public libraries in the United States and other English-speaking countries, founded the Carnegie Institute of Technology (now Carnegie Mellon), and built Carnegie Hall in New York City. His mansion in New York City is now the Cooper Hewitt National Design Museum, at Fifth Avenue and Ninety-first Street.

ANDREW "RUBE" FOSTER (1878–1930) founded baseball's Negro Leagues. He began his career at age seventeen pitching for the Waco Yellow Jackets, then played for the Chicago Union Giants. He earned his nickname when he defeated Hall-of-Famer Rube Wadell in an exhibition game, but he was denied the opportunity to play in the major leagues because of his race. After he retired from the mound he organized the National Negro League, which he ran until 1926. Andrew was inducted into the Baseball Hall of Fame in 1981.

ANDREW JACKSON (1767–1845) was born in the Carolinas but moved to Tennessee, where he worked as a lawyer. He became wealthy enough to build a mansion near Nashville; known as the Hermitage, it still stands. He was elected to the House of Representatives and the Senate, then served as a major general in the War of 1812. The seventh president, he was elected in 1829 and served for eight years before retiring to the Hermitage. His portrait appears on the twenty-dollar bill. Quick to anger and quick to protect his honor, he once killed in a duel a man who had insulted his wife.

"Any man worth his salt will stick up for what he believes is right, but it takes a slightly better man to acknowledge instantly and without reservation that he is in error." —Andrew Jackson

---

ANDREW JOHNSON (1808–1875) became the seventeenth president of the United States after Abraham Lincoln was assassinated. A courtly Southerner, Johnson was considered to be too lenient on the South during Reconstruction. He removed Edwin Stanton as secretary of war and was accused of violating the Tenure-of-Office Act (the act was later declared unconstitutional). The House of Representatives voted to impeach him, but he was acquitted by the Senate.

ANDREW MELLON (1855–1937) was a banker, industrialist, secretary of the treasury, and philanthropist. He started a lumber business when he was only seventeen, then joined his father's banking firm, and by the time he was twenty-seven he had assumed control of it. His genius was recognizing the potential of a person or an idea, and this helped him to build a fortune in the steel, oil, construction, and shipbuilding industries. Two of the companies he founded were the Aluminum Company of America (today called ALCOA) and Carborundum Steel. During World War I Andrew gave generously to the American Red Cross and the YMCA, and he later endowed Ohio Wesleyan University and the Mellon Institute (now Carnegie Mellon University); his art collection forms the core of the National Gallery's archives. Warren Harding appointed Andrew to his cabinet as secretary of the treasury in 1921. A fiscal conservative, Andrew believed in a "trickle-down" economy, as Ronald Reagan described it sixty years later.

ANDREW WYETH (b. 1917) is one of America's most popular and beloved painters. A sickly child, Andrew was homeschooled in every subject by his parents; his father, the illustrator N. C. Wyeth, taught him art. His first one-man show was presented in 1937, and his first one-man museum exhibition was held at the Farnsworth Art Museum in

1951. Andrew's primary media are watercolors and egg tempera, and his meticulous realism is at its peak in his most famous work, *Christina's World*. He was born in Chadds Ford, Pennsylvania, where the Brandywine River Museum has a large collection of his work.

"Watercolor perfectly expresses the free side of my nature." —Andrew Wyeth

---

ANSEL: from the Old French for protector of a nobleman. Anselm, the German variation, comes from God's helmet.

ANSEL ADAMS (1902–1984) was famous for his black-and-white photographs of the landscapes at Yosemite National Park. He was also an environmentalist: he joined the Sierra Club in 1919 and was the organization's president for thirty-four years. In 1932 he founded Group f/64 with such photographers as Edward Weston and Imogen Cunningham, and in 1936 he held a one-man show at Alfred Stieglitz's gallery in New York City. He moved to Yosemite in 1937, and throughout his life he published several books—some were beautiful volumes of his work, others were technical instruction manuals.

"The understanding of the inanimate and animate world of nature will aid in holding the world of man together." —Ansel Adams, responding to criticism that he took pictures of rocks while the world was falling apart

---

ANTHONY: from the Latin for praiseworthy. Anton is the German and Russian variation; Antoine is French, and Antonio is Spanish and Italian. It is usually shortened to Tony.

ANTHONY QUINN (1915–2001) was born Antonio Rodolfo Quinn Oaxaca to a half-Irish father and Mexican-Indian mother. One of the few Hollywood stars of Mexican ancestry, he played forceful characters with a passion for living. He won two Academy Awards, for *Viva Zapata!* and *Lust for Life*, but he is most associated with his role as Zorba in *Zorba the Greek*. A self-educated high school dropout and a talented painter and sculptor, Anthony created a lithograph to commemorate the fortieth anniversary of the Universal Declaration of Human Rights for the United Nations.

ANTHONY WAYNE (1745–1796) was nicknamed "Mad Anthony" for

his reckless courage and quick temper. A general in the Revolutionary War, Anthony assisted General Benedict Arnold in his retreat from Quebec, captured the English garrison at Stony Point in New York, and aided General Nathanael Greene in pursuing the British from Georgia and South Carolina. In 1792 George Washington recalled him to fight the Indians in Ohio and Indiana; his victory at the Battle of Fallen Timbers led to Wayne's Treaty of Greeneville, which in turn led to exploration in the Pacific Northwest.

ARCHIBALD: from the Old French and Old German for brave or bold. Arch and Archie are the most common nicknames.

ARCHIBALD MACLEISH (1892–1982) started out as a lawyer but discovered he had a talent for writing. A native of Illinois, Archibald attended Yale University, served in World War I as an ambulance driver and captain of artillery, then practiced law. In 1923 he moved to Paris with his wife; they became part of the expatriate community that included Gertrude Stein, F. Scott and Zelda Fitzgerald, and Ernest Hemingway. Five years later they returned to the United States, where Archibald worked as a magazine editor. Two books, *Conquistador* and *Collected Poems 1917–1952*, won Pulitzer Prizes for poetry; his play *J.B.* won a Tony and a Pulitzer for drama. Franklin Roosevelt appointed him Librarian of Congress, and he also taught at Harvard and Amherst Universities.

ARCHIE MOORE (1913–1998) was born Archibald Lee Wright. In and out of reform schools until he was twenty-one, Archie went on to become one of the greatest boxers of the twentieth century. He began boxing as an amateur in 1935 and turned pro as a middleweight the following year. By 1946 he was a light heavyweight, known for his punching and for winning by knockouts. He complained that none of the champs would risk their titles by fighting him, but in 1952 he beat Joey Maxim in fifteen rounds, winning a title at the age of thirty-nine. He challenged the heavyweight champion, Rocky Marciano, and came within seconds of winning in round two when he knocked Marciano down, but the champ got up and won by a knockout in the ninth round. He kept his title until 1962, when the young Cassius Clay knocked him out in four rounds.

ARTHUR: from the Irish for stone; it may also be from the Old German for Thor. Arturo is one variation; it is used in Spanish- and Italian-speaking countries. Art and Artie are diminutives.

ARTHUR ASHE (1943–1993) helped to break the color barrier in tennis. He played at UCLA, and in 1968 won the U.S. Open; by 1970 he had two Grand Slams under his belt, and to this day he is the only black player to win the men's singles at Wimbledon, the U.S. Open, and the Australian Open. When he beat Jimmy Connors at Wimbledon in 1975 he became the number-one player in the world. Denied a visa to play in South Africa, Arthur took a stand against apartheid and called for the country's expulsion from the professional circuit. He discovered he had AIDS in 1988; he had contracted the disease during open heart surgery. In the years before his death he helped to lessen the stigma associated with the disease, and he founded the Arthur Ashe Institute for Urban Health. The tennis stadium that is home to the U.S. Open is named for him.

"I could never forgive myself if I elected to live without a humane purpose, without trying to help the poor and unfortunate, without recognizing that perhaps the purest joy in life comes with trying to help others."
—Arthur Ashe

ARTHUR MACARTHUR (1845–1912) was a Civil War hero. An eighteen-year-old soldier with the Twenty-fourth Wisconsin Infantry, Arthur was one of the Union troops at the bottom of a hill known as Missionary Ridge. His unit led the charge up the hill; the soldier carrying the unit's colors was shot down, as was the corporal who picked it up. Arthur grabbed the fallen flag, yelled, "Follow me! On, Wisconsin!" and charged up the ridge, alone, into enemy fire. The Union army took Missionary Ridge, and Arthur was awarded the Medal of Honor and attained the rank of lieutenant general. Fifty years later he attended a reunion of the Twenty-fourth Wisconsin; the tattered colors hung behind him. As he stood at the podium, he fell and died; his comrades wrapped his body in the flag. Arthur had two sons: one was a submarine lieutenant in the navy, and the other was the commander of the Pacific during World War II: General Douglas A. MacArthur.

ARTHUR MIDDLETON (1742–1787) signed the Declaration of Independence. Born in Charleston, South Carolina, and educated in England, Arthur became a leader of the American Party and a member of the Council of Safety when he returned home. He served as a delegate to the General Congress in Philadelphia in 1776. As a signer of the Declaration he had committed treason, and when Charleston fell to the British in 1780 he was captured and sent to St. Augustine as a prisoner of war.

ARTHUR C. PARKER (1881–1955) was a Seneca anthropologist and activist for Native American rights. He spent two summers on archaeological digs in New York State, and was so successful at collecting data on the Iroquois that he was offered a position at the New York State Museum. A founder of the Society of American Indians and editor of its journal *American Indian Magazine*, he later helped to found the National Congress of American Indians. He served as the director of the Rochester Museum of Arts and Sciences for twenty years, overseeing its collection of Iroquois materials and artifacts.

ARTIE SHAW (1910–2004) was born Arthur Jacob Arshawsky in New York City, and by the middle of the twentieth century he was one of the biggest celebrities in the country. A clarinetist and bandleader, Shaw was an innovator of the big band era. At a time when bands were segregated, he persuaded Billie Holiday to join his group. During the Depression, Artie was said to earn thirty thousand dollars a week; his cover of "Stardust" and "Begin the Beguine" sold millions of copies each. He enlisted in the navy during World War II. Although his professional life was wildly successful, his personal life was less so. Married eight times, Artie called himself "a very difficult man." In 2004 he was presented with a Lifetime Achievement Grammy Award.

ARTURO ALFONSO SCHOMBURG (1874–1938) was a historian and book lover who helped black Americans recapture their history. He was born in Puerto Rico and moved to New York City in 1891, where he met the journalist and book collector John Edward Brusce. Arturo began collecting books and other materials about African people, and his library came to include more than ten thousand items. He often lent his collection to the New York Public Library's 135th Street branch, and in 1926 his collection was purchased by the library with a grant from the Carnegie Corporation. Schomburg was an advisor of sorts to the artists and writers of the Harlem Renaissance.

ASA, ASAPH: from the Hebrew for doctor or healer. Asa was a popular name among Puritans and early colonists.

ASA GRAY (1810–1888) was a botanist whose area of expertise was the eastern United States. The author or several textbooks, Asa was the Fisher Professor of Natural History at Harvard University; he donated his library and plant collection to help create the botany department there. He authored several textbooks; the most famous, *Manual of the Botany of the Northern United States, from New England to Wisconsin and South to Ohio and Pennsylvania Inclusive*, is still the definitive volume and has gone through several editions.

A. [ASA] PHILIP RANDOLPH (1889–1979) was a labor leader and social activist who was once called the most dangerous black man in America. The son of a Methodist minister, Randolph moved to New York and worked as a waiter, porter, and elevator operator before starting a magazine. The *Messenger* spoke out for civil rights, and, because Randolph urged blacks to avoid joining the armed forces during World War I, he was arrested for breaking the Espionage Act. He became a member of the Socialist Party and a labor organizer; in 1929 he was president of the first successful black trade union, and in 1941 he was among those who prevailed upon Franklin Roosevelt to bar discrimination in federal and defense positions. Through Randolph's work, Harry Truman signed an executive order banning segregation in the armed forces; Randolph also helped to organize the March on Washington, D.C., where Martin Luther King, Jr., delivered his "I have a dream" speech.

ASA YOELSON (1886–1950) is better known as Al Jolson, the first man to talk in the movies. Born to Russian Jews who wanted him to become a cantor, Al ran away and joined the circus, then a vaudeville troupe, before becoming a sensation on Broadway and as a singer. The first person to sell a million records, "Jolie" recorded such hits as "You Made Me Love You," "Swanee," "Toot Toot Tootsie Goodbye," as well as tearjerkers like "Mammy" and "Sonny Boy." Al's trademark was appearing in blackface, and although this was common among white and black performers, Al Jolson's music and movies are today shunned as politically incorrect and racist.

ASAPH HALL (1829–1907) was an astronomer who, although he had little formal education, took a job at the Harvard College Observatory, where he developed a reputation as a brilliant observer. Later he worked at the United States Naval Observatory in Washington, D.C., and when it acquired the largest refractor telescope in the world in the late 1870s, Asaph was the first to see that Mars had moons. He also calculated the mass of Saturn's rings and tracked the orbits of double stars. In 1902 he was elected president of the American Association for the Advancement of Science.

AUGUSTUS: from the Latin for wise or great. August, Augustine, and Austin are alternate forms; Augie and Gus are the most common nicknames. Augustus and its variations were very popular during the Victorian era.

AUGUSTUS SAINT-GAUDENS (1848–1907) was considered America's greatest sculptor. Although he created several public works and monuments, his most frequently seen work was uncredited: Saint-Gaudens created Liberty on the Double Eagle twenty-dollar gold piece. His other sculptures include *Admiral Farragut* in New York City's Madison Square Park, *General Sherman Led by Victory* at the entrance to New York's Central Park, a series of bronzes of Abraham Lincoln in Chicago's Lincoln Park, and the Shaw Memorial on Boston Common.

AVERELL: from the Old English for boar hunter. Averill is perhaps the more common spelling of the name.

AVERELL HARRIMAN (1891–1986) was a governor of New York, a diplomat, and an industrialist. The son of a railway baron, Averell joined the Union Pacific Company and eventually became chairman of the board. A visit to Siberia under the reign of Czar Nicholas II led to a lifelong fascination with Russia; as an adult he served as ambassador to the Soviet Union during World War II. He went into the banking business with his brother Roland, and during Harry Truman's administration served as secretary of commerce. He was a negotiator in both the Nuclear Test Ban Treaty during John F. Kennedy's presidency and the peace talks with North Vietnam. At the end of his political career he was a senior member of the United States delegation to the United Nations' Special Session on Disarmament.

B

BANCROFT: from the Old English for field of beans.

BANCROFT JOHNSON (1864–1931), known as Ban, was the founder and first president of baseball's American League. When he became president of the Western League, it was a junior division of professional ball—at the time, the National League was the only pro league. Rules were sketchy, ballplayers often fought with each other and officials while on the field, and with only one pro league, there was no World Series. Ban changed the Western League's name to the American League, changed it so it was no longer a junior division, and created the World Series. In addition, he created and enforced rules regarding conduct on and off the field. He built better stadiums to bring in more fans and increased players' salaries to attract better players, and without ever playing the game himself changed it into America's pastime.

BARNEY: the familiar form of Barnabas, from the Greek for son of consolation. Barnaby is another variation; Bernabe is the Spanish form. Barney is also a nickname for Bernard.

BARNEY OLDFIELD (1878–1946) was a daredevil and an auto racer. He started out as a boxer, and in 1895 started racing bicycles. In 1902 he met Henry Ford and drove Ford's 999 in a race in Grosse Pointe, Michigan. Disregarding Ford's warnings to drive cautiously, Barney raced the car as he did his bike, sliding through turns rather than braking, and beat the defending champion by a length of a half mile. In 1903 he drove a mile in 55.8 seconds, a record at the time. People loved Barney—he was brash and colorful, and usually had a cigar stuck in the side of his mouth—but the American Automobile Association suspended him for his "outlaw" racing style. He was reinstated several years later and ran the first hundred-mile-per-hour lap in the history of the Indianapolis 500.

BARRY: from the Gaelic for fair-haired; it may also be a nickname for Barrett or Barrington.

BARRY BYRNE (1883–1967) was an architect who quit school at fourteen after his father was killed by a train; to support his mother, he took a job in the mail room at Montgomery Ward in Chicago. He'd been interested in architecture from the time he was ten, and when he saw an exhibition of Frank Lloyd Wright's works he contacted Wright to ask for a job. Barry's lack of formal schooling wasn't a problem for Wright, who hired the young man as an apprentice. Barry worked at Wright's studio until 1907, then entered a partnership with another of Wright's protégés; the two designed dozens of residential and commercial buildings before Barry went out on his own. His major client was the Chicago archdiocese, for whom he designed churches and schools noted for their grace and beauty.

BAYARD: from the French for auburn-haired.

BAYARD RUSTIN (1912–1987) was an early leader in the civil rights movement. A black man and a homosexual, Bayard was reared a Quaker by his grandparents, who instilled in him the principles of equality, nonviolence, and respect for others. During World War II he was imprisoned as a conscientious objector; after his release he was arrested during a protest and was sentenced to a North Carolina chain gang. He spent five years traveling in India and Africa to learn about the principles of nonviolence, and upon his return he became an advisor to Martin Luther King, Jr., and was one of the primary organizers of the 1963 March on Washington. The Bayard Rustin High School for the Humanities, located on West Eighteenth Street in New York City, is a testament to his contributions to humanity.

BENJAMIN: from the Hebrew for son of my right hand. Ben, Bennie, and Benjie are the short forms.

BENJAMIN BANNEKER (1731–1806) was the first black scientist in the United States. Although he earned his living as a tobacco farmer, he was an astronomer and clock maker as well. Something of a mechanical genius, Benjamin carved a clock from wood that kept perfect time for fifty years; he also made timepieces for surveyors. At age fifty-eight, Benjamin learned to predict solar and lunar eclipses, and he published his calculations in *Benjamin Banneker's Almanac*. He was honored in 1980 with a postage stamp, and the Benjamin Banneker Historical Park and Museum stands in Catonsville, Maryland.

BENJAMIN FRANKLIN (1706–1790) was a patriot, author, inventor, printer, and Founding Father. Born in Boston, he spent most of his life in Philadelphia. His achievements are as varied as they are impressive: he founded America's first public library, the Library Company of

Philadelphia, as well as the country's first scholarly society, the American Philosophical Society. He founded the University of Pennsylvania and was a cofounder of the Pennsylvania Hospital. His experiments with electricity are the stuff of legend, and the stove he invented is still used more than two hundred years after his death. He negotiated an alliance between France and the United States during the Revolution, helped to create the Declaration of Independence and to write the Constitution. *Poor Richard's Almanack* is perhaps his best-known work, though he wrote several books, including an autobiography. When Benjamin Franklin died, George Washington proclaimed that the country had lost "a genius, a philosopher, a scientist, a noble statesman, and its first citizen."

BENNY GOODMAN (1909–1986) was a bandleader, clarinetist, and jazz musician whose remarkable talent earned him the nickname the "King of Swing." One of twelve children, Benny grew up in miserable poverty in Chicago. He learned to play clarinet in a boys' band run by a charitable organization. By age twelve he was appearing onstage, and by sixteen he was in one of Chicago's top bands. He moved to New York in his early twenties and started his own band with Bunny Berigan, Jess Stacey, and Gene Krupa, and in 1933 he sat in on Bessie Smith's last recording session and Billie Holiday's first. His appearance at Los Angeles's Palomar Ballroom made him an "overnight" sensation, and many consider the performance to be the birth of the swing era. Benny helped to break music's color line, but he and his black musicians didn't tour the South for fear of arrest.

BENJAMIN HARRISON (1833–1901) was the twenty-third president and the grandson of President William Henry Harrison. He served as a colonel in the Civil War, and then moved to Indianapolis to practice law. He was elected to the U.S. Senate in the 1880s and championed the rights of homesteaders, veterans, and Native Americans, and although he received fewer popular votes in the presidential election than did his opponent, Grover Cleveland, Benjamin carried the Electoral College. His legacy as president includes the Pan-American Union and the Sherman Antitrust Act; he tried to make Hawaii a state but wasn't successful.

BENJAMIN RUSH (1745–1813) was a doctor, social activist, writer, and patriot. He studied medicine in Philadelphia, Edinburgh, and London, and one of his greatest achievements was devising a treatment for yellow fever—at the time, one of the most dreadful and feared diseases. Benjamin was an abolitionist, and he advocated for public medical clinics and scientific education for all people. He was a founder of the Pennsylvania Hospital and Dickinson College, a signer of the Declaration of Independence, and the author of several books.

BENJAMIN WEST (1738–1820) was one of the first American artists to achieve fame on an international scale. One of ten children born to a Quaker family in Springfield (now Swarthmore), Pennsylvania, Benjamin showed early promise and was sent to Philadelphia to study art. By the time he was twenty he was making a living painting portraits in New York City, and after traveling through Italy he settled in London, again as a portraitist. King George III became his patron, allowing Benjamin to paint what he wanted: historical subjects. He helped to establish the realistic movement. His paintings hang in many of the world's premier museums, including Ottawa's National Gallery, the National Gallery of Art in Washington, D.C., and the Metropolitan Museum of Art in New York City.

BERNARD: from the Old German and Old French for strong, brave as a bear. Barnard, Bernardo, and Bjorn are variations; Bernie and Barney are pet forms.

BERNARD BARUCH (1870–1965) was a statesmen, advisor to presidents, and financier. The son of a Confederate surgeon, Bernard grew up in New York City. He attended City College, and by the time he was thirty he had made a fortune speculating on Wall Street. The head of the War Industries Board during World War I, Bernard was an advisor to presidents, from Woodrow Wilson to John F. Kennedy. He served as Roosevelt's personal emissary during World War II and helped the president to fight the Great Depression. He helped to devise a plan to control atomic weaponry with the United Nations Atomic Energy Commission, and continued to counsel leaders on international affairs until his death. Throughout his life, Bernard was subject to anti-Semitism.

BILL, BILLY: familiar forms of William, from the Old German for determined protector.

BILL ROBINSON (1878–1949) is known to most Americans today as Mr. Bojangles, from the song by Jerry Jeff Walker, but he is considered by many to be the greatest tap dancer who ever lived. A child prodigy, Bill ran away from home and survived as a street performer. Soon he was working in clubs and taverns in Washington, D.C., and then headlining at the Hoofer's Club in Harlem. He appeared in movies with costars as diverse as Shirley Temple and Lena Horne, danced on Broadway, and at one point was the highest-paid black entertainer in the world. Famous for his "stair dance" and his ability to run backward, as well as for his generosity and charity, Bill died broke at the age of seventy-one. Ed Sullivan paid for his funeral, and more than half a million people lined the streets of New York to say farewell.

BILLY MITCHELL (1879–1936) was a general known as the Father of the Air Force. He was born in France, grew up in Wisconsin, and in 1897 enlisted to serve in the Spanish-American War. By 1906 he was predicting that wars would eventually be fought in the air, and in 1917 he learned to fly—the army considered him too old to be a pilot, so he took private lessons. He was a commander in France during World War I and led one of the first air offensives in history, winning the Distinguished Service Cross and the Medal of Honor. He showed the same willingness to take on all comers off the battlefield: Billy infuriated his superiors by insisting they take airpower more seriously. He used retired battleships to show that planes could sink ships, infuriating navy brass, and was sent to Hawaii. He was demoted for writing a report predicting a Japanese attack on Pearl Harbor, and he was court-martialed for accusing senior officers of incompetence after a navy dirigible crashed and killed fourteen men. He resigned from the military, and it was only after his death that he was vindicated. Mitchell Field on Long Island is named after Billy.

BLACK HAWK: the American transliteration of the Sauk name Ma-ka-tai-me-she-kia-kiak.

BLACK HAWK (1767–1837) was a great chief of the Sauk, or Osage, Indians. Courageous and honorable, Black Hawk was one of the signers of the Treaty of Greenville in 1795; when a few leaders were tricked into selling the American government 15 million acres of land for a little over two thousand dollars, Black Hawk argued that the treaty wasn't valid; the government ignored him and built a fort on the land. Black Hawk attacked the fort, and, as the rift between the Sauk and the United States deepened, the Sauk sided with the British in the War of 1812. In 1831 the Sauk returned to their land, but American troops engaged them in the Black Hawk War. Dozens of Sauk were killed or captured, and Black Hawk was paraded through the streets. Instead of jeering at him, crowds greeted him as a symbol of the frontier and a hero. The Black Hawk helicopter immortalizes his fighting spirit.

"A few summers ago, I was fighting against you. I did wrong, perhaps, but that is past. It is buried. Let it be forgotten. Rock River was beautiful country. I loved my towns, my cornfields, and the home of my people. It is yours now. Keep it as we did." —Black Hawk, in his last public appearance

---

BOOKER: from the English occupation of bookbinder or bookmaker.

BOOKER T. WASHINGTON (1856–1915) was born a slave in Virginia. After working in a salt furnace and as a coal miner, he attended Hampton Institute; Booker was such an outstanding student and teacher that, when white Alabamans were looking for a white teacher to run a school for local blacks, Booker was hired. When he arrived in Tuskegee he found only a dilapidated building, but he built the Tuskegee Institute into a fine school, then went on to found and run several other schools and colleges throughout the South. Booker was a founder of the National Negro Business League, and he financed legal battles challenging segregation. He holds the distinction of being the first black American to appear on a postage stamp and on a coin.

"I will let no man drag me down so low as to make me hate him."
—Booker T. Washington

BRANCH: from the Latin for paw.

BRANCH RICKEY (1881–1965) had more of an impact on professional baseball than perhaps any other man. He played professionally for a while, then became the manager of the St. Louis Browns and eventually president of the St. Louis Cardinals. He led the Cardinals to six pennants, and created such innovations as the farm system and promotional days. When he was sixty-three he became the president of the Brooklyn Dodgers and did something even more innovative: he hired Jackie Robinson and broke the color line in professional baseball.

BRET: a variation on Brett, from the Latin for Brittany or Britain.

BRET HARTE (1836–1902) was a writer whose short stories about the West captured the imagination of generations of Americans. Born and raised in Albany, New York, Bret moved to California when he was in his early twenties. He worked as a miner and as a writer for the *Californian*, and after his story "The Luck of Roaring Camp" was published he was famous. Another story, "The Outcasts of Poker Flat," cemented his fame. His stories, filled with miners, cowboys, outlaws, and dance hall girls, started a genre that lives on in movies, television series, and books. In 1871 he signed a contract for a record amount with the *Atlantic*

Monthly and left California forever. He was made U.S. consul to Germany and Scotland, and lived in England for the last years of his life.

BRIGGS: from the Old English for bridges.

BRIGGS CUNNINGHAM (1907–2003) was a sailor and race car driver. He started racing yachts while he was a student at Yale University. Although he was good enough to win the America's Cup in 1958, Briggs's first love was cars. He had promised his mother he wouldn't race them—and he kept his word until after her death in 1940, when he began building cars of his own design and racing them. His most successful was the C4R, a two-seater with an overhead-valve V-8 that was the forerunner of the Chevrolet Corvette and the Shelby Cobra. Three C4Rs were built in 1951. Fitted with Chrysler's HEMI V-8 and boasting 325 horsepower, these cars dominated Le Mans for years. In his fifties Briggs switched to Jaguars, and in 1962 he placed fourth at Le Mans driving an XK-E.

BRIGHAM: from the Old English for settlement or homestead by the bridge.

BRIGHAM YOUNG (1801–1877) was a self-educated Vermonter who became a religious and political leader. He joined the Church of Latter-day Saints in 1832 and moved to Ohio to form a church. When the Mormons were expelled from Missouri in 1838, Brigham led the move to Illinois. He ran for president in 1844, and while he was campaigning, the leader of the church, Joseph Smith, was murdered; instead of becoming president of the country, Brigham became president of his church. To avoid persecution for himself and his followers, Brigham sent colonists to establish Mormon communities in Utah and planned Salt Lake City. He founded the University of Deseret (now the University of Utah) in 1850, and served as governor of Oregon Territory as well.

BRONSON: from the Old English for Brown's son.

BRONSON ALCOTT (1799–1888) was an educator and philosopher—as well as father to Louisa May Alcott. As a boy, Bronson was so profoundly influenced by the book *Pilgrim's Progress* that he made it his manual for living. With Elizabeth Peabody he founded the School for Human Culture (known as the Temple School) in Boston, and with Ralph Waldo Emerson was a founding member of the Transcendental Club. In addition, he was one of the founders of Boston's first antislavery society. In

1840 the Alcott family moved to Concord, where Bronson became a philosopher farmer—"Orpheus at the plough." A few years later he bought a farm with the hope of turning it into a utopian community, but it was a dismal failure. He returned to Concord and, with Emerson, became the resident philosopher.

BUCKMINSTER: from the Old English for preacher.

BUCKMINSTER FULLER (1895–1983) was an architect, inventor, and visionary. One of the most brilliant men of the twentieth century, Bucky, as he was known, experienced something of an epiphany after his daughter died in 1927, during which time he decided to dedicate his life to bettering humankind. He was a pioneer in using basic geometrical shapes in design—the geodesic dome is one of his inventions—and developed what he termed "Comprehensive Anticipatory Design Science," which attempted to anticipate and solve problems by providing more support with less resources. He made the terms "synergy" and "Spaceship Earth" household terms, was awarded twenty-five patents, and was the epitome of someone who thought outside the box. *Critical Path* and *Only Integrity Is Going to Count* are two of his books.

BUSBY: from the Scottish for village in the thicket. Busby is also the name for tall fur hats, such as those worn by British guards at Buckingham Palace.

BUSBY BERKELEY (1895–1976) was an innovative cinematographer and film director. The son of a theatrical director and an actress, he was named William Berkeley Enos at birth, and took his showbiz name from Amy Busby, a popular actress of the time. Best known for dance extravaganzas featuring dozens of showgirls, Busby used new and different camera angles to capture the action from perspectives not available to theater audiences. Inventive choreography, water fountains, props, lavish costumes, and the camera set above the action to create a kaleidoscope-like image were the hallmarks of his films: *42nd Street*, *The Gold Diggers of 1933*, *Million Dollar Mermaid*, and *Easy to Love* are just a few of the more than fifty he directed or staged in a career that spanned decades.

BUSTER: American nickname for fighter.

BUSTER KEATON (1895–1966), né Joseph Frank Keaton, was a master at physical comedy. Called the Great Stone Face because of his deadpan

expression, he received the nickname "Buster" from Harry Houdini after taking a nasty fall without complaint. Buster was the son of vaude-
villians and was onstage by the time he was three. Pratfalls were his
specialty, and eventually he was able to pull off the most dangerous
stunts. He began acting in films with Fatty Arbuckle and came to write,
direct, and produce many of the movies he starred in. *The General* is
considered his masterpiece.

**BUTCH: the familiar form of the Old English for butcher;
also an American nickname for a variety of names.**

BUTCH O'HARE (1914–1943) might have been named Edward Henry
at birth, but he's known to generations as the navy ace and war hero
Butch O'Hare. On February 20, 1942, nine Japanese bombers attacked
the battleship *Lexington*. Butch was a twenty-seven-year-old lieutenant
junior grade, piloting an F4F Wildcat; his plane was the only one between
the bombers and the battleship. In four minutes, Butch shot down five
planes and crippled a sixth; the other planes turned and fled. On November 27, 1943, Butch was shot down. He was awarded the Congressional
Medal of Honor. Chicago's O'Hare Airport is named in his honor.

BUTTON: from the American for tough, rugged.

BUTTON GWINNETT (1735–1777) was a signer of the Declaration of
Independence and a governor of Georgia. He emigrated from England
as a young man and settled first in South Carolina and then in Georgia,
where he bought land on St. Catherine's Island. In his adopted state he
served as justice of the peace and in the lower assembly, and in 1772
joined the patriot cause. He was elected commander of Georgia's Continental soldiers, and was one of five elected to the Second Continental
Congress. He signed the Declaration on August 2, 1776, and the following year became governor of Georgia. He died of injuries sustained
in a duel with a political rival.

**BUZZ: the familiar form of Busby, from the Scottish for vil-
lage in the thicket; also an American nickname for a variety of
names.**

BUZZ ALDRIN (b. 1930) was born Edwin Eugene Aldrin, Jr., in Mont-
clair, New Jersey. His father was a pioneer in the field of aviation, and
after graduating from West Point, Buzz fought in the Korean War, where
he flew Sabre jets in sixty-six combat missions. After the war he earned a

Ph.D. in astronautics from MIT, specializing in manned space rendezvous, and he designed techniques that were used on all NASA missions. Aldrin made history on July 20, 1969, when he and Neil Armstrong became the first people to walk on the moon. Buzz received more than fifty awards, including the Presidential Medal of Freedom. He is the author of several books, including *Reaching for the Moon* (with Wendell Minor), *The Return* (with John Barnes), and *Famous First Flights That Changed History*.

★ ★ ★ ★ ★ ★ ★ ★ **C** ★ ★ ★ ★ ★ ★ ★ ★

CABELL: from the Old French for rope maker; Cable is another spelling. Cab is the most common nickname.

CAB CALLOWAY (1907–1994) was born Cabell Calloway III in Rochester, New York. Although he was expected to follow in his father's footsteps and become a lawyer, Cab went onstage as a teenager and never looked back. By the time he was twenty he was leading an orchestra, and a few years later he was appearing in such movies as *International House* and *Stormy Weather*. A singer and songwriter, some of the tunes he is best known for are "Minnie the Moocher," "It Ain't Necessarily So," and "Jumpin' Jive." In the late 1960s he appeared on Broadway with Pearl Bailey in *Hello, Dolly!*, and more than a decade later he was featured in *The Blues Brothers*. He continued touring and performing into his eighties.

───────────────

"I'll tell you who my heroes are. My heroes are the notes, man. The music itself. You understand what I'm saying? I love the music. The music is my hero." —Cab Calloway

───────────────

CAESAR: from the Latin for head of hair; the title of the Roman emperors Julius Caesar and Augustus Caesar. Cesar (or César) is the Spanish variation; Cezar is Slavic, and Cesare is Italian.

CAESAR RODNEY (1728–1784) was a signer of the Declaration of Independence, a delegate to the Continental Congress, and a leader in the Colonial militia. Like Paul Revere, Caesar Rodney is remembered for a midnight ride. On June 30, 1776, delegates voted about declaring independence. Nine colonies were for fighting Britain, two were against, one abstained, and the delegates from Delaware were split. Caesar, a brigadier general, was quelling a riot and wasn't present for the vote. Late in the evening of June 30, he heard of the vote and rode the eighty miles through a thunderstorm to Independence Hall in Philadelphia to cast the deciding vote for Delaware.

CÉSAR CHAVEZ (1927–1993) was a labor leader. He was born in Arizona and, after his family lost their ranch in the Great Depression, moved to California. They lived in camps and slept in cars; César went to more than thirty elementary schools and left school entirely after eighth grade. After serving in the navy during World War II he again became a migrant worker. In 1948 he was involved in his first strike; eight years later he had formed the National Farm Workers Association, which later became the United Farm Workers. Influenced by the nonviolent aspects of the civil rights movement, César prevailed upon Americans to boycott table grapes in support of striking union members. Two decades later he championed another boycott of grapes, this time protesting the use of toxic pesticides.

CALVIN: from the French for little bald one. Cal is the short form.

CALVIN COOLIDGE (1872–1933) was America's thirtieth president. Born in Vermont, he attended Amherst College, then became a lawyer. He entered politics, eventually becoming governor of Massachusetts. He was Warren G. Harding's vice president and, when Harding died in 1923, was sworn in by his father (a notary public). Quiet by nature, he became even more so when his younger son died of an infection, though he was known for his dry wit. When a dinner guest made a bet that she could get him to say three words during the meal, Calvin responded, "You lose." Nevertheless, he gave more speeches than any president before him and held 520 press conferences. Elected to the presidency in 1924, Coolidge lowered taxes and reduced the national debt. He retired to Northampton, Massachusetts, and wrote his autobiography.

CARL: a variation of Charles, from the Old German for free man. Karl is another spelling.

CARL ROGERS (1902–1987) was a groundbreaking psychotherapist. He received his Ph.D. in psychology from Columbia University and worked with abused children early in his career. He believed that psychoanalysis—where therapists analyze clients and dictate to them the correct responses—hindered clients from growth. He thought that each person needed to understand himself or herself and make appropriate choices when coming to terms with problems. The author of sixteen books and more than two hundred articles, Carl is best remembered as the father of client-centered therapy.

CARL SAGAN (1934–1996) was an astronomer and writer who helped to make the mysterious and distant understandable. He attended the University of Chicago and taught at Cornell University and Harvard

University. In the 1950s he became a consultant to NASA. He helped to figure out why Venus had such high temperatures, why Mars had seasonal changes, and why Titan had a red haze. Carl also contributed to the Voyager unmanned space probes. He wrote several books, including *Cosmos* (the best-selling science book ever published), *Dragons of Eden*, *Contact*, and *The Demon-Haunted World*; he also appeared on the PBS series *Cosmos*.

CARL SANDBERG (1878–1967) is perhaps best remembered as a poet. He began his writing career with the Chicago *Daily News*. In the early 1920s he wrote two books of fairy tales for his sick daughter, and between 1926 and 1939 wrote a six-volume biography of Abraham Lincoln, for which he won the Pulitzer Prize in history. His poems champion the working men and women of America; "Chicago" is perhaps his best-known poem, but he wrote several volumes over the years. He collected folk songs in *The American Songbook* and also wrote an autobiography, *Always the Young Strangers*.

CARL STOKES (1927–1996) was the first black American to be elected mayor of a major city. Carl was only two when his father died; his mother worked as a domestic, and Carl dropped out of school to work in a foundry. He served in the army and earned his high school degree when he was twenty, then put himself through college and law school working as a waiter. He was elected to the Ohio legislature in 1962, and in 1967 was elected mayor of Cleveland and served two terms. When he retired, he moved to New York and became an anchorman with WNBC for eight years, then returned to Cleveland and became a judge. During President Clinton's administration, Carl was ambassador to the Seychelle Islands.

"By electing Carl Stokes . . . we have shown the nation, indeed the world, that Cleveland is today the most mature and politically sophisticated city on the face of the earth." —The *Cleveland Plain Dealer* upon Carl Stokes's election in 1967

CARTER: from the Old English for transporter of goods.

CARTER BRAXTON (1736–1797) was a wealthy planter from Virginia who used his fortune to support the Revolution. He represented King William County in the Virginia House of Burgesses, and in 1769 he joined the radical faction who supported Virginia's sole right to tax inhabitants. When the House of Burgesses was dissolved he joined the Committee of Safety, and he represented King William County again at the Virginia Convention. A member of the Continental Congress, Carter signed the Declaration of Independence and lent £10,000 sterling to the cause of freedom, but never recouped the money; in 1786 he had to give up his country estate. He died in Richmond.

CARTER GLEN STANLEY (1925–1966) was one of the Stanley Brothers. Born in Big Straddle Creek, Virginia, Carter and his brother, Ralph, were bluegrass musicians who were contemporaries of Bill Monroe. Carter played guitar and sang lead in a voice filled with emotion and resonance. After serving in the army during World War II, Carter sang in the Blue Ridge Mountain Boys, and later he and Ralph formed a band called the Clinch Mountain Boys. Their recordings included gospel and honky-tonk, as well as a number of original songs. Although Carter died at age forty-one, Ralph continued to perform, and even sang in the movie *O Brother, Where Art Thou?*

CHARLES: from the Old German for free man. Carl, Karl, Carlo, Carlos, Charlton, and Karol are variations; Chuck, Chad, Chas, Charlie, Charley, and Chip are nicknames and pet forms.

CHARLES BULFINCH (1763–1844) was one of the first great American architects. Born in Boston, he did most of his best work in his home city. After attending Harvard, Charles designed the old Federal Street Theater and the Massachusetts State House, as well as the nation's Capitol; the latter two buildings have become the model for state capitols throughout the country. The First Church of Christ in Lancaster is one of the most beautiful churches he designed. Charles also designed drainage systems and street lighting, straightened and widened Boston's streets, and supported the first round-the-world voyage of an American ship. The hallmarks of his work are simplicity, elegance, and refinement.

CHARLES CARROLL (1737–1832) was a Marylander who signed the Declaration of Independence. He left home for France at age eight and didn't return until twenty years later, but he immediately identified with the radical cause and independence. In 1772 he penned a series of anonymous articles protesting taxation without representation, and he served on the Committee for Safety, in the Provisional Congress, and in the Continental Congress. He was integral in drafting the state of Maryland's constitution, and served first in the Maryland senate and then in the country's first Federal Congress; after two years he returned to the state senate. At the time of his death he was the last surviving signer of the Declaration.

CHARLES W. CHESNUTT (1858–1932) was a biracial author (both of his grandfathers were white) who was one of the first to write stories in black dialect. His works are powerful and controversial: they primarily take place in the South, and the predominant themes are how light-skinned black people pass for white and interracial sex. *The Conjure Woman* is perhaps his best-known work. In the early twentieth century he stopped writing fiction, turning his efforts to civil rights and the po-litical and economic exploitation of blacks. He was a member of the NAACP's General Committee; in 1928 the organization awarded Charles its Spingarn Medal for his life's work.

CHARLES CURTIS (1860–1936), a native of Topeka, Kansas, was the first person of Native American descent to be vice president; he was also the first vice president from west of the Mississippi. His mother died when he was three and he was reared on the Kaw Reservation. He studied law, was admitted to the bar in 1881, and became a prose-cuting attorney. In 1893 he was elected to the U.S. House of Repre-sentatives and served for sixteen years, then served as a senator from 1907 to 1913 and from 1915 to 1929. He was Herbert Hoover's run-ning mate, and after Hoover's term Charles practiced law in Washing-ton, D.C. His mansion in Topeka is an architectural marvel; it is located at 1101 SW Topeka Blvd.

CHARLES DREW (1904–1950) was a black doctor and surgeon whose ideas saved an incalculable number of lives and have indeed revolution-ized how medicine is practiced. Educated at Amherst, McGill University, and Columbia, Dr. Drew taught at Howard University, then became chief surgeon at the Freedmen's Hospital. While at Presbyterian Hospital in New York, Dr. Drew researched blood plasma for transfusion and devel-oped a system for long-term preservation of plasma. He came up with the idea for blood banks, and was the first director of the Red Cross's blood bank, but resigned when the U.S. War Department issued a state-ment stipulating that blood from white people should not be mixed with blood from blacks. A postage stamp was issued in his honor in 1981.

CHARLES A. LINDBERGH (1902–1974) is the most famous aviator in history. The son of a lawyer and congressman, Charles grew up in Min-nesota and then attended the University of Wisconsin before going to flight school in Nebraska. In 1926 he heard of a twenty-five-thousand-dollar prize for the person who made the first nonstop solo flight be-tween New York and Paris. Charles found businessmen to finance his effort. In a specially built plane called *The Spirit of St. Louis*, Charles took off at 7:52 a.m. on May 20, 1927, and landed thirty-three and a half hours later at Le Bourget Field outside of Paris. He was awarded the Congressional Medal of Honor. He later married Anne Morrow, the daughter of the ambassador to Mexico; their first child was abducted and murdered in 1932. During World War II, Charles flew in fifty combat missions and was made a brigadier general.

"There were times in an aeroplane when it seemed I had escaped mortality to look down on earth like a God." —Charles A. Lindbergh, 1927

CHARLIE "BIRD" PARKER (1920–1955) was one of the premier saxophonists of the twentieth century. A founder of bebop, Bird approached melody, rhythm, and harmony with a novel style that broke utterly new ground. He began playing sax as a teenager in Kansas City, Missouri, and in 1930 moved to New York City. There he played with Earl Hines, and he joined Dizzy Gillespie and Thelonius Monk in the mid-1940s. By 1950 he was the musician others tried to emulate. Although he was a jazz superstar and an icon of the Beat Generation, Charlie Parker was a fan of classical music and recorded *Charlie Parker with Strings*; it is one of his many CDs still available. Several books have been written about him, and *Bird*, a movie based on his life, was directed by Clint Eastwood.

CHARLES M. SCHULZ (1922–2000) created *Peanuts*, one of the most successful comic strips ever. The son of a barber, Charles was born in Minneapolis. His childhood dog, Spike, became the inspiration for Snoopy. Charles enrolled in a correspondence course in cartooning when he was in high school; a stint as a machine-gun squad leader delayed the start of his professional career until 1947, when his cartoon *Li'l Folks* debuted in the *St. Paul Pioneer Press*. He sold the strip to United Features Syndicate in 1950; the syndicate renamed it. By the 1960s, *Peanuts* was everywhere: on the cover of *Time* magazine in 1965, on TV in the Peabody Award–winning *A Charlie Brown Christmas* special feature, and off Broadway in 1967 in the musical *You're a Good Man, Charlie Brown*. In the mid-1970s, more than 90 million people read the comic strip, and in 1984 it entered the *Guinness Book of World Record's* for appearing in two thousand newspapers. Charles Schulz continued to draw his beloved cartoon until shortly before his death.

CHESTER: from the Old English for camp of soldiers; it may also be short for Rochester. Chet is the most common nickname.

CHESTER ALAN ARTHUR (1829–1886) became the twenty-first president after James Garfield was shot four months into his term. A lawyer who specialized in civil rights work on behalf of slaves, Chester had become an officer in the Union army during the Civil War. When it ended, Ulysses Grant appointed him collector of the Port of New York.

As president, Chester was known for creating the Civil Service system, with examinations and a nonpolitical merit system, as well as for his fashionable style of dress and courtly manner. Despite his wild popularity at the end of his term, he did not seek a second term: Chester had been diagnosed with a kidney disease, and he died two years after he left office.

CHESTER HIMES (1909–1984) started writing in prison. Born into a middle-class black family (his parents were schoolteachers) in Jefferson City, Missouri, Chester started getting into trouble when his family moved to Cleveland. He was arrested for armed robbery, convicted, and sentenced to twenty to twenty-five years in the Ohio Penitentiary. He was paroled in 1936 and later was pardoned. During World War II he published his work in *Crisis* and *Opportunity* magazines, and he wrote the novel *If He Hollers Let Him Go*. An editor persuaded Chester to write detective fiction. He created a series known as the "Harlem Cycle," which featured the first two black detectives, Coffin Ed and Gravedigger Jones; two books in the series are *Cotton Comes to Harlem* and *Blind Man with a Pistol*. In 1972, Chester was honored by the Carnegie Endowment for International Peace.

CHESTER WILLIAM NIMITZ (1885–1966) was a naval war hero who played a crucial role in defeating Japan during World War II. A native of Fredericksburg, Texas, Chester attended the United States Naval Academy; after graduation he rose rapidly through the ranks. In the First World War, he was chief of staff to the commander of the submarine division, and after the war he taught naval science at the University of California, Berkeley and continued his military career. After Pearl Harbor, Chester was made admiral and commander in chief of the Pacific Fleet. A brilliant strategist, Nimitz authorized strikes on Japanese positions and fleets that ultimately led to victory. By the end of the war he was a five-star fleet admiral. When Japan surrendered in August 1945, Admiral Nimitz signed the instrument of surrender.

CHISWELL: a surname used as a first name.

CHISWELL DABNEY LANGHORNE (1843–1919) was a tycoon and the father of five famous beauties. Chillie (pronounced Shilly), as he was known, married Anne Witcher Keene in 1864; despite the privations during wartime, the festivities went on for a week. He lost everything during the war but recouped it by investing in railroads. The Langhornes bought a lavish estate called Mirador and reared their daughters. Irene married Charles Dana Gibson and became the model for the Gibson Girl; Nancy became Lady Astor, the first woman in the British Parliament.

CHRISTOPHER: from the Greek for bearer of Christ. Christofer and Christoffer are the German spellings; Cristofer is Spanish; Christophe is French. Chris is the most common nickname, but Kip and Kit are sometimes used.

CHRISTOPHER LUDWICK (1720–1801) was a patriot and baker. He emigrated from Germany to Philadelphia in 1754. Twenty years later he donated £200 to the revolutionaries for weapons, and in 1776 he joined the army. At first he served as a soldier, then became a spy. He infiltrated the Hessians—German mercenaries who were helping the British—and convinced them to join the revolutionaries. He later returned to baking; as superintendent of bakers for the Continental army he supplied bread to the troops. When the war ended Christopher subsidized the education of more than fifty children; after his death he left an estate that has become the Christopher Ludwick Foundation, which to this day provides scholarship money for poor children in Philadelphia.

CHRISTOPHER LATHAM SHOLES (1819–1890) was an inventor. A descendant of John and Priscilla Alden, Christopher apprenticed as a printer and worked for newspapers until the 1860s, when President Lincoln appointed him collector for the Port of Milwaukee. With fewer demands on his time, Christopher was able to work on various inventions. He and a friend were granted a patent for a page-numbering device in 1864, and another colleague suggested he refine it into a letter-printing machine. By 1873, he had devised a typewriter. The first typewriters tended to jam. Christopher rearranged the keys so the most common ones were spread across the keyboard rather than organized alphabetically. It's still used today as the Sholes QWERTY keyboard.

CLARENCE: from the Latin for one who lives near the river Clare.

CLARENCE BIRDSEYE (1886–1956) was dubbed "the Father of Frozen Food." A college dropout, he went to work with the U.S. Biological Survey and was sent to the Arctic to do research on Indians. During the five years he spent on the Peninsula of Labrador, he realized that foods that were frozen during the coldest months tasted better than those that were frozen in the spring and fall. When he returned home, Clarence devised a machine that was able to freeze foods quickly. He founded the General Seafoods Company, and when he sold it became a millionaire. The company was renamed General Foods, but Clarence's contribution lives on in the trade name Birds Eye. In addition to the Quick Freeze Machine, Clarence invented heat lamps and a method of dehydrating food, and he held the patents to nearly three hundred other devices and procedures.

CLARENCE DARROW (1857–1938) is remembered as a great lawyer. He was admitted to the bar in Ohio in 1878 and worked as a small-town lawyer until he moved to Chicago in 1887. A brilliant speaker who could move juries and judges to tears, Clarence lost only one murder case out of more than one hundred. The case that made him a celebrity was known as the Monkey Trial, in which John T. Scopes was tried for teaching evolution as the origin of man. Clarence wrote several books, including *Crime, Its Cause and Treatment* and *The Story of My Life*.

"Inside every lawyer is the wreck of a poet." —Clarence Darrow

CLARENCE DAY (1874–1935) was a humorist and writer. Born into a life of privilege, Clarence was a Yale graduate who received a seat on the stock exchange from his father. He joined the navy, but in 1899 he was stricken with crippling arthritis. Soon he was partially paralyzed in his arms and hands and completely paralyzed from the hips down. Despite constant pain, he created funny verses, stories, and drawings that appeared in a variety of publications. Even after the stock market crashed and he was financially ruined, Clarence remained cheerful and upbeat. His semiautobiographical book *Life with Father* became a best seller, as well as a smash hit on Broadway and a movie.

CLAUDE: from the Latin for lame.

CLAUDE McKAY (1890–1948) was an early figure in the Harlem Renaissance. Born in Jamaica, he published his first book of poetry, *Songs of Jamaica*, in 1911, and came to the United States a year later. He studied at the Tuskegee Institute and Kansas State University before moving to New York City, where he worked as a porter. *Harlem Shadows* was published in 1922, and Claude also worked as associate editor of the socialist magazine *Liberator*. His other books include his autobiography, *A Long Way from Home*; *Home to Harlem* was on the best-seller list. Claude's best-known poem was a sonnet entitled "If We Must Die"; Winston Churchill quoted it during World War II.

"Like men we'll face the murderous, cowardly pack / Pressed to the wall, dying but fighting back!" —Claude McKay, the last lines of "If We Must Die"

CLEMENT: from the Latin for merciful. Clem is the most common short form.

CLEMENT C. MOORE (1779–1863), the author of "A Visit from St. Nick," better known as " 'Twas the Night Before Christmas," was more popular for his scholarly books during his lifetime. A professor of Oriental and Greek literature at General Theological Seminary, Clement wrote a two-volume Hebrew Dictionary. A graduate of Columbia University and the son of the institution's president, Clement wrote his beloved poem in the 1850s. He made handwritten copies: one copy is in the Harris Collection at Brown University, and an original is at the Strong Museum in Rochester, New York.

W. CLEMENT STONE (1902–2002) was a writer, businessman, and philanthropist who helped thousands to "think and grow rich." A go-getter from the start, this native of Chicago owned a newsstand when he was thirteen; by sixteen he was earning a hundred dollars a week selling insurance. He founded an insurance company and soon employed more than one thousand agents. In the 1960s he published two books, *Success Through a Positive Attitude* and *The Success System That Never Fails*, which emphasized his belief that a positive mental attitude could lead to riches and a healthy, productive life. Clement gave away more than $275 million during his lifetime; for his one hundredth birthday he gave $100,000 to the University of Illinois at Chicago.

CLINTON: from the Old English for fenced settlement, Clinton was originally a surname. Clint is the short form.

CLINTON J. DAVISSON (1881–1958) won the Nobel Prize in Physics in 1927. He won a scholarship to the University of Chicago, where he found a mentor in a professor named R. A. Millikan, but had to quit for lack of funds. Millikan helped Clinton find an assistantship at Purdue University and later an instructorship at Princeton University. Clinton worked for the Carnegie Institute and Bell Laboratories. He and G. P. Thomson demonstrated that electrons could behave as waves as well as particles, which led to the Nobel Prize. Clinton helped to develop the electron microscope, and after he left Bell he worked as a visiting professor at the University of Virginia.

CLINTON HART MERRIAM (1885–1942) was a naturalist. He grew up on an estate in Locust Grove, New York, then studied medicine at Yale. In 1886 he left medicine and joined the U.S. Biological Survey as director. One of his first exploratory projects was of the Colorado Plateau; he also went to California to study the San Francisco Peaks, then later explored the Grand Canyon and the Painted Desert. Through his research and study he developed the concept of Life Zones, which detail the relationship between temperature patterns and the distribution of plants and animals.

COLE: from the Middle English or Old French for dark, swarthy, or coal black. Cole may be a short form of Nicholas, Colbert, Coleman, or Colson.

COLE PORTER (1891–1964) was one of the greatest American composers and songwriters. Born in Peru, Indiana, Cole started violin lessons at six, piano at eight, and wrote his first operetta at ten. He went to Yale and then Harvard Law School, but he switched to Harvard's School of Music instead. His best-loved songs include "Night and Day," "Let's Do It, Let's Fall in Love," and "You're the Top"; his musical comedies include *Anything Goes, Can-Can,* and *Kiss Me, Kate.* Cary Grant played him in *Night and Day,* the movie version of his life.

COLEMAN: from the English for coal miner. Coleman may also be an Irish variation on Columba, from the Latin for dove. Cole is a common nickname.

COLEMAN HAWKINS (1904–1969) was a legendary jazz musician and a child prodigy. He learned the piano at five, the cello at seven, and the tenor sax at nine—this last instrument became his signature—and was performing professionally by the time he was twelve. His first regular gig was with the Kansas City Jazz Hounds, but in 1923 he joined the Fletcher Henderson Band. Before Coleman, the tenor sax had been something of a novelty instrument; his big sound and heavy vibrato made it a standout in solos. As the band toured New England and the Midwest, Coleman became a star. He left the band and played in Europe for most of the 1930s, but returned to New York. His masterpieces include "Body and Soul" and "Woody'n You," and he appeared on television as well as in live performances up until his death.

COLIN: from the Irish for young cub.

COLIN KELLY (1915–1941) was the first hero of World War II. A captain in the air corps, Colin grew up in Florida and graduated from West Point. In 1941 he was a commander of a B-17 Flying Fortress in the Philippines. Three days after the attack on Pearl Harbor, Colin and his crew put the Japanese cruiser *Ashigara* out of commission. As they returned to Manila, his plane was attacked by four Japanese fighter jets. He ordered his crew to bail; the men were later rescued, but Colin's body was found near the wrecked plane. He received the Distinguished Service Cross posthumously.

CONRAD: from the German for wise counselor.

CONRAD WISE CHAPMAN (1842–1910) was the son of an artist and an artist himself. He grew up in Rome, Italy, but returned home to fight for the Confederate side in the Civil War. He was wounded at Shiloh, and a family friend persuaded General P. G. T. Beauregard to have Conrad paint the defense of Charleston. The young artist ignored exploding shells while he sketched the bombardment, and his series of thirty-one paintings today hangs in Richmond, Virginia's, Museum of the Confederacy. He wrote a memoir of his military service in 1867. After the war, Conrad went to Mexico, then lived and painted in Hampton, Virginia. His paintings also hang in the Gibbes Museum of Art in Charleston, South Carolina.

CONRAD HILTON (1887–1979) created one of the largest hotel chains in the world. His father, a Norwegian immigrant who owned or operated the post office, bank, telegraph office, and hotel in a small mining town in New Mexico, taught Conrad about business. He went to Texas at thirty-one to strike it rich in the oil fields with $5,000 pinned to the lining of his coat; his goal was to buy a bank, but he bought a hotel instead. He bought two more, then lost nearly everything during the Great Depression. By 1937 he was repaying his debts, and in 1938 he bought the Sir Francis Drake Hotel in San Francisco—it had cost the owners $4 million to build, and Conrad purchased it for $275,000. In 1947, Hilton Hotels became the first hotel chain listed on the New York Stock Exchange, and by the end of the century Hilton's empire was worth $6.2 billion.

CORDELL: from the Old French for rope maker.

CORDELL HULL (1871–1955) has been called the Father of the United Nations. Born in a log cabin in the mountains of Tennessee, he attended a one-room school until he was fifteen. He decided to become a lawyer and was admitted to the bar when he was eighteen, then later became a circuit judge. Cordell was elected to the U.S. Congress, first in the House of Representatives and later in the Senate. In 1933, President Roosevelt appointed him secretary of state. After World War II, he worked to bring to fruition his vision: an organization of nations united in the goal of peace.

COTTON: originally a surname. May be spelled Cotten.

COTTON MATHER (1663–1728) was a minister who helped to shape life among the Puritans in Colonial America. He graduated from Harvard University at age fifteen, then became an assistant at Boston's Old North Church. Cotton supported the Massachusetts charter of 1691 and wrote a biography of the governor, Sir William Phips. A prolific writer, he wrote more than 450 books and pamphlets about religious and secular matters. His religious writings were used in the Salem witchcraft trials (though he believed witchcraft should be fought with prayer and fasting), and his secular writings detail, among other things, his experiments with plant hybridization.

COUNT: from the English title.

COUNT BASIE (1904–1984) was born William Basie in Red Bank, New Jersey. His mother was a music teacher; she taught him piano, and his organ teacher was Fats Waller. In 1935 he started the Count Basie Orchestra; its style was based on Kansas City swing. Count Basie's band rivaled Duke Ellington's in popularity and influence. He wrote songs as well: "Jumpin' at the Woodside" and "Lester Leaps In" were written for his saxophone player, Lester Young. He's the subject of several biographies, and most of his music is still available on CD.

CRISPUS: from the Latin for curly haired. Crispin is another variation.

CRISPUS ATTUCKS (1723–1770) was the first American to die for the cause of independence. Born and raised a slave, he escaped by joining a whaling ship. By his late forties he was back in Boston. Supposedly a British soldier, taunted by a crowd, shot a young boy. Crispus went to the front of the crowd and talked about striking back. On March 5, 1770, Crispus was in the lead of a group of men heading toward the British garrison, and, although none of the men were armed, they were yelling that the way to get rid of the soldiers was to attack the main guard. Soldiers opened fire. Eleven colonists were shot; five, including Crispus Attucks, died in what came to be known as the Boston Massacre. A statue of Crispus Attucks by Augustus Saint-Gaudens stands in Boston Commons.

CYRUS: Persian, from the Greek name Kyros. May also be related to the Greek word *kyrios*, or Lord. Cy is the nickname.

CYRUS FIELD (1819–1892) started out as a delivery boy in New York. By the time he was in his early thirties he had amassed a fortune, and in 1854 Fredrick Gisborne approached Cyrus about financing an underwater cable from Nova Scotia to Newfoundland. According to published reports, Cyrus went to his globe and, while studying it, contemplated whether the telegraph might span the Atlantic Ocean. His first attempt failed: the cable snapped. He used heavier cable the second time, but it leaked. The third cable, from Ireland to Newfoundland, had a weak signal but failed after three weeks. In 1866, two cables spanned the Atlantic Ocean, and transmissions across the wires were successful. Cyrus Field's impossible dream had come true.

CYRUS McCORMICK (1809–1884) was an inventor. He grew up on a farm, where he watched his father try to devise a machine that would harvest grain. Cyrus built on his father's attempts and, in June of 1834, received a patent for his "Improvement in Machines for Reaping Small Grain." The horse-drawn reaper did the work of ten men, but the noise it made scared horses, so farmers shunned it. Cyrus worked to improve the machine, and it slowly caught on as farmers realized that it could increase crop yields while reducing labor costs. Though competitors tried to steal his patents, though he extended credit to farmers and never took the nonpayers to court, and though his factory was destroyed in the Great Chicago Fire, Cyrus McCormick overcame adversity and revolutionized the farming industry.

CY YOUNG (1867–1955) was born Denton True Young. Nicknamed "Cyclone" for his blinding fastball, Cy was the greatest pitcher in the history of baseball. He began his career with the Cleveland Spiders, and by the time he retired at age forty-four in 1911 he was one of the Boston Red Sox greats. Cy won 511 games—nearly 100 more than any other pitcher—and pitched the first perfect game in American League history; his other records include most complete games and most innings pitched—751 and 7,356, respectively. The Cy Young Award is given in his name to award excellence in pitching.

★ ★ ★ ★ ★ ★ ★ ★ **D** ★ ★ ★ ★ ★ ★ ★ ★

DANIEL: from the Hebrew for God is my judge. Danilo is the Spanish spelling; Dan and Danny are nicknames.

DANIEL CARTER BEARD (1850–1941) was a woodsman, illustrator, naturalist, and founder of the Sons of Daniel Boone, the forerunner of the Boy Scouts of America. Born in Cincinnati, Daniel grew up in Kentucky. Tales of Daniel Boone's famous exploits were part of his boyhood. Daniel Beard became a civil engineer and surveyor, but earned a living as an illustrator; his pictures appeared in Mark Twain's books *A Connecticut Yankee in King Arthur's Court* and *Tom Sawyer Abroad*. He also wrote a how-to manual that told boys how to do everything in the out-of-doors; it sold more than 300,000 copies and was the basis of the *Boy Scouts Manual*. He founded the Boy Pioneers—Sons of Daniel Boone in 1905, and in 1910 he merged his group with a new organization called the Boy Scouts of America. Daniel became the national scout commander, designed the Boy Scout emblem and developed the system of merit badges, and was awarded the only gold Eagle Scout badge ever. He also received the Roosevelt gold medal for distinguished service.

———

"I would rather be a Boy Scout than a dictator, a king or even President of the United States." —Daniel Carter Beard

———

DANIEL BOONE (1734–1820) was a frontiersman and explorer. Born in Pennsylvania, Daniel moved to North Carolina as a young man. He heard about Kentucky from an old hunter, and although he had work and a wife in North Carolina, he dreamed of moving west. In 1767 he led his first expedition, blazing a trail through the Cumberland Gap. He established the settlement of Boonesborough and built a fort as protection from Indians. Despite his precaution, his daughter was captured by Shawnees—but Daniel rescued her—and he himself was captured. He escaped and walked 140 miles in four days to alert settlers of an Indian attack. He lost his land in Kentucky and left for Missouri (then Upper Louisiana, a Spanish colony). Renowned for his bravery, loyalty, strength, and honesty, Daniel Boone was a real hero as well as a folk hero.

D'ARCY: from the French for from Arcy. When spelled without the apostrophe, Darcy is from the Gaelic for dark.

D'ARCY MCNICKLE (1904–1977) was an author and an advocate for Native Americans. The son of an Irish rancher and a Flathead (originally the Cree tribe) mother, D'Arcy attended the University of Montana and Oxford University; he financed his education by selling his tribal allotment of eight acres. His first novel, *The Surrounded*, was written while he lived in New York City; over the course of his life, several more works of fiction and nonfiction followed. He joined the Bureau of Indian Affairs, and was a founder of the National Congress of American Indians, a congressional lobbying group. D'Arcy resigned from the Bureau of Indian Affairs and moved to the University of Saskatchewan, where he chaired the anthropology department, and later was the first director of the Newberry Library's Center for the American Indian—now called the D'Arcy McNickle Center for American Indian History—in Chicago.

DASHIELL: of unknown origin.

DASHIELL HAMMETT (1894–1961) was one of the great mystery writers. Dash, as he was known, worked for the Pinkerton Detective Agency for six years, and his experiences provided him with the material for the hard-boiled detective stories that became his forte. His story "Arson Plus" appeared in the crime fiction magazine *Black Mask*; it introduced his first famous detective, the Continental Op. A novel featuring the Continental Op was published in 1928, and in 1930 Dash published his first book featuring Sam Spade, *The Maltese Falcon*. *The Glass Key*, another Sam Spade novel, and *The Thin Man*, which introduced the duo Nick and Nora Charles, followed. Movies and radio shows came next, and by the 1940s Dash was making thirteen hundred dollars a week. Accused by the House Un-American Activities Committee of being a communist, Dashiell refused to testify and spent five months in jail for contempt. He spent his last years in New York and on Martha's Vineyard.

"If it were my life, I would give it for what I think democracy is . . . [but] I don't let cops or judges tell me what I think democracy is." —Dashiell Hammett

------

DAVID: from the Hebrew for beloved. Dave and Davy are the most common nicknames. Davyn is the Welsh variant; Davis and Dawson mean David's son.

DAVID BELASCO (1853–1931) was born to Portuguese-Jewish parents in San Francisco and was educated in a monastery. As a child he ran away and joined the circus, and by the time he was twelve he was acting professionally and writing plays. He honed his craft performing on the frontier and in mining camps, and by age twenty-nine he'd played more than two hundred different roles and written more than one hundred plays. He moved to New York and worked as a stage manager; by 1906 he was working at a theater located at 111 West Forty-fourth Street that today is named for him. Among the four hundred or so plays he collaborated on or wrote are *The Girl of the Golden West* and *Madam Butterfly;* his other contributions to theater include innovations in staging, sets, and lighting.

DAVY CROCKETT (1786–1836) was born on the Tennessee frontier, the fifth of nine children. He ran away from home at age twelve to avoid a "licking" from his father and got a job driving cattle to Virginia. He didn't return home for two and a half years. An expert marksman, Davy won shooting competitions. Despite only four days of formal schooling, Davy was a commander in the Creek Indian War of 1813, and was elected to the Tennessee legislature in 1821 and the United States Congress in 1827. In March of 1836 Davy was killed in the massacre at the Alamo. His first gun is in Jefferson County, Tennessee; his rifle, "Betsy," is in Nashville, and his tomahawk is in the Smithsonian Institution.

DAVID DUBINSKY (1892–1982) was a prime architect of the American labor movement. He was born in Russian Poland and was later arrested by the Bolsheviks; he escaped and came to America in 1911. David found work as a cutter in the garment industry. He joined the International Ladies Garment Workers Union and was elected its president in 1920, and served as president and secretary-treasurer until 1959. David was an advisor to President Roosevelt in the 1930s and pioneered legislation for social and labor reforms, such as minimum wage, unemployment insurance, Social Security, and the thirty-five-hour workweek.

"Yes, we were dreamers when we advocated legislation for unemployment insurance, for social security, for minimum wages. They laughed at our crazy ideas. Although we have not reached perfection, many of our 'wild dreams' have now become realities of everyday life." —David Dubinsky

---

DAVID GLASCOW FARRAGUT (1801–1870) was a Civil War hero. Born in Tennessee, he first went to sea when he was eight, and by nine and a half had received his first naval appointment as midshipman. By the time he was eleven he'd seen combat, and he was commander of a vessel at age twelve. In 1862 he was the commander of the West Gulf Blockading Squadron; his orders were to capture New Orleans. Camouflaging his ships' hulls, he ran past Fort Jackson and Fort St. Philip. New Orleans fell, and David was promoted to admiral—the first in the United States Navy. He later took Vicksburg and Mobile Bay, and when he died at age sixty-nine his funeral procession was headed by none other than President Ulysses S. Grant.

"Damn the torpedoes. Full speed ahead!" —Admiral David G. Farragut

DEAN: from the Latin for leader of a school or church official.

DEAN ACHESON (1893–1971) was a statesman and diplomat. Born in Connecticut, he attended Groton, Yale, and Harvard Law School, then clerked for the Supreme Court justice Louis Brandeis. He served as secretary of state under Franklin Delano Roosevelt and Harry Truman, and was one of the architects of NATO, the Truman Doctrine, and the Marshall Plan. Dean also played a lead role in developing America's postwar foreign policy. He served as an advisor to President Kennedy, and wrote several books, including *Morning and Noon*, *Grapes from Thorns*, and the Pulitzer Prize winner *Present at the Creation*.

"Always remember that the future comes one day at a time." —Dean Acheson

DEAN RUSK (1909–1994) served as secretary of state under two presidents, John F. Kennedy and Lyndon B. Johnson. Born in Georgia, he was a Rhodes scholar and served in Burma during World War II. He joined the United States Department of State, and in 1950 was made assistant secretary of state for Far Eastern affairs. His belief that military action was necessary and appropriate to fight communism helped to shape America's foreign policy in Asia. After he retired from public service he taught international law at the University of Georgia and wrote several books.

DELMORE: a variation of Delmar, from the Spanish for of the sea.

DELMORE SCHWARTZ (1913–1966) was a poet of the Beat Generation. Born in Brooklyn, Delmore was the youngest winner of the Bollingen Prize and published dozens of poems, stories, and plays. His best-known work, "In Dreams Begin Responsibilities," was published in 1937; it and "Calmly We Walk Through This April's Day" were the inspiration for a Star Trek movie. He taught creative writing at Syracuse University (one of his students was Lou Reed), but mental instability, hastened by alcoholism and amphetamine use, created a downward spiral that led to an early death. Saul Bellow's novel *Humboldt's Gift* is based on his life.

"Into the Destructive element . . . that is the way." —Delmore Schwartz, on a note found after his death

---

DE WITT: from the Flemish for blond. Witt and Dwight are variations.

DE WITT CLINTON (1769–1828) was called the Father of the Erie Canal. A mayor of New York City and governor of New York State, De Witt favored building a canal to connect the Great Lakes with the Hudson River, linking the Western states to the East. His opponents derided the notion as "Clinton's Folly" or "Clinton's Ditch," but when the Erie Canal opened in October 1825, it was the engineering marvel of the nineteenth century, and its role in the growth of the country cannot be overstated. The Erie Canal spurred westward migration, giving settlers access to the rich land and resources west of the Appalachian Mountains.

DEXTER: from the Latin for adroit, dexterous. Dexton is a variation; Dex is the short form.

DEXTER GORDON (1923–1990) was the only jazz musician to be nominated for an Academy Award. His father was a doctor whose patients included Lionel Hampton and Duke Ellington, and Dexter joined Hampton's band when he was only seventeen. A bebop tenor saxophonist, Dexter played with everyone from Hampton and Charlie Mingus to Louis Armstrong and Billy Eckstine. In 1962 he went to London for a two-week gig; he stayed for fourteen years, returning to New York in 1976. Ten years later he starred in *'Round Midnight*, for which he earned a nomination for Best Actor.

DIZZY: a nickname meaning zany or wild.

DIZZY DEAN (1910–1974) was christened Jay Hanna Dean when he was born in Lucas, Arkansas. A naturally gifted pitcher, Dizzy was playing pro ball by the time he was twenty-two. In 1934 he and his brother, Paul, nicknamed "Daffy," led the "Gas House Gang" to the World Series; Dizzy was 30–7 for the season. In five seasons he won four strikeout awards and averaged twenty-four wins, and he is the last National League pitcher to finish the season with thirty wins. His career ended after an injury in the 1937 All-Star Game. Dizzy went on to become a sports announcer.

"As a ballplayer, Dizzy Dean was a natural phenomenon, like the Grand Canyon or the Great Barrier Reef. Nobody ever taught him baseball and he never had to learn. He was just doing what came naturally."
—Red Smith, on Dizzy Dean

DIZZY GILLESPIE (1917–1993) was born John Birks Gillespie in Cheraw, South Carolina, and earned the nickname "Dizzy" for his antics onstage. He was playing the piano by the time he was four; by twelve he picked up the instrument that would win him world fame: the trumpet. Dizzy joined Cab Calloway's orchestra in 1939, but his style was so distinctive that he was fired. Collaborations with Earl Hines and Charlie Parker led to explorations in bebop. "Night in Tunisia," "Manteca," "Birk's Work," and "Con Alma" are just a few of the songs he composed. Many of his recordings are still available; Dizzy also wrote two books: *To Be or Not to Bop* and *Dizzy Gillespie*.

DONALD: from the Scottish for great chief or ruler. Donal and Donnell are variants; Don and Donny are diminutives.

DONALD BARTHELME (1931–1989) was a writer. He began his career in his hometown of Houston, writing pieces on culture for the *Post*, then moved to New York City in 1962. Although he is perhaps most associated with the stories and essays he wrote for the *New Yorker*, where his incisive wit and mocking style were a perfect fit, Donald also wrote fourteen books—in fact, he won a National Book Award for a children's book, *The Slightly Irregular Fire Engine*.

DOUGLAS: from the Scottish for dark water. Doug is the most common nickname. In the 1940s and 1950s, Douglas was one of the most popular names for boys.

DOUGLAS "WRONG WAY" CORRIGAN (1907–1995) was an aviator who dreamed of emulating Charles Lindbergh and his transatlantic flight. Douglas was of Irish ancestry and wanted to fly to Ireland, but his application to fly across the ocean was denied because authorities didn't think his plane would make the trip. His OX5 Robin monoplane was, however, certified for cross-country flights, so on June 17, 1938, Douglas took off from Brooklyn's Floyd Bennett Field, ostensibly for California. Instead, he headed due east, and after twenty-eight hours and thirteen minutes landed at Baldonnel Airport in Dublin. Until his death he insisted that visibility was so poor he didn't notice he was over water and that he'd gone the wrong way by mistake. When he returned to New York he was a hero; more than a million people lined the street for a ticker-tape parade.

DOUGLAS FAIRBANKS (1883–1939) was one of Hollywood's first great movie stars. Handsome and athletic, he began his career in silent movies and made the transition to talkies. He did his own stunts in such swashbuckling features as *The Mark of Zorro*, *The Three Musketeers*, *Robin Hood*, *The Black Pirate*, and *The Thief of Bagdad*. He married Mary Pickford in 1920, and together with Charlie Chaplin they founded United Artists. Douglas was one of the founders of the Academy of Motion Picture Arts and Sciences and served as its first president. The Douglas Fairbanks Museum is located in Austin, Texas.

DOUGLAS MACARTHUR (1880–1964) was the supreme commander of the Allied forces in the Pacific theater during World War II. The son of the Civil War hero Arthur MacArthur, Douglas was a military genius who was as controversial as he was popular. He had a brilliant career during World War I and served in the Philippines before retiring from the army in 1937, but was recalled to active duty when the Second World War became imminent. Though he withdrew from Bataan under orders from President Roosevelt, he vowed, "I shall return"—and he did. General MacArthur accepted the Japanese surrender on September 2, 1945, then led the occupation of Japan during its reconstruction. He led the United Nations forces in Korea, helping to drive the North Korean invaders back. Despite MacArthur's bold and brilliant maneuvers, President Truman thought he had gone too far and relieved the general of his command. The MacArthur Memorial stands in Norfolk, Virginia, and the MacArthur Museum of Arkansas Military History is located in Little Rock.

"Old soldiers never die, they just fade away." —Douglas MacArthur, in his address to Congress after being relieved of his command

---

DREW: from the Welsh for wise; Drew is also the short form of Andrew.

DREW PEARSON (1897–1969) was a muckraking journalist and radio commentator. Born Andrew Russell Pearson to a Quaker family in Illinois, Drew went to Swarthmore College. After graduation he went to Europe, where he rebuilt houses destroyed in the First World War, then traveled throughout Asia and Australia. He wrote for the Baltimore *Sun* from 1926 to 1941, then joined the *Washington Post*. He wrote an exposé during the HUAC investigations accusing chairman J. Parnell Thomas of rewarding friends with cushy federal jobs, and stood up to Joseph McCarthy. After John Kennedy was assassinated, Drew uncovered information indicating that Fidel Castro was involved, but Earl Warren and his investigative committee rejected it.

DUANE: from the Irish for dark. Dwayne and Dewayne are alternate spellings.

DUANE HANSON (1925–1996) was a sculptor whose materials and methods were as contemporary as his themes. Using fiberglass and vinyl, he made casts of people, then dressed them in clothing and painted them with the normal human complement of blemishes and imperfections. His earlier works were known for their violent themes—*Accident* shows a motorcycle crash—but later works were more benign. Recognizable for their startling realism, Duane Hanson's works showed Americans as they were, not as they wished to be.

DUKE: from the Latin for leader. A short form for Marmaduke, Duke is also a nickname inspired by the English title.

DUKE ELLINGTON (1899–1974), christened Edward Kennedy Ellington, was a pianist, bandleader, arranger, and composer. He played piano at seven and was composing music at fifteen, and at twenty-four he moved to New York and formed a band that endured for fifty years. Duke wrote music for revues, movies, Broadway productions, ballets, his band, and other artists; some of his most famous songs are "Don't Get Around Much Anymore," "Mood Indigo," and "Sophisticated Lady."

Duke Ellington was the first jazz musician to be elected to the Royal Music Academy in Stockholm; he was awarded the Presidential Medal of Freedom as well as honorary degrees from Yale and Howard Universities.

DWIGHT: a variation on De Witt, from the Flemish for blond.

DWIGHT F. DAVIS (1879–1945) was a tennis champion and statesman. A graduate of Harvard University, Dwight won the intercollegiate singles championship in 1899; that same year, he thought that an international tennis competition would promote goodwill. Calling the event the International Lawn Tennis Challenge Bowl, Dwight commissioned a large bowl made of silver as a trophy. The competition and the trophy are today known as the Davis Cup. Dwight also served as Calvin Coolidge's secretary of war, and later was governor general of the Philippines and director general of the Army Specialist Corps.

DWIGHT DAVID EISENHOWER (1890–1969) was a man of integrity, leadership, and vision. Known as Ike, he grew up in Texas and Kansas, then attended West Point. He rose through the ranks and by World War II was a general. As leader of the Allied troops in Europe, Eisenhower commanded the landing in North Africa in November of 1942 and was supreme commander of the troops that invaded France on D-day. When the war ended he became president of Columbia University, until 1951, when he was appointed supreme commander of NATO. He ran against Adlai Stevenson for president in 1952 and 1956; as president, he won a truce in Korea, and worked to desegregate the armed forces.

★ ★ ★ ★ ★ ★ ★ ★ **E** ★ ★ ★ ★ ★ ★ ★ ★

EARL: from the Old English for nobleman. Erle, Earle, and Errol are variations.

EARL "FATHA" HINES (1903–1983) was an innovative jazz pianist. His father played cornet and his mother was a church organist. Earl started playing piano professionally in the early 1920s, and by 1926 he was in the vanguard of Chicago's Hot Jazz movement. He collaborated with Louis Armstrong in the late 1920s. By the 1930s and 1940s he was leading his own band; Billy Eckstine joined them on vocals in 1940; Dizzy Gillespie and Charlie Parker in 1943. Earl's influence can be seen in musicians who came after him, such as Teddy Wilson, Joe Sullivan, Art Tatum, and Nat King Cole. Earl's compositions include "Rosetta," "You Can Depend on Me," and "My Monday Date."

EARL W. SUTHERLAND, JR. (1915–1974) was a medical researcher who won the Nobel Prize in Physiology or Medicine in 1971. He earned his master of science degree from Washington University School of Medicine, and spent his life as a teacher and researcher: he was a professor at his alma mater and at Vanderbilt University's School of Medicine; most of his research was done under the auspices of the American Heart Association. His area of specialty was hormones, specifically the location of chemical receptors in cell membranes and the connection between stress, epinephrine, and blood sugar and its effects on diabetes and heart disease.

"I am fully convinced that medical research can offer one a happy and productive life. And if one has a little Viking spirit he can explore the world and people as no one else can do." —Earl Sutherland, in his Nobel Prize acceptance speech

---

EBENEZER: from the Hebrew for foundation stone. Eb or Eben are familiar forms of the name.

EBENEZER D. BASSETT (1833–1906) was of black and Pequot Indian ancestry. Born in Connecticut, he attended Yale University. During the Civil War he wrote appeals to black men to enlist in the army. His contributions to the war effort were rewarded by Ulysses S. Grant; the president appointed Ebenezer the ambassador to Haiti in 1869. Ebenezer became U.S. consul general in 1874.

EDGAR: from the Old English for powerful spear. Ed and Eddie are the most frequently used nicknames.

EDGAR RICE BURROUGHS (1875–1950) was one of the most popular authors of the twentieth century. He created the character Tarzan, and his novels were translated into fifty-six languages and sold more than 100 million copies. *Tarzan of the Apes* was his second story; it was published in 1914. Twenty-six Tarzan novels followed, as did several movies. The first one appeared in 1918 and was silent; later films featured the Olympic swimmer Johnny Weissmuller in the title role. The University of Louisville Libraries has a wonderful collection of Tarzan and Burroughs memorabilia.

EDGAR ALLAN POE (1809–1849) was a master storyteller whose appeal is undimmed more than 150 years after his death. Adopted after his mother died when he was two, Edgar attended schools in England and Virginia and briefly attended West Point. He lived in Boston and Baltimore, and by 1844 he was married to his cousin, Virginia Clemm, and working in New York for the *Evening Mirror*. After Virginia's tragic death in 1846 Edgar began drinking. Three years later he was back in Baltimore and was found unconscious; he was taken to a hospital, where he died. Throughout his adult life, and despite problems familial and financial, Edgar wrote poems ("The Raven" is perhaps his best known) and tales of horror and mystery.

"Depend upon it, after all, Thomas, Literature is the most noble of professions. In fact, it is about the only one fit for a man. For my own part, there is no seducing me from the path." —Edgar Allan Poe, in a letter to Frederick W. Thomas written nine months before his death

---

EDMUND: from the Old German for protector. Eamon is the Irish variant; Edmond, Edmondo, and Edmon are sometimes seen. Ed, Eddie, or Ned may be used as the short form.

EDMUND SIXTUS MUSKIE (1914–1996), a governor and senator from Maine, was often compared to Abraham Lincoln both in appearance and intellect. Born to a Polish-American family in a mill town in Maine, Edmund graduated from Cornell University and served in the navy during World War II. In the 1960s he was presidential candidate Hubert

Humphrey's running mate, and his commanding presence and even-handedness won him fans from both political parties. He was a front-runner for the Democratic nomination in 1972; after Edmund cried in public, people and the press doubted he "had what it takes" to run the country, and he lost the nomination to George McGovern. Four years later he served as secretary of state in President Carter's administration.

EDMUND WILSON (1895–1972) was a writer and literary critic. A native of New Jersey, Edmund went to Princeton and then served in World War I. After the war he worked as a reporter for the *New York Sun*, then wrote for *Vanity Fair*, the *New Republic*, and the *New Yorker*. Two books, *Axel's Castle* and *To the Finland Station*, brought him literary acclaim. He was a critic of America's cold war policies and a tax protestor. A brilliant man who spoke several languages, he learned Hebrew when he studied the Dead Sea Scrolls. He was awarded an honorary doctorate from his alma mater, and received the National Medal for Literature.

EDWARD: from the Old English for guardian. Eduard and Eduoard are French; Eduardo is Spanish and Portuguese. Nicknames include Ed, Eddie, Ned, and Ted.

EDWARD HOPPER (1882–1967) was an artist. He was born in Rockland County, New York, and studied art in New York City and Paris. Until he was forty-three he made his living as a commercial artist and illustrator. When he began painting full-time he captured on canvas scenes that other artists ignored: a bored usherette at a movie theater, a storefront in the early morning, commuters waiting for a train. All of his works—of people and of buildings—are known for their haunting loneliness, and for his ability to capture the isolation of even the most crowded places.

EDWARD VERNON RICKENBACKER (1890–1973) was a World War II fighter pilot. A high school dropout, Eddie was fascinated by cars and speed: he set a record of 134 miles per hour at Daytona, and later was part owner of the Indianapolis Speedway. He volunteered for service when World War I broke out. Too old to train as a pilot, Eddie lied about his age, and earned his wings in a mere seventeen days. As commander of the Hat-in-the-Ring Ninety-fourth Aero Squadron, Eddie shot down twenty-six German planes and was awarded the Medal of Honor, the Croix de Guerre, the French Legion of Honor, and the Distinguished Service Cross. In World War II he and seven crew members were lost over the Pacific and given up for dead; they were actually on three life rafts, without food or water. Eddie kept the men going for twenty-four days, until they were found. He was honored with a postage stamp in 1995.

EDWARD RUTLEDGE (1749–1800) signed the Declaration of Independence; at twenty-six, he was the youngest to do so. He left the Continental Congress shortly after signing and joined the Charleston Battalion of Artillery and rose to the rank of captain. He was captured during Britain's third invasion of Charleston and was imprisoned in St. Augustine until July 1781. He returned to South Carolina and became a legislator and, in 1789, governor.

EDWARD ROBINSON SQUIBB (1819–1900) was a physician, pharmacist, and chemist. Orphaned at the age of thirteen, Edward was raised by his grandmothers. He wanted to go to medical school, and he financed his education by apprenticing with a pharmacist. He enlisted during the Mexican War; as a medical officer, he was shocked at the quality of medications given to soldiers. After the war he worked to make pure, effective medications, and he perfected the formulas for many common drugs. He opened his laboratory in September of 1858; today the Squibb Company is part of Bristol-Myers.

EDWARD WESTON (1886–1958) was one of the preeminent photographers of the twentieth century. A native of Illinois, Edward began taking photographs as a boy. He moved to California in 1906 and worked printing photographs and taking pictures as a door-to-door photographer. In 1915 he saw an exhibit of modern art at the San Francisco World's Fair. He quit portraiture and began to develop the style and form that became his trademark: common items and landscapes photographed in natural light and composed in such a way as to appear abstract. His apprentice and lover, Tina Modotti, was a model for nude studies over the years. Weston was a founder of Group f/64 with Ansel Adams and Imogen Cunningham, and he received the first Guggenheim Fellowship for Photography in 1937. Several of his photographs are part of the collection at the Museum of Modern Art in New York City; the Weston Gallery is located in Carmel, California.

"His work illuminates man's inner journey toward perfection of the spirit."
—Ansel Adams on Edward Weston's work

EDWIN: from the Old English for prosperous friend. Edwyn is an alternate spelling; Ed, Eddie, Ned, and Ted are diminutives.

EDWIN POWELL HUBBLE (1889–1953) was an astronomer. Fascinated as a child by science and the science-fictional worlds created by Jules Verne and Henry Rider Haggard, Edwin became a lawyer, then quit within a year. He returned to school and received his Ph.D. from the

University of Chicago. After World War I he went to work at the Mount Wilson Observatory in Pasadena, California. Using the one-hundred-inch reflecting Hooker Telescope, Edwin took photographs of the Cepheid variables and proved that they were outside our galaxy—and that other galaxies existed. He calculated the size of the universe, developed the idea of an expanding universe, and devised Hubble's law, which helped to determine the age of the universe. The Hubble Space Telescope is named in his honor.

EDWIN HERBERT LAND (1909–1991) invented the Polaroid camera. Fascinated by polarized light as a freshman at Harvard University, he took leave from college to develop a new kind of polarizer using crystals in a plastic sheet; he called it Polaroid. He returned to school but left before graduating. He founded a laboratory with other scientists that eventually became the Polaroid Corporation; Edwin was its president. Working with light filters, optical devices, and motion picture processes, Land and his colleagues applied polarizing principles and invented infrared filters, dark-adaptation goggles, and target finders. He also invented a microscope to view cells in their natural color, and in the late 1940s the Polaroid Land camera was on the market.

ELBRIDGE: from the Old English for old bridge.

ELBRIDGE GERRY (1744–1814) signed the Declaration of Independence and later served his country as vice president under James Madison. He became involved with the revolutionary cause when he met Samuel Adams in 1772; Elbridge attended the first and second provincial congresses, served on the Council of Safety, and was the chairman of the Committee of Supply. His areas of expertise were financial and logistical matters, and he worked to get better pay and better equipment for soldiers. Elbridge served as governor of Massachusetts from 1810 to 1813.

ELEAZAR: from the Hebrew for God has helped. A variation of the name Lazarus, Eleazar may be shortened to Eli, Ely, or Elie.

ELEAZAR WHEELOCK (1711–1779) founded Dartmouth College. After studying the classics at Yale, he became a Congregationalist minister. He became swept up in the Great Awakening, a religious revival movement of fervent, fire-and-brimstone sermons. Reverend Wheelock's preaching was popular with the public, but not so much with his church, and he lost his position. He started tutoring, then decided to open a school for Native American boys. By 1762 he had twenty students, and decided to expand his school to include a college. He opened the school in Hanover, New Hampshire, and in 1771 the first class of four students graduated.

ELI: from the Hebrew for uplifted. Elie and Ely are alternate spellings. Eli may be the short form of Elias, Elijah, Eleazar, or Elliott.

ELI WHITNEY (1765–1825) is remembered as the inventor of the cotton gin, but his greatest contribution was really a system of manufacturing. A mechanical genius, Eli went to Yale when he was in his mid-twenties. He accepted a position working at the plantation of Catharine Littlefield Greene, and while there he created the prototype of one of Mrs. Greene's ideas: a machine that removed the seeds from cotton. Eli received the patent in 1794, and in 1798 he started producing muskets for the government. Rather than have one man make each weapon, however, Eli divided their manufacture into a series of tasks, with one man responsible for one component. This assembly-line system cut manufacturing costs considerably, primarily because it didn't require skilled labor. It revolutionized industry.

ELIAS: the Greek form of Elijah, from the Hebrew for the Lord is my God.

ELIAS HOWE (1819–1867) invented the sewing machine. Working in a textile mill as a machinist's apprentice, Elias devised a machine that would automate sewing; his first successful one debuted in 1845 and could sew 250 stitches in one minute—more than five hand sewers. He obtained a patent in 1846, and although he had difficulty finding buyers for the machine in the United States and England, the design was pirated by others. He sued and won, earning royalties on every machine made in the United States; in thirteen years he earned nearly $2 million. During the Civil War he joined the infantry as a private and used part of his wealth to equip his regiment.

ELIJAH: from the Hebrew for the Lord is my God.

ELIJAH LOVEJOY (1802–1837) was a minister, newspaperman, and vehement abolitionist. A native of Maine, he moved to St. Louis, became pastor of a church there, and started publishing the *St. Louis Observer*. After seeing a slave burned at the stake, his editorials became even more scathing in their indictment of slavery. His opponents destroyed his press in 1836, so he moved to Alton, Illinois, where he worked to support the Anti-Slavery Society of Illinois and began publishing the *Alton Observer*. The Alton citizens were enraged and destroyed three more presses, and in November 1837 Elijah was killed while guarding a new printing press.

ELISHA: from the Hebrew for the Lord is my salvation.

ELISHA GRAVES OTIS (1811–1861) can be credited for an invention that made skyscrapers possible. The inventor of the safety elevator, Elisha designed a hoist that couldn't fall: if the rope lifting the hoist broke, a safety catch opened automatically. He patented his invention, though there wasn't much demand for it, and was about to go west to pan for gold when he received two orders. In 1854 he demonstrated the safety elevator at the Crystal Palace Exposition. He cut the elevator's cable with an ax, and when it didn't plummet to the ground, word of his invention spread. The passenger elevator and steam elevator were later refinements.

ELLIOTT: an English variation on Elijah, from the Hebrew for the Lord is my God. Eliot and Elliot are alternate spellings; Eli is sometimes used as a nickname.

ELLIOTT COUES (1842–1899) was a naturalist, author, and ornithologist. He received a Ph.D. and a medical degree from Columbian University, and as a student the Smithsonian Institution sent him to Labrador to collect birds, an association that lasted nearly all his life. Later he served as an army surgeon in the Carolinas and Arizona; in both regions, he studied birds. Eventually he quit practicing medicine and became a naturalist with the U.S. Northern Boundary Commission, surveying the forty-ninth parallel from Lake of the Woods to the Rockies. The books he wrote, *Birds of the Northwest*, *Fur Bearing Animals*, and *Birds of the Colorado Valley*, won him the respect of his peers; in 1877 he became the youngest member of the Academy of National Sciences and the chairman of anatomy at the National Medical College. He was a founder of the American Ornithologist's Union.

ELLIOTT P. JOSLIN (1869–1962) was a doctor whose passion to fight diabetes came about when his mother developed the disease. The founder of the Joslin Diabetes Foundation and the Joslin Clinic, Elliott researched cures and treatments, advocating patient education, diet, and exercise as important methods of controlling the disease. He also started a summer camp for diabetic children. The book he wrote in 1916, *Joslin's Diabetes Mellitus*, has been updated and revised but is still in print today.

ELLIS: an English variation on Elias, from the Greek for Elijah, the Lord is my God.

ELLIS WILSON (1899–1977) was an artist from Kentucky. Born in a segregated neighborhood, he worked as a janitor in a women's clothing shop and one day drew a portrait in soap on the store's window. The owner loved it and asked him to do one every week. Ellis went to Chicago to study at the Art Institute and worked as a commercial artist, then moved to New York City in 1928. He became famous painting for the WPA, then received a Guggenheim Fellowship in 1944. He traveled the South and painted blacks doing the ordinary tasks of their lives, at work and home. Today his work is in many museums; the University of Kentucky Art Museum and the Smithsonian Art Museum are two good places to start.

ELWOOD: from the Old English for ancient woods. Ellwood is an alternate spelling. Woody is a common nickname.

ELWOOD HAYNES (1857–1925) was a pioneer in the alloy and automotive industries. In the early 1890s he was sketching vehicles powered by a gasoline engine, and in 1894 he built a one-cylinder car with the help of Elmer and Edgar Apperson. The Haynes-Apperson Company, formed in 1895, produced seventy-one hundred cars a year at its peak. These luxury vehicles sold for thousands of dollars at a time when Henry Ford's Model T cost less than nine hundred dollars. Elwood also worked with metals; he combined tungsten with cobalt-chromium alloys to create stellite. The Stellite Corporation manufactured an early form of stainless steel; he built it into a multimillion-dollar company before merging it with Union Carbide.

EMMETT: from the Old German for industrious, strong.

EMMETT KELLY (1898–1979) was the most famous clown in the world. His character, Weary Willy, was a sad hobo based on a character Emmett had created while working as a cartoonist for a silent film company. As a boy, Emmett had dreamed of joining the circus, and trained as an aerialist. He got a job as a trapeze artist and doubled as a clown. Weary Willy captured the sentiments of the nation during the Great

Depression. Emmett joined Ringling Bros. and Barnum & Bailey Circus in 1942 and later the Shrine Circus; he appeared in such movies as Fellini's *The Clowns* and *The Greatest Show on Earth*.

ERLE: a variant of Earl, from the Old English for nobleman.

ERLE STANLEY GARDNER (1899–1970) created one of the most famous lawyers ever, Perry Mason. With no formal training he was admitted to the California bar in 1911, but legal practice bored him. He began to write detective stories for pulp magazines. Perry Mason, his most famous character, was the subject of more than fifty novels, as well as Hollywood movies and a television series starring Raymond Burr. Many of the novels are still in print.

ERNEST: from the Old English for earnest, sincere. Ernst is the German variation; Ernesto is Spanish. Ernie is the most common diminutive.

ERNEST HEMINGWAY (1898–1961) was a man's man, a legend in his own time, and one of the great writers of the twentieth century; his honors include the Pulitzer Prize and the Nobel Prize in Literature. Born in Illinois, he was an ambulance driver in Italy during World War I. After the war he lived in Paris as part of the Lost Generation that included Gertrude Stein and F. Scott Fitzgerald, and was a foreign correspondent with the Third Army during World War II, commanding a battalion of more than two hundred troops. Some of his stories and novels drew on his experiences: *The Sun Also Rises* and *A Farewell to Arms* about World War I, *The Green Hills of Africa* from his safaris in the 1930s. *For Whom the Bell Tolls* is set in the Spanish Civil War. Several of his works were made into movies.

ETHAN: from the Hebrew for strong.

ETHAN ALLEN (1738–1789) was a rebel, Revolutionary War hero, and guerrilla fighter. A folk hero of Colonial New England, Ethan was the commander of the Green Mountain Boys, and at one time had a bounty of £60 on his head. He led the expedition that captured Fort Ticonderoga—the first victory for the Colonial troops—but was captured when he attempted an assault on Montreal. After the war Ethan worked on behalf of statehood for Vermont, but it didn't happen in his lifetime. The Ethan Allen Homestead Museum stands in Burlington, Vermont.

EUBIE: a nickname for Hubert, from the Old German for bright mind.

JAMES HUBERT "EUBIE" BLAKE (1883–1982) was a composer and musician. Ragtime, jazz, and popular music were his specialties, and his hits include "Charleston Rag," "Love Will Find a Way," "I'm Just Wild About Harry," and "You Were Meant for Me." With the bandleader Noble Sissle he wrote *Shuffle Along*, the first Broadway musical directed and written by blacks. Eubie earned a degree in music after the Second World War. He came out of retirement at age eighty-nine, and in 1978 the musical *Eubie* opened on Broadway. Twelve years after his death a postage stamp was issued in his honor.

"If I'd known I was going to live this long, I would have taken better care of myself." —Eubie Blake, shortly before his one hundredth birthday

EUGENE: from the Greek for noble born. Eugenio is the Spanish spelling; Efegenio is Greek, and Yevgeny is Russian. Owen is the Welsh variation. Gene and Gino are nicknames.

EUGENE V. DEBS (1855–1926) was a labor leader and humanitarian. He dropped out of school at fourteen to work on the railroad, becoming a charter member of the Brotherhood of Locomotive Firemen. He became active in local politics, and by the time he was thirty he was a state representative. Eugene organized the first industrial union in the country; the American Railway Union went on strike in May 1894, and he was arrested in July 1894 and again the following year. He ran as the Socialist Party's candidate in five presidential elections, including one from prison. Eugene had been arrested for espionage after making an antiwar speech and sentenced to ten years in prison; he was disenfranchised and stripped of his citizenship. Fifty years after his death, his citizenship was restored.

"Your Honor, years ago I recognized my kinship with all living beings. . . . While there is a lower class, I am in it; while there is a criminal element, I am in it; while there is a soul in prison, I am not free." —Eugene V. Debs, to the judge when he was sentenced for espionage

EUGENE O'NEILL (1888–1953) wrote some of the greatest plays in American literature. He grew up in a theatrical family in Connecticut; as a young man he was hospitalized for six months with tuberculosis.

After his recovery, he joined the Provincetown Players and began writing plays. His first, *Beyond the Horizon*, opened on Broadway in 1930; it won the Pulitzer Prize for drama. He wrote forty-five plays, including *Long Day's Journey into Night, A Moon for the Misbegotten, Ah, Wilderness!*, *The Iceman Cometh*, and *Mourning Becomes Electra*. Eugene won the Nobel Prize in Literature in 1936.

EVERETT: from the Old English for courageous.

EVERETT DIRKSEN (1896–1969) was a senator from Illinois. He was influential in passing two key acts of the civil rights movement: the Civil Rights Act of 1964 and the Open Housing Act of 1968. His rumpled appearance, beautiful voice, and sense of humor were legendary: Everett was known for diffusing tempers in the Senate by proposing that the marigold be named the national flower. He recorded four record albums; *Gallant Men* won a Grammy Award in 1968. After his death, one of the Senate buildings was named after him.

★ ★ ★ ★ ★ ★ ★ F ★ ★ ★ ★ ★ ★ ★

FIORELLO: from the Italian for little flower.

FIORELLO HENRY LA GUARDIA (1882–1947) was one of the most famous mayors the city of New York has had. Elected in 1933, he fought patronage and bossism, introduced slum-clearance projects, and helped to draft a new city charter. Besides helping to clean up corruption, he joined firemen to help put out fires and he read comic strips over the radio. After he retired as mayor, he was the director general of the United Nations Relief and Rehabilitation Administration. La Guardia Airport was named for him.

FITZHUGH: from the Irish for son of Hugh.

FITZ HUGH LANE (1804–1865) was a painter who specialized in maritime subjects. Paralyzed in the legs after a bout with polio, he learned to sketch; his drawings of the Massachusetts coastline led to an apprenticeship with a lithographer in New York City. Fitz Hugh was influenced by Dutch painters; he studied their use of light to create a feeling of calm, and his style in turn has influenced subsequent painters of ships and the sea.

FLETCHER: from the Old English for arrow maker.

FLETCHER HENDERSON (1897–1952) began playing piano at six. Thought to be the first jazz musician to form a band, Fletcher was also the recording director and accompanist for Black Swan recording company. He toured with the Black Swan Troubadours and created arrangements for Benny Goodman; among the other musicians he worked with were Art Blakey, Ethel Waters, Louis Armstrong, and Henry Allen.

FLOYD: from the Welsh for gray-haired, holy.

FLOYD BENNETT (1890–1928) was the first aviator to fly across the North Pole. He quit school to work on cars, and enlisted in the navy in 1917. He met Richard E. Byrd, the polar explorer, in flight school and became Byrd's personal pilot. The two flew from Spitsbergen to the Pole and back in a three-engine Fokker monoplane and were awarded the Medal of Honor. They planned to cross the Atlantic, but Floyd was injured in a plane crash. He contracted a fatal bout of pneumonia flying before he had fully recovered. Floyd Bennett Field in Brooklyn, New York, was named for him.

FRANCIS: from the Latin for free. Franz is the German spelling; Francisco is Spanish; Francesco is Italian, and François is French. Frank and Fran are common nicknames in English; Pancho and Paco are Spanish nicknames.

FRANCIS HOPKINSON (1737–1791) was a signer of the Declaration of Independence, but he is best known for his literary and musical contributions. He represented New Jersey in the Continental Congress; after the war he wrote some of the new country's first secular music, including an attempt at opera, as well as poems, essays, and satire. His best-known work is *Battle of the Kegs*.

FRANCIS SCOTT KEY (1779–1843) was a lawyer practicing in Washington, D.C. During the War of 1812 a friend of his was captured by the British; Francis went to Baltimore to meet with an agent who arranged prisoner exchanges; while he was there, the British bombarded Fort McHenry. Francis wrote a poem, "Defence of Fort McHenry," which was soon set to the music of an old drinking song and renamed "The Star-Spangled Banner." In 1931 it became the national anthem.

FRANCIS LIGHTFOOT LEE (1734–1797), known as Frank, signed the Declaration of Independence. Born into a prominent Virginia family, Frank had been involved with the fight for independence from the days of the Stamp Act. He was a member of the Virginia Conventions as well as the Continental Congress. The town of Leesburg, Virginia, is named for Frank and his brother, Philip. He was the grandfather of Robert E. Lee.

FRANCIS LEWIS (1713–1802) signed the Declaration of Independence. After his "act of treason," British soldiers came to his estate on Long Island. His house was destroyed and his wife was imprisoned. Though she was released after three months, she never recovered from her ordeal, and died in 1779. Francis used most of his fortune to support the Revolution and the fight for independence.

FRANK O'HARA (1926–1966) was a poet of the Beat Generation. Ironic and urbane, Frank's amusing poetry documents the vagaries of daily life, from buying cigarettes to traffic jams. He worked as an editor and as a ticket taker at the Museum of Modern Art, and he wrote as he worked. "The Day Lady Died," about Billie Holiday, is his best-known poem. His works have been collected into several volumes; *Selected Poems* won the National Book Award.

FRANK LLOYD WRIGHT (1867–1959) was one of the most influential architects of the last century. His houses and commercial buildings are works of art, recognizable for their clean lines and the unassuming way they blend into the landscape—one, called Fallingwater, was designed around and actually built over a stream. Not content to just design a structure, he designed furnishings, windows, and other treatments as well. The Solomon R. Guggenheim Museum, built in the round and featuring a long spiral ramp, is perhaps his most recognizable building.

FRANKLIN: from the Middle English for free landowner. Frank is the short form.

FRANKLIN PIERCE (1804–1869) was the fourteenth President, serving from 1853 to 1857. Known as New Hampshire's favorite son (the phrase was the title of a biography of Pierce), Franklin was a member of the New Hampshire legislature before serving in the House of Representatives and then the Senate. He was nominated for the presidency as a dark-horse candidate and won the election by a narrow margin, but tragedy befell the Pierce household before Franklin took office: he and his wife, Jane Appleton Pierce, saw their eleven-year-old son die in a train wreck, and Pierce entered the White House grief-stricken. Increasing tensions between the North and South are the hallmark of Pierce's administration. The Kansas-Nebraska Act repealed the Missouri Compromise, and the subsequent battle over the territory led to its nickname "Bleeding Kansas," and was a prelude to the Civil War. Pierce was not nominated to a second term and returned to New Hampshire.

FRANKLIN DELANO ROOSEVELT (1882–1946) was the only president to be elected for four terms. Born into an old New York family, FDR was brilliant and liberal and took office during the Great Depression and led the country through World War II. The architect of the New Deal, he created work programs such as the WPA, and within three years of his inauguration the economy was beginning to recover. He was the first president to speak on television (in 1939) and his "Fireside Chats" aired weekly on the radio. FDR resisted entering World War II until Pearl Harbor was attacked.

"The only thing we have to fear is fear itself." —Franklin Delano Roosevelt, in his 1933 inaugural address

---

FRANZ: from the German for Francis, from the Latin for free.

FRANZ BOAS (1858–1942) was the father of modern anthropology. Born in Germany, he moved to the United States and worked as assistant curator at the American Museum of Natural History before joining the faculty of Columbia University; his students included Margaret Mead, Ruth Benedict, Edward Sapir, and Zora Neale Hurston. His 1911 book *The Mind of Primitive Man* dispelled the notion of "superior" and "inferior" races; in it he outlined his belief that learning and habits are the result of society and culture, not of instinct or racial heritage.

FREDERICK: from the Old German for peaceful ruler. Frederik is a Scandinavian form; Frederic is French. Fritz, Fred, Freddy, Rick, and Erick or Eric are used as nicknames.

FRED ASTAIRE (1899–1987) was an unlikely movie star. His long face, slim build, and weak voice caused one movie studio executive to write, "Can't act. Can't sing. Balding. Can dance a little." But Fred, born Frederick Austerlitz, and his sister Adele had started in vaudeville when they were young children, and he went on to star in more than thirty movie musicals with a number of female costars, most memorably Ginger Rogers. His best-known movies include *Holiday Inn*, *Top Hat*, *Daddy Long Legs*, and *Shall We Dance*, and some of the songs he helped to make famous are "Night and Day," "Cheek to Cheek," and "Nice Work If You Can Get It."

FREDERICK DOUGLASS (1818–1895) was the most prominent black American of the nineteenth century. Born a slave in Maryland, he never knew his father; his mother died when he was nine. Frederick was taught to read by his master's wife (she broke the law in teaching him), and in 1838 he escaped. He met William Lloyd Garrison and became involved with the Massachusetts Anti-Slavery Society, then later was a newspaper publisher. Frederick was also a stationmaster on the Underground Railroad and helped to recruit blacks for the Union army. After the war he was appointed ambassador to Haiti and the Dominican Republic.

★ ★ ★ ★ ★ ★ ★ ★ **G** ★ ★ ★ ★ ★ ★ ★ ★

GAIL: from the Irish for foreigner. Alternate spellings include Gale, Gael, Gaill, Gayle, and Gaille.

GAIL BORDEN (1801–1874) was an inventor. Born in Norwich, New York, he moved to Texas in 1829 to work as a surveyor for Stephen Austin. He started a newspaper with his brother, and after Texas won its independence, Gail helped to write the constitution. After his wife and children died from contaminated food, Gail vowed to find a way to preserve food safely. He devised a method of condensing milk in 1851 and formed the New York Condensed Milk Company in 1856; today it is known as the Borden Company. He patented a process for condensing fruit juices, as well as for condensing tea, coffee, cocoa, and beef extracts. The town of Borden, Texas, is named in his honor.

GARRETT: from the Irish for brave spearman.

GARRETT AUGUSTUS MORGAN (1877–1963) was an important African-American inventor; two of his patents are for the traffic signal and the gas mask. Born in Kentucky to former slaves, Garrett left school at age fourteen, having completed only the fifth grade. He moved to Ohio, opened a repair shop, and soon had several shops. He invented and patented the first chemical hair straightener, which brought in enough money that he could spend his time inventing. When he used the gas mask to rescue thirty-two men trapped in a tunnel beneath Lake Erie, it made headlines, and soon fire departments across the nation were ordering it; the military used it during World War I.

GENE: a short form of Eugene, from the Greek for noble born.

GENE KELLY (1912–1996) was a dancer, choreographer, and movie star. Born in Pittsburgh, Gene was playing semiprofessional hockey by the time he was fifteen years old; he also took dance lessons, and ultimately his love for the theater won out over the ice rink. He moved to New York City and within a week was dancing on Broadway; in 1940 he was cast as the lead in *Pal Joey*. Other films, and stardom, followed: *For Me and My Gal*, *Anchors Aweigh*, *Cover Girl*, *Invitation to the Dance*, and *Singin' in the Rain*.

GEORGE: from the Greek for farmer. Although the only nickname associated with this name is Georgie, there are several foreign forms: Jorge is Spanish; Jurgen and Joren are Scandinavian; Jerzy is Polish; Georges is French; Giorgio is Italian; Egor, Igor, and Yuri are Russian.

GEORGE HERBERT WALKER BUSH (b. 1924), the forty-first president of the United States and the father of the forty-third, was the son of a senator and was a navy fighter pilot during World War II. After the war, he married Barbara Pierce and went to Yale, then became active in politics. Richard Nixon appointed him ambassador to the United Nations, and under Gerald Ford he headed the CIA. Chosen as Ronald Reagan's running mate, he served two terms as vice president, then was elected president in 1988. Since leaving office, he has acted as a goodwill ambassador and philanthropist.

GEORGE WALKER BUSH (b. 1946) is the forty-third president of the United States, and the second president who is also the son of a president. Born in Connecticut, George grew up in Texas. After graduating from Yale he returned to Texas, where he met his wife, Laura. He went into the oil business, invested in the Texas Rangers baseball team, and became governor of Texas before running for president. His administration has been dominated by the terrorist attacks of September 11, 2001, and the war in Iraq.

GEORGE EASTMAN (1854–1932) founded the Eastman Kodak Company and made a fortune by inventing roll film and a camera that used it. George donated more than $100 million, often anonymously; the Massachusetts Institute of Technology, the Tuskegee Institute, the Hampton Institute, and the University of Rochester are just a few of the recipients. In 1954 a postage stamp was issued in his honor.

GEORGE GERSHWIN (1898–1937) composed some of the most beloved songs of the twentieth century. Born Jacob Gershvin to Russian-Jewish immigrants, George learned to play the piano from his older brother and collaborator, Ira. By the time he was sixteen, George was writing songs for Tin Pan Alley; his first hit song was "Swanee," sung in 1919 by Al Jolson. George wrote twenty-two musicals, including the first to win a Pulitzer Prize, *Of Thee I Sing,* as well as the opera *Porgy and Bess* and the score for the movie *Shall We Dance.*

GEORGE SMITH PATTON, JR. (1885–1945), known as Old Blood and Guts, was one of the commanders of World War II. A graduate of West Point, George competed in the 1912 Summer Olympics in Stockholm; his event was the pentathlon. As part of General Black Jack Pershing's unit in World War I, George was one of the first to use tanks in battle; he was placed in charge of the First U.S. Armored Corps, and in World War II he commanded the First U.S. Army in North Africa and the Seventh Army's invasion of Sicily. After D-day, he commanded the U.S. Third Army and blitzed through Europe, taking Germany and moving into Czechoslovakia before he was ordered to halt. Shortly after, he was in a fatal car accident. George C. Scott played him in the movie *Patton*.

"The object of war is not to die for your country, but to make the other bastard die for his." —General George S. Patton

---

GEORGE READ (1733–1798) was a signer of the Declaration of Independence. Although he was the only delegate to vote against going to war, he signed the Declaration and narrowly escaped capture once the fighting started. He became president of the state of Delaware and was part of the Constitutional Convention; because of his efforts, Delaware was the first state to ratify the Constitution.

GEORGE ROSS (1730–1779) was a signer of the Declaration of Independence. A lawyer with Loyalist leanings, George wasn't a member of the Congress that voted for independence on July 2, 1776, but he had been elected by August 2, when the document was signed, and thus became part of this historic group.

GEORGE HERMAN RUTH (1895–1948) was known as Babe, the Bambino, and the Sultan of Swat, and he is one of the greatest players in baseball's history. Although his total of 714 career home runs has been surpassed, his record of 457 total bases has endured since 1921, and his three home runs in one game wasn't equaled until 1977. He signed as a pitcher with the Boston Red Sox in 1914, and was traded five years later to the New York Yankees, where he played right field. The Babe led the Yankees to seven pennants and four World Series titles, and in the early 1930s he earned $80,000 a year. He returned to Boston at the end of his career, playing for the Braves.

GEORGE TAYLOR (1716–1781) was a signer of the Declaration of Independence. He came from Ireland as an indentured servant and worked in an iron forge; by 1742 the owner had died and he'd married the widow. He was elected by the Pennsylvania assembly to the Continental Congress, and he produced cannons, cannonballs, and shot for the army.

GEORGE WALTON (1741?–1804) was a signer of the Declaration of Independence. Orphaned at a young age and reared by an uncle, George moved to Savannah, Georgia, in 1769 and became involved in the patriot cause. He participated in the Continental Congress until the British attacked his adopted state, then he returned home to fight. Wounded, captured, and imprisoned, George survived the war and served as chief justice, governor of Georgia, and senator afterward.

GEORGE WASHINGTON (1732–1799) was considered by many to be the Father of the new nation. The first president and the commander of the Continental army during the Revolutionary War, George was the son of a Virginia planter. He served with the Virginia militia during the French and Indian Wars, and under his leadership the ragtag militia—unevenly trained and poorly equipped—defeated the greatest military power of the time. After his eight years as president, George retired to Mount Vernon with his wife, Martha.

GEORGE WHYTE (1726–1806) was a signer of the Declaration of Independence. His parents died when he was young, and George, who went to live with an uncle who was a lawyer, became a lawyer himself at age twenty. He became the mayor of Williamsburg, Virginia, in 1768, and taught law to Thomas Jefferson; later, as a professor at the College of William and Mary, his students included John Marshall and James Monroe. George was one of the first to propose the idea of separate nationhood for the colonies. After he signed the Declaration he went to work drafting Virginia's constitution, then sat on the state's high court of chancery for twenty-eight years.

GERALD: from the German for mighty spearman. Garrett, Jarrett, Geraldo, Jared, and Garrard are variations; Gerry is the most common nickname.

GERALD R. FORD (b. 1913) was the thirty-eighth president of the United States. He was appointed to the vice presidency after Spiro Agnew resigned, and after Richard Nixon resigned as president on August 9, 1974, Gerald Ford was sworn in—making him the first president who was never on a ballot. Born Leslie Lynch King, he was adopted by his mother's second husband. He was the first Eagle Scout to become president, and he served in World War II. As president, Ford tried to run a country that was reeling from inflation and a depressed economy, the Vietnam War, the Watergate Scandal, and the cold war. It was a thankless and nearly impossible task, and he lost the 1976 election to Jimmy Carter.

———————

"For myself and for our Nation, I want to thank my predecessor for all he has done to heal our land." —Jimmy Carter, in his inaugural speech

———————

GILBERT: from the French for bright promise. Gilberto is Spanish; Gil and Bert are nicknames.

GILBERT STUART (1755–1828) was a portrait painter whose best-known work was of George Washington. Born in Rhode Island to Loyalist parents, Gilbert and his family were in London when the war broke out. He returned to America in 1792, deeply in debt despite renown as London's premier portraitist. He painted three versions of George Washington; each presents a man larger than life, yet completely American. His Washington is an elder statesman without the trappings of rank or wealth. He painted the next five presidents.

GLENN: from the Irish for valley. Glen, Glyn, Glynn, and Glin are alternate spellings.

GLENN MILLER (1904–1944) was the most popular bandleader of the swing era. His Glenn Miller Orchestra broke records all over the East Coast, playing such hits as "Chattanooga Choo Choo," "In the Mood," and "Tuxedo Junction." He joined the army in 1942; in December of 1944, Glenn took off on a flight from Bedford, England, to Paris. The plane disappeared, and America lost one of its greatest musical talents.

GOUVERNEUR: from the French for governor.

GOUVERNEUR MORRIS (1752–1816) signed the U.S. Constitution and is the author of its preamble. He also was a visionary who put an indelible stamp on the new nation: he conceived of a citizenry of "Americans," rather than of separate states; he recommended the first national currency; and he was a tireless advocate for improving the conditions of soldiers. After the war, he served as U.S. minister to France, and later was a founder of the Erie Canal Commission.

GROVER: from the English for lives in a grove.

GROVER CLEVELAND (1837–1908) served two nonconsecutive terms as president of the United States—the only man to do so. He clerked for a law firm in Buffalo, New York, and was admitted to the bar in 1859. He was elected mayor of Buffalo, then ran for governor of New York in 1882. He ran for president in 1884 and won; while in office he married—the only president to do so. In 1888 he won the popular vote against Benjamin Harrison but lost in the Electoral College, but won against him four years later.

GUNNING: from the Scandinavian for warrior.

GUNNING BEDFORD, JR. (1747?–1812) was a signer of the U.S. Constitution. He graduated from the College of New Jersey (now Princeton) in 1771 and studied law. He was a delegate from Delaware to the Constitutional Convention, where he advocated for the rights of smaller states and sought to limit the powers of the executive branch. In 1789 he was appointed a federal district judge.

★ ★ ★ ★ ★ ★ ★ ★ **H** ★ ★ ★ ★ ★ ★ ★ ★

HAROLD: from the Scandinavian for army ruler. Herrold and Harald are alternate spellings, and Harry and Hal are the most common nicknames.

HAROLD "DOC" EDGERTON (1903–1990) revolutionized photography. A scientist and faculty member at the Massachusetts Institute of Technology, Harold experimented with light and photography. He invented the stroboscope, which allowed photographers and cinematographers to take extremely high-speed, stop-motion pictures, and multiflash techniques that changed sports photography. His photographs of the atomic bomb, hummingbirds in flight, and the "crown" formed by dropping one liquid into another are among the first of their kind. Working with Jacques Cousteau, Harold created a camera for use underwater, as well as a sonar device that was used to locate the USS *Monitor*. The Massachusetts Institute of Technology Museum has an exhibit of his work and inventions.

HAROLD LLOYD (1893–1971) was a silent-screen star. A master of physical comedy, he created a persona of a shy, nervous young man caught in misadventures. Born in Nebraska, he moved to California and began acting in movies in 1913. *The Freshman* is probably his best film, but the two scenes for which he is most remembered are in *Safety Last*, where he hangs from the hands of a giant clock, and *High and Dizzy*, where he clings to a skyscraper. He appeared in more than five hundred movies, and did most of his own stunts.

HARRY: familiar form of Harold or Henry.

HARRY JAMES (1916–1983) was a bandleader and trumpet player. His father was the bandleader of a circus and his mother was a trapeze artist. Harry learned to play the drums at seven and the trumpet at nine; he was soon performing in the circus band. Harry joined Benny Goodman's band in 1937, and left it the following year to form his own band. He became famous for his ear-shattering sound, his hit songs—"The Flight of the Bumblebee," "I Cried for You," and "You Made Me Love You"—as well as for his marriage to pinup girl Betty Grable.

HARRY HOUDINI (1874–1926) was born Erich Weiss in Budapest, but emigrated with his family to America. Magic was his passion, and his feats of prestidigitation and escape captured the imagination of the world. He took the name Houdini when he was seventeen, and began making movies in 1918. He died on Halloween in 1926 from injuries sustained from a blow to the abdomen (he hadn't prepared to take the hit). Before he died, he promised his wife he would contact her from the other side; every Halloween she held a séance.

"No prison can hold me; no hand or leg irons or steel locks can shackle me. No ropes of chains can keep me from my freedom." —Harry Houdini

---

HARRY S. TRUMAN (1884–1972) became the thirty-third president after Franklin Delano Roosevelt died. A Midwesterner, Harry's no-nonsense maxims were "The buck stops here" and "If you can't stand the heat, get out of the kitchen." He grew up in Independence, Missouri, and married Bess Wallace, whom he'd known since grade school. After fighting in France during World War I, he became active in local politics; he was elected senator in 1934. One of his first acts as president was to issue the order to bomb Hiroshima and Nagasaki; Japan surrendered, and the Second World War ended soon after. He witnessed the signing of the charter for the United Nations, and, later, ordered troops to Korea. Among his domestic actions, Truman expanded Social Security and signed antidiscrimination laws.

HARVEY: from the Old French for warrior. Herve is the modern French.

HARVEY CUSHING (1869–1939) was a great neurosurgeon whose innovations in medicine have saved thousands of lives. Alarmed by the number of deaths caused by improper amounts of anesthesia, he created "the ether chart" early in his career. Later, he devised methods of controlling bleeding during brain surgery, reducing the mortality rate from almost 100 percent to about 10 percent. Within a year of Röntgen's discovery of X-rays, he was working on using them in clinical settings. He also won the Pulitzer Prize for his biography of Sir William Osler.

HARVEY WASHINGTON WILEY (1844–1930) is the man to thank for getting labels on packaged foods and getting toxins out of foods. As chief chemist for the U.S. Department of Agriculture, Harvey looked into America's food supply and found distressing, if not alarming, news: coal-tar dye and borax in sausage, formaldehyde in pork and beans, alum in bread. It took him more than twenty years, but in 1906 the Pure Food and Drug Act was passed. Harvey came under attack by food manufacturers, and he resigned from the USDA because of government concessions to them.

HAYM: a variation on Chaim, from the Hebrew for life. Haim, Hayyam, and Hyman are other variations.

HAYM SALOMON (1740–1785) isn't a name in the history books, but without his patriotism and generosity America might not exist. Born in Russian Poland, he emigrated to America and made a fortune of $600,000—and then gave it all to the new government. He was arrested by the British, and while serving as an interpreter for the Hessian troops he worked to persuade them to switch sides. He negotiated with France and Holland to send aid to the revolutionaries, served as a spy, and died nearly penniless.

HENRY: from the Old German for household ruler. Heinrich is the German; Enrique is Spanish; Henri is French; Hendrick is Dutch, and Henryk is Polish. Hank is the most common nickname; Hal and Harry are sometimes used.

HENRY CLAY (1771–1852) saw the British ransack his house when he was a child; it turned him into an ardent Unionist. He was a brilliant orator and was elected to the House of Representatives in 1811, where he served as Speaker of the House. He ran for president four times but never won, and served in the Senate from 1825 until his death. Although he considered slavery "the deepest stain upon the character of the country," he tried to keep the country united. He wrote the Missouri Compromise and the Compromise Act of 1850. His estate, Ashland, still stands in Lexington, Kentucky.

HENRY JOHNSON (1850–1904) belonged to the Ninth U.S. Cavalry, the black regiment known as buffalo soldiers, and was awarded the Congressional Medal of Honor. Sergeant Henry Johnson fought in a bloody siege that started after another cavalry division had been ambushed and massacred by Ute Indians. The siege lasted from September 29 to October 5, 1879; Henry's citation reads: "Voluntarily left fortified shelter under heavy fire at close range; made the rounds of the pits to instruct the guards; fought his way to the creek and back to bring water to the wounded."

HENRY KNOX (1750–1806) was a general in the American Revolution. In the winter of 1775, George Washington and his troops needed cannons to keep the British from taking Boston. Henry and his men built sledges and transported the guns from Fort Ticonderoga. One gun fell through the ice crossing the Mohawk River, but Henry retrieved it and delivered more than fifty tons of artillery in the form of cannons and mortar. Washington drove the British from Boston, and Knox and his artillery were in every major engagement thereafter—including at Yorktown, where the British surrendered.

HENRY WADSWORTH LONGFELLOW (1807–1882) was one of America's best, and best-loved, poets. His poems immortalized America's history and heritage, its people and landscapes: "Song of Hiawatha," "Evangeline," "The Village Blacksmith," "The Wreck of the Hesperus," and "The Courtship of Miles Standish."

"Life is real! Life is earnest! / And the grave is not its goal; / Dust thou art, to dust returnest, / Was not spoken of the soul." —Henry Wadsworth Longfellow, "A Psalm of Life"

HENRY DAVID THOREAU (1817–1862) changed the way we think and live. In 1845 he built a cabin on the shores of Walden Pond; the journal he kept during his two years there became the book *Walden*. An abolitionist who helped slaves escape to Canada, Henry wrote on civil disobedience, and his ideas can be seen in the words and work of Martin Luther King, Jr., and Mohandas K. Gandhi. His books about nature and travel, *The Maine Woods*, *Cape Cod*, and *A Week on the Concord and Merrimack Rivers*, speak of the importance of protecting the environment and natural resources.

HERBERT: from the German for soldier. Rigoberto is the Spanish variation; Bert is the most common short form.

HERBERT HOOVER (1874–1964) was America's thirty-first president. The son of a Quaker blacksmith, Herbert attended Stanford University and became a mining engineer. He and his wife lived in China during the Boxer Rebellion; he built barricades while she worked in a hospital. They were in London at the start of World War I; Herbert helped 120,000 Americans return home, delivered food to starving people on the Continent, and served as the head of the U.S. Food Administration. After the war he helped to distribute food throughout Europe and the famine-ravaged Soviet Union. He was president when the stock market crashed and was unfairly blamed for the Depression; he served one term as president, and later worked in Truman's and Eisenhower's administrations.

HERMAN: from the German for soldier. Armin ("army man") is one variation; Armand is French.

HERMAN MELVILLE (1819–1891) wrote some of the greatest novels of the nineteenth century. One of eight children, Herman left school at eleven after his father died. At twenty-two he went to sea on a whaling ship; he jumped ship in the Marquesas Islands, signed on with another ship bound for the Sandwich Islands, and then joined the navy. He moved to Pittsfield, Massachusetts, and wrote prolifically until debts forced him to return to New York, where he worked as a customs inspector. Among his best-known works are "Bartleby the Scrivener" and the novels *Typee, Omoo, Redburn, Mardi,* and the epic *Moby-Dick; Billy Budd* was published more than thirty years after his death.

HIRAM: from the Hebrew for most noble.

HIRAM BINGHAM (1875–1956) was an explorer. Born in Hawaii to missionary parents, he went to South America in 1905. Three years later he followed the Spanish trade route from Buenos Aires to Lima, where he heard about the legendary "lost city of the Incas." In 1911, he took a mule train and discovered the ruins of Machu Picchu, then located the lost capital of the Incas, Vitcos, and a third site called Espiritu Pampa. His final expedition was in 1915. Hiram served as governor of Connecticut, and from 1925 to 1933 he was a U.S. senator.

HOAGLAND: a surname used as a first name.

HOAGLAND "HOAGY" CARMICHAEL (1899–1981) composed some of America's best-loved standards; he also was an actor. His songs include "Stardust" (it's the most recorded song ever written), "Georgia on My Mind," "Heart and Soul," and "Riverboat Shuffle," which he wrote for his friend Bix Beiderbecke. In 1935 he went to Hollywood as a songwriter, and won an Academy Award for "In the Cool, Cool, Cool of the Evening." Later he appeared in the television series *Laramie.*

HORACE, HORATIO: from the Latin family name Horatius.

HORACE GREELEY (1811–1872) was a newspaper editor and founder of the *New York Tribune.* He was an abolitionist and public speaker, then won a seat in Congress. He made a bid for president but lost to Ulysses S. Grant. Today, he is best remembered for his advice, "Go west, young man!"

HORACE MANN (1796–1859) was an educator who established the American public school system. A Massachusetts native, he started out as a lawyer and then entered politics; he founded the first state mental hospital as well as a state board of education. He then turned to creating public high schools and schools for teacher training that were nonsectarian and open to all students, regardless of race or gender. The system he founded was copied by other states.

HORATIO ALGER (1832–1899) wrote tales that captured the American dream. He grew up in genteel poverty as the son of a minister, then graduated with honors from Harvard University. Unable to serve in the army due to his poor eyesight and short stature, he wrote patriotic stories instead. After the war he moved to New York. His first novel was *Ragged Dick; or, Street Life in New York with the Boot-Blacks*; it was published in 1868, and more than one hundred rags-to-riches novels followed.

HOSEA: from the Hebrew for salvation.

HOSEA WILLIAMS (1926–2000) was a leader of the civil rights movement. His mother died giving birth to him and he was reared by his grandparents. When he was fourteen, he came close to being lynched because he was friendly with a white girl. He served in France during World War II and had two more brushes with death: his platoon was wiped out when it was hit by a shell, and the ambulance taking him to the hospital was hit; in both instances he was the sole survivor. After the war he was beaten for drinking from a whites-only fountain and was left for dead; the undertaker discovered he had a pulse. Hosea became involved with the NAACP and by the 1950s was working alongside Martin Luther King, Jr. He led the march in Selma, Alabama, and was with King when he was assassinated.

HOWARD: from the English for watchman; Howie and Ward are the short forms of this name.

HOWARD HAWKS (1896–1977) was one of the great directors of Hollywood. He started in the story department at Paramount and by 1925 he was directing; he is known for such feature films as *The Big Sleep*, *Bringing Up Baby*, *Scarface*, *To Have and Have Not*, and *His Girl Friday*. Known for comedies, gangster movies, and Westerns, Hawks's signature style included heroes and antiheroes, visual imagery, and atmospheric lighting.

HOWARD MAYS (b. 1931) might not ring any bells, but say Willie Mays and you've got the Say Hey Kid. Born in Alabama, Willie was playing semipro baseball when he was sixteen; the New York Giants signed him in 1950. Known for his trademark basket catch, he was also a slugger. In 1954 he batted .345 and hit forty-one home runs; he led the league in home runs in 1955, 1962, 1964, and 1965, and by 1966 he was the highest-paid player in the sport. He made the All-Star team twenty times, and has been inducted into the Baseball Hall of Fame.

HUGH: from the German for bright. Hugo and Hughes are variations; Huey (or Hughie) is the familiar form.

HUEY LONG (1893–1935) was governor of Louisiana and a U.S. senator whose slogan was "Every Man a King." In his home state he built roads, hospitals, the Louisiana State University Medical School, and a new state capitol, and he provided schoolchildren with free textbooks. A modern-day Robin Hood, Huey was a radical populist who wanted to take from the rich and give to the poor: he was elected to the Senate on a platform he called Share Our Wealth, and wanted to guarantee every family an income of five thousand dollars and everyone over age sixty a pension. He ran for president but was assassinated before the election.

HUGH WILLIAMSON (1735–1819) was a signer of the U.S. Constitution. A member of the first graduating class of the College of Pennsylvania, Hugh was on his way to London when he witnessed the Boston Tea Party. While in London he testified before the Privy Council. He told its members that repression would inspire a rebellion. Hugh had trained as a doctor; during the war he was appointed physician and surgeon general. He smuggled medicine from the West Indies through Britain's blockades, averted a smallpox epidemic, and kept the troops in the Dismal Swamp free of disease. He represented North Carolina in the Constitutional Convention, then served in Congress.

HUMPHREY: from the German for peaceful strength.

HUMPHREY BOGART (1899–1957) was one of the great film stars of the twentieth century. Laconic, charismatic, and the epitome of cool, "Bogie" became a star with his performance as Sam Spade in *The Maltese Falcon*. He won his first Best Actor nomination for his role as Rick in *Casablanca*, and won the Academy Award for his performance in *The African Queen*. He was cast opposite Lauren Bacall in *To Have and Have Not*; they fell in love and were together until his death. One of his finest roles was as the insane captain in *The Caine Mutiny*; other memorable films were *The Treasure of the Sierra Madre* and *The Harder They Fall*, his last film.

★ ★ ★ ★ ★ ★ ★ ★ ★   **I**   ★ ★ ★ ★ ★ ★ ★ ★ ★

IRVING: from the Old English for sea friend. Earvin, Erwin, and Irvine are variations; Irv is the short form.

IRVING BERLIN (1888–1989) wrote more than one thousand songs. Born Israel Isadore Baline in Siberia, he moved to New York and found work as a singing waiter. By 1911 his song "Alexander's Ragtime Band" had sold more than a million copies. After his first wife died on their honeymoon, he wrote "When I Lost You"; other songs include "Cheek to Cheek," "Easter Parade," and "God Bless America"; he donated the royalties from the last song to the Boy Scouts and the Girl Scouts. During World War II he entertained the troops overseas and gave more than $2 million to the Army Relief Fund.

ISAAC: from the Hebrew for he will laugh. Ytzhak, Itzak, Izaac, and Isaak are alternate spellings; Ike is the most common diminutive.

ISAAC HULL (1773–1843) was a naval hero of the War of 1812. As captain of the *Constitution*, he found himself becalmed and surrounded by five warships from the greatest navy in the world. Using every trick he knew he outmaneuvered the British ships and sailed into Boston Harbor. A week later he captured three ships and burned two, then went after the British frigate *Guerriere*. Within thirty minutes the frigate's hull had taken thirty shots; its masts were down and the ship surrendered. The *Constitution* had taken no hits, and was renamed *Old Ironsides*.

ISAAC BASHEVIS SINGER (1902–1991) was born in Poland and came to New York in 1935; he became a U.S. citizen in 1943. He started writing for the *Forward*, a Jewish newspaper, and even after the war continued to write in Yiddish. His stories are humorous yet poignant; the best known is *Gimpel, The Fool*, which was translated into English by Saul Bellow. He wrote eighteen novels, fourteen children's books, and several volumes of short stories. He won the Nobel Prize in Literature in 1978.

ISAIAH: from the Hebrew for salvation of God.

ISAIAH MONTGOMERY (1847–1924) was born a slave; he was owned by Joseph Davis, the older brother of Jefferson Davis, and went on to found one of the first incorporated black towns in the United States. He joined the Union navy and helped to capture Vicksburg; after the war he went into business with his father. The two men bought Joseph Davis's plantation. Isaiah later helped to found the National Negro Business League with Booker T. Washington. In 1886 Isaiah bought 840 acres in Mississippi and named it Mound Bayou; the settlement eventually grew to 30,000 acres with a population of four thousand. Today it is a historic site.

ISRAEL: from the Hebrew for wrestled with God.

ISRAEL PUTNAM (1718–1790) was a general in the Revolutionary army. He'd been plowing his fields one April morning when he heard of the attack at Lexington; he left the oxen in the field and rode off to summon the militia. Israel rode one hundred miles in eighteen hours and led the battles at Breed's Hill and Bunker Hill.

"Don't fire until you see the whites of their eyes." —General Israel Putnam at the battle of Bunker Hill

---

★ ★ ★ ★ ★ ★ ★ ★ J ★ ★ ★ ★ ★ ★ ★ ★

JACK: familiar form of Jacob or John.

JACK DEMPSEY (1895–1983) was one of the great heavyweight boxers. Born William Harrison Dempsey, he was the son of sharecroppers. He lived in hobo jungles from the time he was sixteen to nineteen, and boxing was his way out of poverty. He earned $2.50 in his first fight; for his first match with Gene Tunney eleven years later he earned $711,000, and throughout his career he made more than $3.5 million. He finally lost his title in a bout with Tunney and left the ring. He served with the Coast Guard in World War II and later ran a restaurant on Broadway.

JACK JOHNSON (1878–1946) was the first black heavyweight champion. Born in Galveston, Texas, John Arthur Johnson quit school in fifth grade, and started boxing when he was twenty-two. In a career that spanned forty-three years, he was knocked out only three times, but racism dogged him. At first, whites refused to fight him. When the defending champion agreed to a bout in 1908, Jack beat him. He became a hero among blacks, while whites looked for a "great white hope" to win the title, which he held until 1915.

JACK LONDON (1876–1916) wrote more than fifty books. He grew up in the slums of Oakland and did odd jobs; as a young man he was jailed for vagrancy, which proved to be a turning point in his life. He went back to school and decided to become a writer, then went to the Klondike in search of gold. He nearly died, but the adventure gave him fodder for the stories that made him famous: "To Build a Fire," *The Call of the Wild*, and *White Fang*.

JACK ROOSEVELT ROBINSON (1919–1972) was called Jackie. The first black major league ballplayer, Jackie joined the Brooklyn Dodgers in 1947 and played for them until 1956. He was chosen Rookie of the Year in 1947 and Most Valuable Player in 1949, and the Dodgers won the pennant in six of the ten years Jackie wore uniform number 42 for them. When he retired from baseball, every major league team retired his number.

JACKSON: from the Old English for Jack's son.

JACKSON POLLOCK (1912–1956) was a major figure in abstract expressionism. Born in Wyoming, he grew up in Arizona before moving to

New York. He married Lee Krasner, an artist from Brooklyn, and the two moved to the east end of Long Island. While they collaborated on some paintings, Jackson's "action paintings" were a sensation. He flung and dripped paint on huge canvases spread on the floor. They were an immediate success, but the pressure of meeting the demands of collectors proved to be overwhelming; he died in an alcohol-related car accident.

"On the floor I am more at ease, I feel nearer, more a part of the painting, since this way I can walk around in it, work from the four sides and be literally 'in' the painting." —Jackson Pollock, 1947

JACOB: from the Hebrew for he who supplants, and a variation on James. Giacomo is the Italian variation; Jacques is French; Yakov is Russian, and Jacobo is Spanish. Jake, Jay, and Jock are nicknames.

JACOB RIIS (1849–1914) was born in Denmark and moved to New York in 1870. His first three years there were spent on the street, but in 1873 he found work as a photojournalist with the *New York Evening Sun*. His photographs of living conditions in the slums and of young children working in factories are a graphic yet moving depiction of life for the working poor. He collected them into a book called *How the Other Half Lives*. Theodore Roosevelt said of Jacob, "No man has ever more vitally and faithfully expressed and interpreted the American spirit. He was a brother to all men and especially to the unfortunate."

JAMES: a variation on Jacob, from the Hebrew for he who supplants. Hamish is Scottish; Iago, Diego, and Jaime are Spanish; Seamus is Irish. Jim, Jimmy, Jamie, and Jem are nicknames.

JAMES BUCHANAN (1791–1869) was the fifteenth president of the United States. The only unmarried president and the only Pennsylvanian, he served as a congressman and a senator, as well as in various cabinet positions, before he was elected president. Unable to stop the Civil War or the legal right of states to secede, he sent the *Star of the West* to carry reinforcements to Fort Sumter shortly before he left office.

JAMES EARL CARTER, JR. (b. 1924) was America's thirty-ninth president. Known to all as Jimmy, he was born in Plains, Georgia, attended the Naval Academy, and served on submarines, eventually becoming a nuclear engineer. Elected to the Georgia senate in 1962, he served three terms before becoming governor in 1970. As president, Jimmy Carter battled double-digit inflation, rising unemployment, and the energy crisis. He expanded the national park system and established the Department of Education, and his foreign policy saw the Camp David Accords between Egypt and Israel. He lost the 1980 election to Ronald Reagan, and after leaving the Oval Office he founded Habitat for Humanity. In 2002 he was awarded the Nobel Peace Prize in recognition of his work for human rights.

JAMES FENIMORE COOPER (1789–1851) wrote fiction about the frontier. He grew up in Cooperstown, New York (his father founded the town), hearing tales of wilderness adventures and Indian life. Expelled from Yale, he was sent on a merchant ship by his father. After he got married, his wife challenged him to write a novel, so he did. His "Leather-Stocking Tales" include *The Last of the Mohicans*, *The Pathfinder*, and *The Deerslayer*; he wrote several other books and essays as well.

JAMES ABRAM GARFIELD (1831–1881) was the twentieth president of the United States. The last of the log cabin presidents, he was born in Ohio. His father died when he was two, but he put himself through college, then served in the Ohio senate. He made the rank of major general during the Civil War and in 1862 was elected to Congress, where he served eighteen years. He was shot on July 2, 1881, six months and fifteen days after he took office, and died of an infection in September. His term was the second shortest.

JAMES MADISON (1751–1836) was a Founding Father and America's fourth president. A Virginian who owned slaves, Madison abhorred slavery. He was a close friend of Thomas Jefferson, and was an ardent federalist. He collaborated with John Jay and Alexander Hamilton in writing the *Federalist Papers*, and he was a major contributor to the writing of the Constitution. He also wrote George Washington's first inaugural address. James served in the House of Representatives and as secretary of state before he won the presidency.

JAMES MONROE (1758–1831) was America's fifth president and one of the youngest Founding Fathers. A Virginia native, he left college to join the war and was seriously wounded at Trenton. He returned to his family's plantation, and after the war joined the Virginia legislature. James worked with James Madison and Thomas Jefferson to create the Republican Party. During George Washington's presidency he served as minister to France, and under Jefferson he returned to negotiate the Louisiana Purchase; he also served as Madison's secretary of state.

Elected president in 1816, Monroe created the Monroe Doctrine and also won Florida from the Spanish.

JAMES KNOX POLK (1795–1849) served as the nation's eleventh president. Born in North Carolina, he grew up in Tennessee and joined the Tennessee House of Representatives when he was twenty-eight. At the urging of his mentor, Andrew Jackson, James ran for governor of Tennessee and, in 1844, for president. Though he only served one term, James Polk was responsible for greatly expanding the United States: he made Texas the twenty-eighth state, and extended the country's borders to the forty-ninth parallel from the Rockies to California; he also engaged Mexico in a war for California.

JAMES SMITH (1719?–1806) was a signer of the Declaration of Independence. An Irish immigrant, he settled in York, Pennsylvania, with his family. He joined the rebellion in 1774 and raised a militia, serving as its captain. James helped to draft Pennsylvania's constitution, and although he was elected to the Continental Congress too late to vote on it, he arrived in time to put pen to the document.

JAMES EWELL BROWN STUART (1833–1864) was known familiarly as Jeb, from his first three initials. A West Point graduate, Jeb was a Virginian first and a U.S. soldier second: when Virginia seceded from the Union, Jeb resigned from the United States Army to join Stonewall Jackson. He became one of the Confederate army's most colorful generals. As head of the cavalry, Jeb led some daring exploits. He was mortally wounded at Yellow Tavern in July of 1864.

JAMES FRANCIS THORPE (1887–1953), called Jim, is widely acknowledged as the greatest athlete of the twentieth century. Half Irish and half Indian, Jim played college football and was an All-American. In the 1912 Summer Olympics in Stockholm, King Gustav said, "Sir, you are the greatest athlete in the world," after he won gold medals in both the pentathlon and the decathlon. Jim was stripped of his medals the following year because he'd played semiprofessional baseball and was in violation of amateur status rules. Thirty years after he died, his medals were restored.

JAMES WILSON (1741?–1806) signed the Declaration of Independence. He came to Reading, Pennsylvania, from Scotland in 1765. While serving on the Continental Congress, he voted with John Morton and Benjamin Franklin for independence; the majority of the Pennsylvania delegates voted against it. During the war James speculated on land, and he used his wealth to create the Bank of North America. James helped to draft the Constitution, and through his counsel Pennsylvania became the second state to ratify it.

JEFFERSON: from the English for Jeffrey's son. It is a surname used as a first name, often in honor of Thomas Jefferson. Jeff is the short form.

JEFFERSON DAVIS (1808–1889) was the president of the Confederate States of America. Born in Kentucky, he attended West Point and graduated in 1828. He served in the Mexican-American War, and then was appointed secretary of war in Franklin Pierce's cabinet. Jefferson was elected president of the Confederacy on February 22, 1862. When the Civil War was nearing its end, he fled from the capital of Richmond but was captured and spent two years in jail on charges of treason; he was never tried. After his release, he and his wife, Varina, moved to Mississippi, where he spent the rest of his life.

JOEL: from the Hebrew for God is willing.

JOEL CHANDLER HARRIS (1848–1908) was the author of the Uncle Remus folktales. He worked at various newspapers as a newsman and wrote stories for adults and children, but he never forgot the stories he'd heard plantation slaves tell. After reading an article on African-American folklore he created Uncle Remus, a folksy character full of stories, sayings, and songs. He wrote nearly two hundred Uncle Remus stories; the first collection of them was published in 1880, and within a few months had sold ten thousand copies.

JOHN: from the Hebrew for God is gracious. John is often combined with other names, and may be spelled John or Jon. Jean is the French spelling; Juan is Spanish; Ian and Iain are Scottish; Gian is Italian; Yannis and Yanni are Greek; Ivan is Russian; Johan is German; Sean is Irish; Evan is Welsh; Jan is Danish, and Jens is Scandinavian. Hans is used in Germany and Scandinavia. Jack and Johnny are familiar or pet forms.

JOHN ADAMS (1735–1826) was the first vice president and the second president of the country he helped found. One of the masterminds of America's fight for independence, Adams helped draft the Declaration of Independence, which he signed; he was also part of the Constitutional Convention in 1779 and negotiated the Treaty of Paris in 1783 with Benjamin Franklin and John Jay. He traveled to Europe on diplomatic missions, and after serving as president he retired to his home in Quincy, Massachusetts. He died on July 4, 1826, the same day as his rival, Thomas Jefferson.

JOHN QUINCY ADAMS (1757–1848) was the sixth president of the United States and the son of the second president. He watched the battle of Bunker Hill from his family's farm in Braintree (now Quincy), Massachusetts. Elected to the U.S. Senate in 1802, he was appointed minister to Russia when James Madison was president; he served as James Monroe's secretary of state and helped to draft the Monroe Doctrine. He became president in 1824; during his time in office he built roads and canals, financed scientific exploration, and proposed a national university and a national observatory. He was defeated in 1828 by Andrew Jackson, but was elected to represent Massachusetts in Congress, where he served until his death.

JOHN JAMES AUDUBON (1785–1851) was a naturalist and artist whose passion was wildlife, particularly birds. He traveled the country studying and drawing birds, with the goal of painting every variety of bird he found. When he couldn't find a publisher for his paintings, he commissioned an engraver to create the 435 life-size copperplates, and lined up subscribers to finance the printing. His four-volume set, *The Birds of America*, took more than twelve years to complete.

JOHN BROWN (1800–1859) was an abolitionist whose raid at Harpers Ferry was a catalyst for the Civil War. Brown was part of a group of abolitionists who stormed the U.S. Arsenal at Harpers Ferry. The goal was to use the arms to liberate slaves. He was captured, tried, and hanged. Although he was considered a murderer in the South, Northerners deemed him a hero, and the song "John Brown's Body" was a marching song for the Union army.

"I, John Brown, am quite certain that the crimes of this guilty land will never be purged away but with blood. I had, as I now think, vainly flattered myself that without very much bloodshed it might be done."
—John Brown, shortly before his execution

JOHN CALDWELL CALHOUN (1782–1850) was a South Carolina man known for his strong will and passionate states' rights stance. When South Carolina tried to nullify federal tariffs, the navy sent warships to coerce the state into obeying them; Andrew Jackson made a famous toast: "Our federal Union—it must and shall be preserved." Calhoun shot back: "Our Union, next to our liberties, most dear." He served in the state and federal senates, as secretary of state and secretary of war, and was John Quincy Adams's vice president. In 1957, the U.S. Senate honored Calhoun as one of the five greatest senators of all time.

JOHN C. FRÉMONT (1846–1901) was an explorer of the American West. He discovered the best route to Oregon, then made a trek to the

Great Salt Lake, up to Washington State, down through California's San Joaquin Valley, then along the Old Spanish Trail. His account of this second trip, written with his wife, Jessie Benton Frémont, was a best seller. Frémont settled on forty-four thousand acres in California and later became a senator.

JOHN HANCOCK (1737–1793) was one of the richest men of Colonial America. The first man to sign his name to the Declaration of Independence, John Hancock signed it large enough so that the king would be able to see it without his spectacles. He joined the Adams cousins, John and Samuel, as revolutionaries shortly after the Stamp Act of 1765: Hancock defied it and was charged with smuggling; John Adams got the charges dismissed. John Hancock organized the Minute Men, started the boycott that led to the Boston Tea Party, and after the war served nine terms as governor of Massachusetts.

JOHN HART (1713–1779) was a signer of the Declaration of Independence. A farmer from Hopewell, New Jersey, he served in the state legislature and protested the Stamp Act. When the British invaded New Jersey they laid siege to his farm. John's wife was dying and he refused to leave. After she died he escaped and lived for a year in the woods, avoiding capture. Despite his advanced age, he joined the army as a private after the battle of Princeton but died before the war ended.

JOHN LEE HOOKER (1917–2001) was an influential musician. Born in Clarksdale, Mississippi, he ran away from home at fourteen. By 1943 he was living and performing in Detroit; he made his first record, "Boogie Chillen," in 1948; hits like "Crawling King Snake," "In the Mood," "Rock House Boogie," and "One Bourbon, One Scotch, One Beer" followed. John Lee Hooker's music and style of guitar playing were discovered by British bands like the Rolling Stones and the Animals in the early 1960s and continue to influence musicians today.

"I don't like no fancy chords. Just the boogie. The drive. The feeling. . . . It's a deep feeling—you just can't stop listening to that sad blues sound. My sound." —John Lee Hooker

---

JOHN JAY (1745–1829) was the first chief justice of the United States Supreme Court. Born to a wealthy family in New York, he attended Kings College (now Columbia University), and in 1774 was part of a revolutionary group called the New York Committee of Fifty-one, a forerunner of the Continental Congress. He played a leading role in drafting New York's constitution, and in 1778 was the Continental Congress's president. A key negotiator of the Treaty of Paris, John Jay also contributed to the *Federalist Papers* before accepting George Washington's request to become chief justice. After he stepped down in 1796 he served two terms as governor of New York.

JOHN PAUL JONES (1747–1792) was one of the great naval heroes of the Revolutionary War. In his most famous battle, the fifty-gun British frigate *Serapis* attacked John Paul's ship the *Bon Homme Richard*. Fires raged on board, but when the British captain asked if he surrendered, John Paul yelled back, "I have not yet begun to fight!" Though they were outnumbered and outgunned, John Paul's crew outfought the British crew, who surrendered.

JOHN FITZGERALD KENNEDY (1917–1963) was America's thirty-fifth president. He was the youngest man to be elected to the office, and after he was assassinated in November of 1963 he became the youngest to die in office. A graduate of Harvard, Kennedy served in the navy in World War II. He married Jacqueline Bouvier, and wrote *Profiles in Courage*, which won a Pulitzer Prize. He was elected to the Congress and then to the Senate in 1953; he won the presidency in 1960. During his three years in office he oversaw the creation of the Peace Corps, called for civil rights legislation, and created programs that supported creative arts, physical education, and the economy.

"Ask not what your country can do for you; ask what you can do for your country." —John F. Kennedy, in his inaugural address

------

JOHN PIERPONT MORGAN (1837–1913) was a banker and railroad tycoon who became one of America's richest men. During two monetary crises, in 1893 and 1907, J. P. Morgan stepped in to stop financial panic and bail out the government. He donated his personal art collection to the Metropolitan Museum of Art and founded the U.S. Steel Corporation, but his actions with Northern Pacific railroad stock led the government to pass the Sherman Antitrust Act.

JOHN JOSEPH PERSHING (1860–1948) was known as Black Jack. He graduated from West Point in 1886 and became one of the army's highest-ranking officers. He fought against the Apaches and Sioux, won the Silver Star in the Spanish-American War, and fought in the Philippines Insurrection. While he was on duty in 1915, his wife and children died in a fire. To allay his grief he threw himself into his career. In charge of American troops in France during World War I, Black Jack insisted his men be adequately trained before going into battle. He wrote his memoirs after the war; the book won a Pulitzer Prize for history.

JOHN D. ROCKEFELLER (1839–1937) was the first billionaire in history. He founded Standard Oil (now ExxonMobil), the largest oil refining business in the world, and was as notorious for his ruthless business dealings as he was respected for his philanthropy. Among the institutions he endowed or funded: Rockefeller University, the University of Chicago, and the Great Smoky Mountains National Park.

JOHN STEINBECK (1902–1968) was a Nobel Prize–winning novelist. Born in Salinas, California, Steinbeck wrote such stories as "The Red Pony" and "Tortilla Flat," as well as the novels *Cannery Row*, *Of Mice and Men*, and the Pulitzer Prize–winning *The Grapes of Wrath*. Shunned in his hometown for writing about labor strife and working conditions, John moved to New York and settled in Sag Harbor. He wrote *East of Eden* while living on the East Coast; many of his books have been made into movies.

JOHN TYLER (1790–1862) was the tenth president, and the first to assume the office due to the death of his predecessor. Born in Virginia, Tyler was strongly for states' rights. He served in Congress and as governor of Virginia, aligning with other Southern states' rights proponents to fight Andrew Jackson's nationalist programs. Tyler passed the "Log Cabin" bill, which allowed settlers to buy 160 acres for $1.25 per acre. He served in the Confederate House of Representatives after Virginia seceded from the Union.

JOHN WAYNE (1907–1979) was born Marion Robert Morrison in Winterset, Iowa, but throughout his life he was called Duke. He went to the University of Southern California on a football scholarship, and worked on the Fox movie lot during summer vacations. There he met the director John Ford, who recommended him for the lead in the Western *The Big Trail*. For nine years, Wayne worked in B movies, then got his big break when Ford cast him as the Ringo Kid in *Stagecoach*. He went on to star in 142 movies in a career that spanned fifty years, and was nominated for three Academy Awards; he won the Best Actor award for his work as Rooster Cogburn in *True Grit*. He helped to found the Motion Picture Alliance for the Preservation of American Ideals in 1944. Whether in Westerns or war movies, John Wayne played—and personified—the ultimate American hero.

JONAS: a variation on Jonah, from the Hebrew for dove.

JONAS SALK (1914–1995) was the scientist who developed the first safe and effective polio vaccine. Poliomyelitis, or infantile paralysis, had crippled thousands of children and adults during the 1940s and 1950s. Jonas created the vaccine in 1947, but it was first used on a mass scale in 1955; since then, polio has been virtually eradicated. Salk received no money for his vaccine and refused to allow it to be patented. At the time of his death he was working on a vaccine for the AIDS virus.

JOSEPH: from the Hebrew for Jehovah increases. José is Spanish; Josephe is French; Giuseppe is Italian; Jozef is German and Polish, and Iosef is Russian. Joe, Joey, Jody, and Joss are nicknames; Che and Pepe are Spanish nicknames.

JOSEPH PAUL DiMAGGIO (1914–1999) was "the Yankee Clipper," one of the best baseball players of all time. He played with the Yankees from 1936 to 1951, though he only played eleven seasons (he missed four seasons because he served in World War II). He was voted the Most Valuable Player in three seasons; his lifetime batting average was .325, he hit 361 career home runs, and he played in ten World Series and won nine of them. In 1941 he had a fifty-six-game hitting streak, a record that still stands.

JOSEPH HEWES (1730–1779) was a signer of the Declaration of Independence. A Quaker merchant, he supported a boycott of British goods even though it hurt him financially; and when he could not reconcile the Quakers' belief in pacifism with his support for the war, he left the faith. He was elected to the Continental Congress in 1774, and although he resisted voting for independence at first, he changed his mind.

JOSEPH STILWELL (1883–1946) was a four-star general in the United States Army. Known as Vinegar Joe, he inspired the world with his courage in battle during World War II. Fighting in Burma, Stilwell and his men were outmanned and outequipped by Japanese forces. They left Burma for India, traveling on foot most of the way. Food was scarce and the heat was oppressive, but as soon as they made it to India Stilwell planned for them to go back and take Burma—and they did.

JOSHUA: from the Hebrew for Jehovah is salvation. Josh is the most common short form.

JOSH GIBSON (1911–1947) was a catcher in the Negro Leagues. One of the best power hitters in baseball's history, Josh often hit home runs in excess of 500 feet—one was measured at 575 feet! He led the Negro National League in home runs for ten straight years. He suffered a stroke when he was thirty-five and died a few hours later.

JOSHUA LOGAN (1908–1988) was a director, producer, actor, and playwright with an astonishing number of hits. He won seven Tony Awards, two Academy Awards, and a Pulitzer Prize. On Broadway, he directed *Annie Get Your Gun*, *South Pacific*, *Fanny*, and *Mister Roberts*; he took over directing the film version of *Mister Roberts* after John Ford got sick, then directed such movies as *Bus Stop*, *Sayonara*, and *South Pacific*, as well as *Camelot* and *Paint Your Wagon*.

JOSIAH: from the Hebrew for fire of the Lord.

JOSIAH BARTLETT (1729–1795) was a signer of the Declaration of Independence. A delegate from New Hampshire, he was the first to vote for independence and the second to sign the document; later, he was the first to sign the Articles of Confederation. He was a physician, and during the war he provided the troops with medical supplies. After the war he became governor of New Hampshire.

JUSTIN: from the Latin for just.

JUSTIN MORRILL (1810–1898) was the senator from Vermont who wrote the Morrill Land-Grant College Act of 1862: this law created a college in each state that provided a liberal yet practical education—in addition to the liberal arts courses offered to clergymen, teachers, lawyers, and doctors, Justin's colleges would provide practical courses in science, engineering, and agriculture for farmers, mechanics, and laborers. He served in the Senate from 1867 until 1898; he also was responsible for the construction of such landmark buildings as the Library of Congress.

★ ★ ★ ★ ★ ★ ★ ★ **K** ★ ★ ★ ★ ★ ★ ★ ★

KING: from the Old English for king.

KING CAMP GILLETTE (1855–1932) was named for Judge King, a friend of his father's. King dreamed of starting a utopian community, but in real life he worked at a bottle cap company and tinkered on various inventions in his basement. The president of the company told him he should invent something that people would throw away so they'd have to buy more. One morning while shaving he had the idea of a safety razor. He founded the Gillette Safety Razor Company in 1901 and two years later invented disposable blades.

KIT: a nickname for Christopher, from the Greek for bearing Christ inside.

KIT CARSON (1809–1868) was a legend of the American West. He left home at age seventeen and landed in Taos, New Mexico; he became famous as John Frémont's guide on his expeditions to California. Kit had two wives, both Indian, and became an Indian agent in northern New Mexico, where he worked to keep the peace between Indians and settlers and make sure that the Native Americans received fair treatment.

KNUTE: a variation on Canute, from the Scandinavian for knot.

KNUTE ROCKNE (1888–1931) was the winningest coach in the history of college football. He was a Lutheran at a Catholic school, first as a student at Notre Dame and then as the coach. In his thirteen seasons as head coach the Fighting Irish won 105 games, lost twelve, and tied five, with five unbeaten seasons and three national championships. Among his innovations was the forward pass. Knute also was famous for his halftime pep talks, including one in which he pleaded with his team to remember a dead teammate, George Gipp, and exhorted them to "Win one for the Gipper!" He died at age forty-three in a plane crash.

★ ★ ★ ★ ★ ★ ★ ★ **L** ★ ★ ★ ★ ★ ★ ★ ★

LANGSTON: from the English for long town.

LANGSTON HUGHES (1902–1967) was a poet, writer, and playwright of the Harlem Renaissance. He grew up in Missouri in a family of activists (one ancestor died at Harpers Ferry) and was a political radical for most of his life. His poetry crackles with rhythms as diverse as bebop and gospel. He wrote the lyrics for the Broadway musical *Street Scene* and used the proceeds to buy a house in Harlem. Perhaps his most famous line of poetry is "What happens to a dream deferred? Does it dry up—like a raisin in the sun?"

LARRY: a familiar form of Lawrence, from the Latin for crowned with laurel. An alternate spelling is Laurence.

LARRY DOBY (1924–2003) was the first black baseball player to play in the American League; he joined just four months after Jackie Robinson started playing in the National League. Bill Veeck signed Larry to the Cleveland Indians in 1947; in 1948, the Indians won the World Series, thanks to Larry's 400-foot home run in game four. In 1952 he led the league with an amazing .541 batting average, and he was selected to the All-Star teams from 1949 to 1954. In 1978 he was the manager of the White Sox—and one of his players was the catcher Larry Doby Johnson, who had been named after him.

LEO: from the Latin for lion.

LEO HENDRIK BAEKELAND (1863–1944) was a chemist who invented Bakelite, one of the first plastics. His first big invention, though, was Velox, the first photographic paper that could be printed in artificial light. He sold the rights to Velox to George Eastman for $1 million in 1899. He used the proceeds to purchase an estate in Westchester County, New York, where he began experiments using coal tar; his goal was to make electric insulators. He instead developed a polymer that was easily moldable and infinitely less flammable than celluloid, and he named it after himself. Bakelite was used to make everything from silverware handles and eyeglass frames to jewelry and buttons.

LEON: from the German for lion.

LEON SHENANDOAH (1915–1996) was a Tadodaho, or wisdom keeper, of the Onondaga Nation. For thirty years this soft-spoken holy man led the Iroquois nations, speaking out against development and gambling casinos on tribal lands and working to restore traditional religions and practices.

"The greatest power is the creator. But if you want to know the greatest strength, that is gentleness." —Leon Shenandoah

---

LEONARD: from the German for lion. Lenard, Lennart, Leonid, and Leonardo are variations; Lee, Lenny, Len, Lon, and Leo are diminutives.

LEONARD BERNSTEIN (1918–1990) was one of the most popular conductors and composers of the twentieth century. He was a protégé of the conductor Serge Koussivitsky, who recommended him for the assistant conductorship of the New York Philharmonic. When the great conductor Bruno Walter became suddenly ill, Leonard took his place with little notice and no time to rehearse, yet his debut was so astounding it was reported on the front page of the *New York Times*. Nearly every major orchestra in the world invited him to be guest conductor over the course of his career. He composed the score of *West Side Story*. He also worked for peace and justice on an international scale: Leonard donated money to Amnesty International, and led concerts to remember the bombing of Hiroshima and to celebrate the fall of the Berlin Wall.

LESTER: from the Old English for from Leicester. Les is a nickname.

LESTER YOUNG (1909–1959) was nicknamed "Pres" by Billie Holiday; he gave her the nickname "Lady Day." Born into a musical family in Woodville, Mississippi, Lester played alto saxophone in his family's band. As a young man he joined Count Basie's orchestra and switched to tenor sax. Brilliant and talented, Lester was known for playing the sax sideways, like a flute, as well as for his compositions "Honeysuckle Rose," "You Can Depend on Me," and "These Foolish Things."

LEWIS: an English variation on Louis, from the Old French for warrior. Variations include Luis, Luigi, Aloysius, and Ludwig; Lew is the familiar form.

LEWIS LATIMER (1848–1928) was the only black man on Thomas Edison's research team. He taught himself mechanical drawing while working in a patent office; when Alexander Graham Bell sought to get the telephone patented, he hired Lewis to do the drawings for it. Lewis worked for Hiram Maxim, Edison's rival, where he devised improvements to the lightbulb, before leaving to join "Edison's Pioneers." During his time with Edison he wrote a book on lighting; he also patented a toilet that could be used on trains.

LEWIS MORRIS (1726–1798) was a signer of the Declaration of Independence. His family owned a three-thousand-acre estate in New York's Westchester County, and despite the all-too-real risk of losing everything, Lewis was an ardent patriot. He served in the Continental Congress and as a brigadier general in the militia, and the British army did indeed destroy his estate during the war. When independence was secured, Lewis worked to rebuild his property, and was a judge and state senator.

LINCOLN: from the Old English for lake colony. Often used in honor of Abraham Lincoln.

LINCOLN STEFFENS (1866–1936) was perhaps the most famous investigative reporter of his time—Teddy Roosevelt coined the term "muckraker" to describe him. Born into a well-off California family, Lincoln attended private schools and traveled through Europe; a secret marriage and political leanings that were on the radical side proved too much for his father, who cut him off. Lincoln became a reporter for the *New York Post*, working the police beat. He later became editor of *McClure's Magazine*, where he started a series of exposés of corruption and graft in America's cities. The book based on this series, *The Shame of Cities*, was on the *New York Times*'s list of one hundred great books of the twentieth century.

"Morality is only moral when it's voluntary." —Lincoln Steffens

---

LINUS: from the Greek for flax.

LINUS PAULING (1901–1994) won the Nobel Prize in Chemistry and the Nobel Peace Prize. A graduate of Caltech, Dr. Pauling was a genius whose contributions to science are legion: he founded the discipline of molecular biology; he was the first to use quantum theory in chemical experiments; his research was used to identify the defect responsible for sickle-cell anemia; he devised the "tinker-toy" models for showing molecules; he demonstrated that anesthesia affects the brain in the same way that extreme cold does; and he advocated vitamin C to protect against and prevent colds. Harassed by the FBI for his liberal politics (he protested the Vietnam War, fought segregation, and declared publicly that he didn't believe in God), Dr. Pauling was a civil libertarian and pacifist throughout his life.

LIONEL: from the French for young lion.

LIONEL BARRYMORE (1878–1954) was an Academy Award–winning actor—and with his sister, Ethel, half of the only brother-sister duo to have won Oscars. His best-known roles are as Scrooge in *A Christmas Carol*, the miserly banker Mr. Potter in *It's a Wonderful Life*, and as Dr. Gillespie in the radio show *Doctor Kildare*. He won the Best Actor Award for his role in *A Free Soul*, and earned a Best Director nomination for *Madame X*. *We Barrymores* is his autobiography.

LIONEL HAMPTON (1908–2002) was a jazz musician and bandleader. He was taught to play the drums by a nun when he was a Catholic schoolboy. During a recording session with Louis Armstrong he taught himself vibraphone; it became his instrument. Lionel joined Benny Goodman's quartet, then started his own band. They played at the White House at Jimmy Carter's invitation, and Bill Clinton hosted a ninetieth birthday party for Lionel. His vibraphone is part of the Smithsonian Institution's collection.

LOREN: from the Latin for crowned with laurel.

LOREN EISELEY (1907–1977) overcame a horrific childhood. He grew up on the Nebraska prairie; his father died when he was young and his deaf, mentally unstable mother communicated with him by pounding on the floor. Loren ran away and lived as a hobo, riding the rails, for ten years, but in 1933 he graduated from the University of Nebraska and later received a Ph.D. from the University of Pennsylvania. His first book, *The Immense Journey*, led to comparisons with Henry David Thoreau. In his writing he reveals the experiences that shaped him and all humanity.

LOUIS: from the Old French for warrior. Variations include Lewis, Luis, Luigi, Aloysius, and Ludwig; Lou is the familiar form.

LOUIS "SATCHMO" ARMSTRONG (1900–1971) was a larger-than-life musician, actor, and celebrity. As famous for his trumpet playing as he was for his gravelly voice, Satchmo was born in New Orleans; he played with local bands, then went to Chicago and on to New York, where he joined Fletcher Henderson's band. He soon went off on his own; the recordings he made are masterpieces of innovation and technique. He toured Europe, played with just about every swing band and jazz orchestra, and acted in more than thirty movies. His most famous recordings include "When the Saints Come Marching In," "What a Wonderful World," and "Hello, Dolly."

LOUIS BRANDEIS (1856–1941) was the first Jewish American to sit on the U.S. Supreme Court. An ardent advocate of civil liberties and a brilliant man, Brandeis was a native of Louisville, Kentucky, who graduated from Harvard Law School at twenty-one; with his classmate Samuel Warren he wrote "The Right to Privacy," one of the country's defining law articles. He was nominated for the Supreme Court in 1916, but because of anti-Semitism he almost wasn't confirmed. Brandeis University in Waltham, Massachusetts, is named after him; he also helped to found the University of Louisville Law School.

LOUIS GEHRIG (1903–1941), called Lou, was one of the greats who left an indelible stamp on baseball. Part of the Yankees' powerful batting lineup called Murderer's Row, Lou batted .361 in seven World Series, and in 1934 won the American League's Triple Crown with 165 RBIs, forty-nine home runs, and a .363 average. He played 2,130 consecutive games—even playing on his wedding day—but his streak ended when he developed ALS, a crippling disease now known familiarly as Lou Gehrig's disease. The Yankees retired his uniform number, making Lou Gehrig the first player to earn that distinction.

"I consider myself the luckiest man on the face of the earth." —Lou Gehrig, in his farewell speech at Yankee Stadium on July 4, 1939

LOUIS L'AMOUR (1908–1988) was one of the most prolific writers of the twentieth century: he penned more than four hundred short stories, one hundred novels, and innumerable scripts and screenplays for television and movies. Born in North Dakota, Louis spent his youth coal mining, prospecting for gold, even living among bandits in Tibet. In World War II he served as a tank officer; when the war ended he started to write the Westerns that won him fans as well as the Congressional Gold Medal and the Medal of Freedom. The first Louis L'Amour novel, *Hondo*, sold 1.5 million copies; it was the first of forty-five of his stories to be made into movies.

LUCIUS: from the Latin for light. Lucian, Lucien, and Luciano are variations; Luke is sometimes used as a nickname.

LUCIUS QUINTUS CINCINNATUS LAMAR (1825–1893) was an influential Southern Democrat and U.S. congressman. Although he worked to avoid secession, he so opposed Abraham Lincoln's election that he resigned from Congress and drafted Mississippi's ordinance of secession. He was a Confederate officer during the Civil War, but returned to Congress in 1872. When his bitter rival, Charles Sumner, died, Lucius paid him tribute and made a plea for reconciliation of the country, still torn asunder by the wounds of war. He was later appointed secretary of the interior and then made a justice of the Supreme Court.

LUTHER: from the Old German for soldier. Often used in recognition of Martin Luther or Martin Luther King, Jr.

LUTHER BURBANK (1840–1926) was a horticulturist, but to call him only that is to understate his genius. A farmer whose experiments with plant hybridization have changed agriculture, Luther developed such oddities as white blackberries, pitless plums, and a cherry tree with more than five hundred varieties on its branches—as well as higher-yielding, hardier varieties of fruits, vegetables, and flowers. The russet Burbank potato, often called an Idaho potato, was one of his first developments; he also created the Shasta daisy, Shirley poppy, and a spineless cactus for feeding cattle in deserts.

LYMAN: from the English for meadow.

LYMAN BEECHER (1775–1863) was a revivalist and religious leader in the nineteenth century, but his greatest legacy to America was his daughters, Catherine Beecher, Isabella Beecher Hooker, and Harriet Beecher Stowe. A graduate of Yale, Lyman became a pastor of a church in Littlefield, Connecticut, before moving to the Hanover Street Church in Boston; he later was president of the Lane Theological Seminary in Cincinnati.

LYMAN HALL (1724–1790) was a signer of the Declaration of Independence. A delegate from Georgia, Lyman had been instructed to get

Britain to recognize the rights of Americans, not to declare independence. He threw his lot in with the rebels, however, and signed the document, then spent the war equipping the Continental army with medical supplies. After the war he resumed his medical practice; he was elected governor of Georgia in 1783.

LYNDON: from the English for linden tree.

LYNDON BAINES JOHNSON (1908–1973) was America's thirty-sixth president, sworn into office on *Air Force One* after John F. Kennedy was assassinated. His social programs reflected his vision of "A Great Society," and he declared a "War on Poverty." Among the legislation and programs enacted during his term were Urban Renewal, Head Start, Job Corps, Food Stamps, Medicare, School Milk and Lunch programs, as well as the 1964 Civil Rights Act and the 1965 Voting Rights Act. The escalating war in Vietnam thwarted his bid for the 1968 Democratic nomination. He bowed out of the race in a televised speech.

★ ★ ★ ★ ★ ★ ★ ★ **M** ★ ★ ★ ★ ★ ★ ★ ★

MALCOLM: from the Scottish for follower of St. Columba. Calum and Colm are variations; Mal is a shortened form.

MALCOLM X (1925–1965) was born Malcolm Little in Omaha, Nebraska. As a young man he was arrested for petty crime and sent to prison. While there, he educated himself—to improve his vocabulary he wrote out the entire dictionary by hand—and joined the Nation of Islam. When he was released, he became a trusted lieutenant of Elijah Muhammed, the head of the Nation of Islam. He traveled the country opening temples, increasing membership, and giving speeches. In 1964 he converted to Islam and made a hajj to Mecca. After his return he began to work for human rights for all races, not just for black nationalism. He was assassinated while giving a speech in Harlem.

MANUEL: from the Spanish for God is with us. Emmanuel, Manolo, and Manuelo are variations; Manny is the nickname.

MANUEL LISA (1772–1820) was a fur trader, explorer, and the first white settler in the Nebraska Territory. He traveled more than twenty-five thousand miles in twelve years, building two forts, establishing the St. Louis Fur Company, and working as an agent for the U.S. government to deal with the Sioux, Yanktonai, and Upper Missouri tribes. He brought seeds, traps, and blacksmithing to the Indians, established guidelines for trade and trading posts, and worked to maintain peace.

MARK: from the Latin for dedicated to Mars, Mark is a biblical name. It is a shortened form of Marcus and Marcellus; variations include Marc, Marco, Marques, Marcel, and Marek.

MARK ROTHKO (1903–1970) was an influential painter in the New York School. Born Marcus Rothkowitz in Russia, he moved with his parents to Oregon when he was a child. He dropped out of Yale and moved to New York; his early works were done on the subway. In the early 1940s, his paintings became filled with symbols and reflected the anxiety of the war years. By the late 1940s his work became more abstract; the anxiety diminished and the symbols became increasingly simplified and, ultimately, rectangles. Shimmering colors gave way in the

1960s to a darker palette reflecting his mental state. Suffering from depression, he killed himself in 1970.

"It is a widely accepted notion among painters that it does not matter what one paints as long as it is well painted. . . . There is no such thing as good painting about nothing." —Mark Rothko

---

MARK TWAIN (1835–1910) was the pen name of Samuel Langhorne Clemens, a Missouri native who grew up to become one of America's most beloved writers. He worked as a riverboat pilot and miner before turning to writing, first as a journalist and then as a novelist. Satirical, humorous, and utterly American in their sensibility, his books include *The Adventures of Tom Sawyer*, *Adventures of Huckleberry Finn*, *The Prince and the Pauper*, and *A Connecticut Yankee in King Arthur's Court*.

"Be good and you will be lonesome." —Mark Twain

MARLON: from the French for falcon.

MARLON BRANDO (1924–2004), arguably the greatest actor of the twentieth century, parlayed a handsome face, a charismatic personality, and extraordinary talent into a career that spanned decades and saw eight Academy Award nominations. One of the first to use method acting, Brando made his name in two films with Elia Kazan: *A Streetcar Named Desire*, playing Stanley Kowalski, and *On the Waterfront*, as Terry Malloy, in which he uttered the famous line "I coulda been a contender." His Best Actor Awards were for *On the Waterfront* and *The Godfather*, playing the Mafia don Vito Corleone.

MARTIN: from the Latin for dedicated to Mars.

MARTIN LUTHER KING, JR. (1929–1968) was a leader of the civil rights movement. Born in Atlanta, Dr. King graduated from Morehouse College and later earned his doctorate from Boston University. As pastor of the Ebenezer Baptist Church, he spoke against segregation and for nonviolent resistance and civil disobedience. Dr. King founded the Southern Christian Leadership Conference, and was a leader of the Montgomery bus boycott and other activities of resistance. He was arrested but continued his efforts, leading marches. The largest was in 1963: he, Bayard Rustin, and Hosea Williams organized the March on Washington, where he gave his most famous speech. He was assassinated in Memphis, Tennessee.

MARTIN VAN BUREN (1782–1862) was the nation's eighth president and the first who was not of Anglo-Saxon heritage (he was of Dutch descent). A native of Kinderhook, New York, Martin practiced law and was active in state and local politics before his election to the United States Senate. He was appointed secretary of state by Andrew Jackson and, in 1832, was Jackson's vice president. When he was elected in 1836 he faced a country on the brink of financial disaster, and he advocated an independent treasury for the federal government.

MATTHEW: from the Hebrew for gift of the Lord. Sometimes spelled Mathew, Mathieu is the French spelling; Matteo is Italian. Matt is the most common short form.

MATTHEW HENSON (1866–1955) was an explorer who, with Robert Peary, helped to discover the North Pole. He ran away to sea at age thirteen. A chance meeting with Lieutenant Peary led to an offer to serve as Peary's valet, but when the lieutenant learned that Matthew Henson had sailing experience he was invited to join the Arctic expeditions, and in 1909 he, Peary, and four Inuits reached the North Pole. Matthew's memoir, *A Negro at the North Pole*, was published in 1912, but it wasn't until 1944 that Congress awarded him with the same medals it had bestowed upon the rest of the expedition.

MATTHEW PERRY (1794–1858) was a naval commander who established trade relations with Japan. A midshipman at fifteen and a commander at thirty-two, Perry was the captain of the first naval steamship, the *Fulton*. He fought in the Mexican War and attained the rank of commodore. In 1853 he sailed to Japan, a country that had not traded with other nations since the seventeenth century, offering a treaty of friendship and commerce; the treaty was signed the following year.

MAX: the short form of Maximilian, from the Latin for the greatest.

MAX WEBER (1881–1961) brought avant-garde art to America. Born in Russia, he emigrated with his family as a ten-year-old. He studied at the Pratt Institute, then moved to Paris, where he studied with Henri Matisse. When he returned to the United States he brought cubism, abstract art, and expressionism with him. His one-man show in 1913 was the first exhibit of modern art at an American museum.

MAXFIELD: from the English for Mack's field.

MAXFIELD PARRISH (1870–1966) was one of the most popular artists of the twentieth century. Called the poor man's Rembrandt, he was named Frederick Parrish at birth. He began working as an illustrator, then turned to painting; his realistic works were out of step among the avant-garde abstract works of his contemporaries, but more than 200,000 prints were sold of his painting *Daybreak*; he also sold calendars and posters of his work.

MAXWELL: from the English for Mack's well.

MAXWELL ANDERSON (1888–1959) was a poet, lyricist, and award-winning playwright. He grew up in North Dakota, and developed a reputation for social justice. Like Shakespeare, he wrote his plays in blank verse (unrhymed iambic pentameter). His play *Both Your Houses* won the Pulitzer Prize in 1933; his plays *Winterset* and *High Tor* won the New York Drama Critics' Circle Award. He also wrote *The Bad Seed*, and did film adaptations of *All Quiet on the Western Front*, *Key Largo*, and *Death Takes a Holiday*.

MELVIN: from the Gaelic for polished chief. Malvin is a variation; Mel is a nickname.

MELVIN OTT (1909–1958) played for the New York Giants for twenty-two seasons, starting when he was sixteen years old. An amazing slugger despite his unorthodox batting style, Mel led the league in home runs six seasons, had a career batting average of .304 and 1,860 RBIs, and made the All-Star team eleven times. After he retired from playing he managed the Giants for seven years. After he was killed in a car accident, the Giants retired his uniform number.

MERCE, MERCER: from the English for shopkeeper.

MERCE CUNNINGHAM (b. 1919) is a major choreographer of modern dance. Born in Centralia, Washington, he studied dance in Seattle, where he met John Cage; the two collaborated for some fifty years. Cage would compose the music independently of Cunningham's choreography. Dancers would rehearse their movements in silence, hearing the music for the first time at dress rehearsal or at the first performance. Cunningham danced with Martha Graham's company as a soloist before forming his own dance company. He still choreographs, but instead of demonstrating the steps himself he uses computer software.

MERIWETHER: from the Welsh for near the sea.

MERIWETHER LEWIS (1774–1809) was part of the team that explored the West and found a route to the Pacific. A Virginia native, he was friendly with Thomas Jefferson. Lewis joined the army in 1794 and met William Clark on frontier duty. Jefferson offered to send Lewis on an expedition to the West Coast; he accepted and invited Clark to be part of it. They left in 1804; in 1805 they found Sacagawea, the sister of a Shoshone chief, who became their guide. They made it to the Pacific, but Lewis died before he returned to Washington.

"I am no coward, but I am so strong, it is so hard to die." —Meriwether Lewis's last words

MICHAEL: from the Hebrew for who resembles God. Micheal is the Gaelic spelling; Miguel is Spanish and Portuguese; Michel is French; Mikael, Mikell, and Mikkel are Scandinavian; Mikhail is Russian, and Michal is Polish. It is often combined with other names, as in Michelangelo. Mitchell is a Middle English variation. The most common nicknames are Mick, Mickey, Mike, and Mikey; Misha is the Russian diminutive.

MICKEY MANTLE (1931–1995) signed with the New York Yankees the day he graduated from high school and played with them from 1951 to 1968. He won the Most Valuable Player award three times and led his team to twelve pennant races and seven World Series. An incredible slugger, he once hit a left-handed homer 656 feet. His popularity remains undimmed: a baseball card from his rookie season sold recently for more than fifty thousand dollars.

MIGUEL JOSÉ SERRA (1713–1784) was a Franciscan priest who took the name Junipero. He was born on Mallorca but left in 1750 to work as a missionary, first in Mexico and then in San Diego and Monterey. He walked more than twenty-four thousand miles throughout California and founded nine missions, teaching Indians to read and write, to farm and raise cattle, as well as teaching them about Christianity.

MILES: from the Latin for soldier.

MILES DAVIS (1926–1991) was a jazz trumpeter and bandleader. The son of a dentist, he left Illinois for New York, attending the Juilliard School by day and playing bebop with Charlie Parker and Dizzy Gillespie by night. In 1949 he released the groundbreaking record *Birth of the Cool*. He developed a heroin addiction in the early 1950s but kicked the habit, and in 1955 he and John Coltrane formed a quintet renowned for its daring and technique. In the 1960s he expanded his repertoire to explore rock and classical music; *Sketches of Spain* is an interpretation of Rodrigo's *Concerto de Aranjuez*. Outrageous and iconoclastic, he was an artist to the core.

MILLARD: from the Old English for guardian of the mill.

MILLARD FILLMORE (1800–1874) was the thirteenth president of the United States, taking the office after Zachary Taylor died. Hailing from upstate New York, he went to a one-room schoolhouse and, as an adult, married his teacher. He was elected to the U.S. Congress in 1823, and in 1848 he became vice president; two years later, he was president. He supported the Compromise of 1850, which made California a free state, settled the Texas boundary dispute, made New Mexico a territory, allowed slaveholders to pursue fugitives with the help of federal officers, and abolished the slave trade. He infuriated abolitionists with the Fugitive Slave Act and lost his bid for reelection.

MILTON: from the English for mill town.

MILTON HERSHEY (1857–1945) built an empire out of chocolate. Born on a farm in Pennsylvania, he became a candy maker's apprentice and by age nineteen had started his own candy business. At first he specialized in caramels and taffy, but by 1894 he had figured out how to mass-produce chocolate and opened the Hershey Chocolate Company. He built more than just a factory—the entire community of Hershey, Pennsylvania, grew out of his generosity.

MOSES: from the Hebrew for savior.

MOSES FARMER (1820–1893) was an inventor from New Hampshire. He made his living as a schoolteacher, but was fascinated with electricity. He invented an electric railroad, a fire alarm system, and a battery-operated electric clock, and he devised a way to electroplate aluminum.

Twenty years before Thomas Edison invented the lightbulb, Moses Farmer lit his house with incandescent lamps.

MOSES FLEETWOOD WALKER (1856–1924) holds the distinction of being the first black man in major league baseball. Jackie Robinson broke major league baseball's color line in 1947, becoming the first black to play on an all-white team, but Moses had played as early as 1884. The son of a doctor, he attended Oberlin College, and in 1883 joined the minor league Toledo Blue Stockings. When the team joined the major league the following year, Moses continued to play for them. Moses faced increasing racism and retired in 1890. He went on to publish a newspaper, own an opera theater, and write a book on racism called *Our Home Colony*.

NATHAN: a variation on Nathaniel, from the Hebrew for gift of God.

NATHAN HALE (1755–1776) was hanged as a spy when he was only twenty-one years old. He graduated from Yale and was teaching school when he heard that the Revolution had begun. He enlisted in the army, and in September of 1776 he volunteered to go behind enemy lines to gather intelligence. He was caught, taken to Manhattan, and hanged the following day, and his body was left on the gallows as a warning. Statues of Nathan Hale stand at the Central Intelligence Agency, at Yale University, and in New York City at Broadway and Murray Street.

"I only regret that I have but one life to give for my country." —Nathan Hale, on the gallows

NATHANIEL: from the Hebrew for gift of God. Alternate spellings are Nathanael and Nathanial, and Nat is the most common short form.

NATHANAEL GREENE (1742–1786) was a general in the Revolutionary War. A self-educated Quaker who walked with a limp, Nathanael became involved with the rebels in 1774, and in 1775 he was made commander of Rhode Island's regiments. He fought at George Washington's side at Trenton, Princeton, Brandywine, and Germantown, and from 1778 to 1780 he was quartermaster general. In 1780 he was sent to the South, where he drove the British from Georgia and the Carolinas, and ultimately into a trap at Yorktown, where they surrendered.

NATHANIEL BOWDITCH (1773–1838) was a mathematician and navigator. Born in Massachusetts, he left school at age ten to go to work. He educated himself by reading books in his employer's library, and developed a passion for navigation. He went to sea in 1795 and determined to revise J. H. Moore's book *The Practical Navigator*. By the third revision he had corrected eleven thousand errors; he retitled the book *The New Practical Navigator* and credited himself as the author. Although it has been revised several times, it is still used today.

NAT "KING" COLE (1919–1965) was born Nathaniel Adams Coles in Montgomery, Alabama, but moved to Chicago as a child. He grew up listening to Earl Hines and Louis Armstrong, and made his first recording while still a teenager. He took the stage name Nat Cole; later a nightclub owner added the "King." His first big hit was "Straighten Up and Fly Right"; his others include "Unforgettable," "Ramblin' Rose," and "Mona Lisa," which was a number-one hit and sold 3 million copies.

NATHANIEL HAWTHORNE (1804–1864) was a master storyteller. The sixth generation of a family from Salem (an ancestor was a judge at the witch trials), he went to Bowdoin College, where Henry Wadsworth Longfellow and Franklin Pierce were classmates and friends. He published his first book of stories, *Twice-Told Tales*, in 1837; his masterpiece, *The Scarlet Letter*, came out in 1850. When Pierce became president, he appointed Nathaniel as consul to Liverpool.

NICHOLAS: from the Greek for victorious. Nicol is the Scottish variation; Nels is the Scandinavian; Nickolaus and Nikolaus are German; Nikolai is the Polish or Russian; Niccolo, Nicoli, and Nicolo are Italian, and Nikolos is Greek. Nick, Nicky, Cole, Claus, Klaus, and Colin are all diminutives or short forms.

NICHOLAS BLACK ELK (1863–1950) was an Oglala Sioux shaman and mystic. Born on the Pine Ridge Reservation, he fought at Wounded Knee and in the Battle of Little Big Horn. In 1881 he became a shamanic healer, and in 1931 he was interviewed by a man looking for survivors of Wounded Knee. The resulting book, *Black Elk Speaks*, reveals the shaman's memories as well as his wisdom and prophecies. Black Elk's book *The Sacred Pipe* outlined the seven traditional rituals of the Oglala Sioux; the book helped to revive traditions that were on the verge of being lost.

NOAH: from the Hebrew for peaceful.

NOAH WEBSTER (1758–1843) was an educator best remembered for the dictionaries that bear his name. A native of Connecticut, he went to Yale and then began teaching. He believed that American children needed American (not English) textbooks, so he wrote his own. The first was *The Blue-Black Speller*; it was used for more than one hundred years and sold more than 70 million copies; grammar, reading, and poetry books followed. With the goal of standardizing American spelling, he published *Webster's Unabridged Dictionary* in 1841. Noah also fought for copyright laws.

NOBLE: from the Latin for aristocratic.

NOBLE SISSLE (1889–1975) was a bandleader and songwriter who was singing professionally before he finished high school. He played in an army band in World War I and introduced ragtime to the French, then formed a vaudeville act with Eubie Blake after the war. The two wrote *Shuffle Along*, which made Josephine Baker a star. He later led a band and, with an unerring sense for spotting talent, hired an unknown singer named Lena Horne and a saxophone player named Charlie Parker. From his early days in Cleveland, Noble and his bands were among the first to play in venues that had previously been whites-only.

NORMAN: from the Old German for Northerner. Norm is the short form.

NORMAN ROCKWELL (1894–1978) was perhaps the most beloved and most popular American illustrator. Born in New York City and educated at the Art Students League, Norman worked as an illustrator and art director before joining the *Saturday Evening Post* in 1916. He painted the magazine's covers for more than fifty years. Reproductions of his paintings continue to be popular; they convey a simpler America, where valor and honor and goodness prevail.

O. HENRY (1862–1910) was the pen name of William Sydney Porter. He was a writer of short stories known for their ironic twists at the end. Indicted for embezzlement, he spent three years in jail. While he was incarcerated he began writing stories. When he got out of prison he moved to New York City, where he wrote a story a week. His best-known work is "The Gift of the Magi."

OGDEN: from the English for oak valley.

OGDEN NASH (1902–1971) was a descendant of the founder of Nashville, Tennessee. He grew up in New York and Georgia. Although he wrote advertising copy and collaborated on the musical comedy *One Touch of Venus*, he is best known for his poetry. It first appeared in the *New Yorker* and was ultimately collected into nineteen volumes. Known for his lighthearted wit and clever turns of phrase, Ogden Nash was called, by no less an authority on writing than the *Atlantic Monthly*, "God's gift to the United States."

OLIVER: from the Latin for olive tree.

OLIVER WENDELL HOLMES (1809–1894) was born into a prominent family in Massachusetts, studied medicine at Harvard and in Paris, then returned to Harvard and worked as a professor for thirty-five years. Among his then-radical ideas were that an individual's behavior was determined in large measure by genetic makeup and by his or her environment; he wrote about this in the *Atlantic Monthly*, which also published his poetry. His light verse became incredibly popular, and today it's what he is remembered for.

OLIVER HAZARD PERRY (1785–1819) was a naval commander. He went to sea at fourteen and saw battle when he was fifteen; by 1812 he was a lieutenant commander. Sent to Lake Erie during the War of 1812, he launched his ships before the British could establish a blockade. Although his flagship was destroyed in the battle, he escaped to another ship and fought the British until they surrendered.

"We have met the enemy and they are ours." —Oliver Perry, after capturing the entire British fleet in Lake Erie

---

OMAR: from the Arabic for highest.

OMAR BRADLEY (1893–1981) was called the Soldier's General. Born in Missouri, he graduated from West Point and, in World War II, fought in North Africa and with General George Patton during the invasion of Sicily. In 1944 he was given command of more than 900,000 men. His troops were taking a beating at the Battle of the Bulge; Patton's Third Army forced the Germans back, allowing Bradley to cross the Rhine. The war in Europe ended soon after. Bradley was promoted to five-star general and served as chairman of the Joint Chiefs of Staff.

ORVILLE: from the Old French for gold town.

ORVILLE WRIGHT (1871–1948) dreamed of building a flying machine. A high school dropout, Orville and his brother, Wilbur, opened a bicycle repair shop in their hometown of Dayton, Ohio, and used their income to pursue their passion for aviation. They made gliders, studied wing design, and by 1903 had filed a patent and built a plane. On December 17, 1903, they made four flights on North Carolina's Outer Banks—the first ever of a heavier-than-air machine operating on its own power. The longest flight that day was 852 feet. Their plane is now in the National Air and Space Museum.

OSCAR: from the Old English for heavenly spearman.

OSCAR CHARLESTON (1896–1954) was perhaps the best all-around baseball player of the Negro Leagues. A left-handed power hitter and center fielder, Oscar was called the Black Ty Cobb by sportswriters of his day. He played for the Indianapolis ABCs, and in 1921 he led the league in doubles, triples, home runs, and stolen bases, and had a batting average of .434; his lifetime average was .353. After he retired from the diamond he managed two teams, and was elected to the Baseball Hall of Fame in 1976.

OSCAR HAMMERSTEIN III (1895–1960) is a name synonymous with the greatest musicals of Broadway and Hollywood. Although he was born into a theatrical family, Oscar was supposed to become a lawyer. He met Richard Rodgers while at Columbia University. Oscar began to write lyrics for Broadway musicals. His first hit, *Rose Marie*, came in 1924; *Showboat* and *Carmen Jones* followed. He collaborated with Rodgers on *Oklahoma!*, which won the Pulitzer Prize, and also wrote the lyrics for *South Pacific*, *The King and I*, and *The Sound of Music*; many of their musicals were made into movies. When Oscar Hammerstein III died, the lights on Broadway were put out in tribute.

★ ★ ★ ★ ★ ★ ★ ★ **P** ★ ★ ★ ★ ★ ★ ★ ★

PATRICK: from the Latin for patrician or noble. Padric and Padraic are the Irish spellings; Patric is French, and Patricio is Spanish and Portuguese. Pat is the most common diminutive.

PATRICK HENRY (1736–1799) was a Virginian whose eloquence helped to stir Americans to revolt against England. His speech against the Stamp Act marked him as a radical, and for the next ten years he led the movement toward independence in Virginia. He was a delegate to the First and Second Continental Congresses and was elected the first governor of Virginia; he served three terms.

"Is life so dear, or peace so sweet, as to be purchased at the price of chains and slavery? Forbid it almighty God! I know not what course others may take, but as for me, give me liberty or give me death!" —Patrick Henry, March 23, 1775

PAUL: from the Latin for small. Pablo is the Spanish form; Paolo is Italian; Paulino and Paulo are Portuguese; Pavel is Slavic, and Pavlik and Pavlo are Russian.

PAUL REVERE (1735–1818) was a master silversmith and ardent patriot. On April 18, 1775, he rode from Boston to Lexington, Massachusetts, to warn Samuel Adams and John Hancock that British troops were on their way to arrest them. Paul had arranged that a signal in the tower of Christ Church would tell him whether the British were coming over land (one lantern hung) or across the Charles River (two lanterns). After seeing two lanterns, Revere set off on his midnight ride. He warned Adams and Hancock, then left for Concord to alert the militia.

PAUL ROBESON (1898–1976) was an actor, singer, and social activist. He graduated as valedictorian from Rutgers University and attended Columbia Law School, but quit and became an actor. He appeared in more than a dozen movies, including *Porgy and Bess*, *Othello*, and *The Emperor Jones*, and made recordings of black folk songs and spirituals. He spoke out for civil rights and briefly joined the Communist Party. Under surveillance by the FBI and hounded by the House Un-American

Activities Committee, Paul Robeson lost his passport and saw irreparable damage to his brilliant career.

"To be free—to walk the good American earth as equal citizens, to live without fear, to enjoy the fruits of our toil, to give our children every opportunity in life—that dream which we have held so long in our hearts is today the destiny that we hold in our hands." —Paul Robeson

---

PEE WEE: an American nickname meaning short, or in reference to the shooter in a game of marbles.

PEE WEE REESE (1918–1999) was named Harold Henry Reese when he was born; he was nicknamed Pee Wee for his prowess at marbles. A Kentucky native, he played baseball with the Louisville Colonels and the Boston Red Sox before moving to the Brooklyn Dodgers. The top shortstop of his day, Pee Wee led the Dodgers to seven National League pennants and made the All-Star team for eight seasons. When Jackie Robinson joined the Dodgers amid racism and uncertainty, it was Pee Wee Reese who put his arm over Robinson's shoulder to indicate to players and the public that he supported his new teammate.

"What a decent human being. How much he helped me. But he refuses to take the credit." —Jackie Robinson, on Pee Wee Reese

---

PETER: from the Greek for rock. Pieter is a Dutch form; Petrov and Pyotr are Russian; Pierre is French, and Pedro is Spanish or Portuguese. Pierce is an English variation. Pete is the most common nickname.

PETER COOPER (1791–1883) was a self-made millionaire. An inventor who used the proceeds to buy or start other businesses, Peter is best remembered today as a philanthropist. He helped to found and finance Cooper Union, helped to build the Croton Reservoir (at a time when New York City's drinking water was deplorable), and was a member of the Public School Society. Among his inventions: the lawn mower, a steam-driven torpedo, and instant gelatin—marketed today as Jell-O.

PHILIP: from the Greek for lover of horses. The name is sometimes spelled Phillip; Philipe is the French spelling, Felipe is Spanish. Phil is the most common diminutive, but Pip is sometimes used.

PHILIP SCHUYLER (1733–1804) was born into a prominent New York family of Dutch ancestry, and served as a major general under George Washington. A veteran of the French and Indian War, where he had commanded a company, Schuyler was a delegate to the Second Continental Congress. Washington appointed him commander of the Northern Department. He became ill and left the army, but was active behind the scenes and in politics. Working with his son-in-law, Alexander Hamilton, he helped to create the Constitution. He also served in the New York and U.S. senates.

POMPEY: a variation on Pompeo, from the Latin for five.

POMPEY FACTOR (1849–1928) was a black man who worked as a Seminole Indian Scout. He won the Congressional Medal of Honor in 1875; his citation reads, "With three others he participated in a charge against twenty-five hostiles while on a scouting patrol." After a deputy sheriff killed another scout a few years later, Private Factor deserted the army; he went to Mexico and fought Indians there, before returning two years later. He was pardoned and returned to service.

POWHATAN: from the Native American for powwow hill.

POWHATAN BEATY (1837–1916) won the Congressional Medal of Honor. He was born a slave but had won his freedom and was living in Cincinnati when he enlisted. His unit, Company G, Fifth Colored Troops, fought at New Market Heights. The unit retreated and the color bearer was killed. Sergeant Beaty went back to pick up the standard; when the white commander was killed, Sergeant Beaty led the company against the Confederates.

★ ★ ★ ★ ★ ★ ★ ★ **R** ★ ★ ★ ★ ★ ★ ★ ★

RALPH: from the English for wise wolf or counselor. Rolf is the German form; Raul is Spanish, and Raoul is French.

RALPH DAVID ABERNATHY (1926–1990) was a leader in the civil rights movement. A close friend of Martin Luther King, Jr., Ralph was the pastor of the First Baptist Church in Montgomery, Alabama; with King and Bayard Rustin he founded the Southern Christian Leadership Conference; after King was assassinated Ralph became leader of the SCLC. He helped to plan the Montgomery Bus Boycott. An advocate of protesting with civil disobedience, Ralph was arrested nineteen times.

RALPH BUNCHE (1904–1971) won the Nobel Peace Prize in 1950. Orphaned at thirteen, he moved in with his grandmother. He went to UCLA and then earned a doctorate at Harvard before going to work for the OSS (the forerunner of the CIA) during World War II. After the war he helped to create the United Nations, where he worked in various capacities until 1971. He won the Nobel Prize for his role in bringing about an Arab-Israeli armistice.

RALPH WALDO EMERSON (1803–1882), called the Sage of Concord, was a philosopher and writer who helped to shape America's national character. He won a scholarship to Harvard when he was only fourteen. As an adult he moved to Concord, Massachusetts, and became part of a community of transcendentalists that included Margaret Fuller, Bronson Alcott, Nathaniel Hawthorne, and Henry David Thoreau. He wrote and lectured about self-reliance, integrity, abolitionism, and trust in oneself.

"What lies behind us and what lies before us are tiny matters compared to what lies in us." —Ralph Waldo Emerson

---

RALPH EDMOND STANLEY (b. 1927) was half of the Stanley Brothers, a bluegrass band that included his brother, Carter. Ralph sang tenor harmony and played banjo; Carter played guitar and sang lead vocals. Their first record was released in 1947, and although Carter died when he was forty-one, Ralph has recorded more than 150 albums. He appeared in the movie *O Brother, Where Art Thou?* in 2000.

RANDALL: from the Old German for wolf shield. Randolph is an alternate spelling; Randy is the familiar form.

RANDALL JARRELL (1914–1965) spent World War II in the U.S. Air Force, but today he is remembered not for his heroics in battle but for his poetry. A Nashville native, he attended Vanderbilt University and then taught at various colleges. He translated such books as *Faust* into English and wrote children's books (which were illustrated by Maurice Sendak). His poems about his time in the service, "Eighth Air Force," "Losses," and "The Death of the Ball Turret Gunner," are among the best and most moving poems of war.

RAYMOND: from the Old German for wise protector. Ramon is the Spanish spelling; Redmond, Raymundo, and Reymond are variations. Ray is the most common diminutive.

RAYMOND CHANDLER (1888–1959) helped to create the genre of hard-boiled detective fiction. He wrote pulp fiction for magazines, but his first novel wasn't published until he was fifty. *The Big Sleep* introduced the detective Philip Marlowe and captured a seedy, noir side of Southern California. He went on to write several more novels, all of which are still in print.

"But down these mean streets a man must go who is not himself mean, who is neither tarnished nor afraid." —Raymond Chandler, in *The Simple Art of Murder*

RICHARD: from the Old German for powerful leader. Ricardo is a popular Spanish and Portuguese form; Riccardo is Italian; Rikard is German. Dick, Rick, and Rich are the most common short forms in English; Rico is common in Spanish, Portuguese, and Italian.

RICHARD HENRY LEE (1732–1794) signed the Declaration of Independence. Born into a prominent Virginia family, Richard was a brilliant orator who introduced the resolution calling for independence in the Continental Congress. He had been involved with the fight for independence from the days of the Stamp Act. After the war Richard opposed the Constitution because he believed it didn't protect individual freedoms; because of him, the Bill of Rights was added.

RICHARD M. NIXON (1913–1994) was the thirty-seventh president of the United States and the only one to have resigned. He served in the Pacific during World War II and entered public service when he came home. He was elected first to Congress and then to the Senate; when he was only thirty-nine he was chosen to be Dwight D. Eisenhower's running mate. He lost his first bid for the presidency to John F. Kennedy but was elected in 1968. As president he established ties with China, but his administration is remembered today for the Watergate scandal. He was on the verge of being impeached when he resigned.

RICHARD WRIGHT (1908–1960) was an important writer of the twentieth century. His novel *Native Son* captures the fear and rage of the dispossessed; it became a best seller and a play on Broadway. *Black Boy* was his next book. It was a semiautobiographical account of the poverty and racism he experienced as a child in Mississippi. In the 1940s he moved to Europe, where he lived the rest of his life.

RING: from the English for ring.

RING LARDNER, JR. (1915–2000), a successful screenwriter in Hollywood's heyday, nearly saw his career derailed by the House Un-American Activities Committee. The son of journalist Ring Lardner, he went to Princeton before going to California. He worked on *Woman of the Year*, *Laura*, and *Forever Amber*, among other films. He'd been a member of the Communist Party for a brief period in the 1930s and was summoned by the HUAC, but he refused to implicate others, invoking his First Amendment rights. He was blacklisted and found guilty of contempt, and was sentenced to twelve months in prison. After his release he worked on *The Cincinnati Kid* and *M*A*S*H*, for which he won an Academy Award.

ROBERT: from the Old German for brilliance. Roberto and Rupert are variations; Rob, Bob, Robin, and Bert are short forms.

ROBERT FROST (1874–1963) was a poet who won the Pulitzer Prize four times. Best remembered for his depictions of rural New England, Frost believed poetry should address things that matter. His most famous poems include "Stopping by Woods on a Snowy Evening," "The Road Not Taken," "Fire and Ice," "Nothing Gold Can Stay," "Birches," and "The Mending Wall"; he read "The Gift Outright" at John F. Kennedy's inauguration. A postage stamp was issued in his honor.

ROBERT FULTON (1765–1815) invented the first steam-powered ship, as well as machines to cut marble and make rope, among other things. His first commercial paddle steamer, the *Clermont*, took two days to go from New York to Albany; it traveled five miles per hour. He also invented a submarine for Napoleon and designed a steam-powered warship.

ROBERT E. LEE (1807–1870) was the commander of the Confederate army during the Civil War. Born into a prominent Virginia family, Robert attended West Point, graduating second in his class (he was the first cadet to graduate without any demerits). He stopped John Brown's raid at Harpers Ferry and, as the Civil War drew near, was offered the opportunity to command the Union troops. He refused to fight against his family members, so he declined; when Virginia seceded, he resigned his commission. He fought valiantly but ultimately surrendered, exhibiting grace in defeat.

ROBERT MORRIS (1733–1806) was a signer of the Declaration of Independence. Born in Liverpool, he came to America, and before the Revolution started he was the richest man in America. He signed the Articles of Confederation and the Constitution as well, and he used his vast resources to help finance the war. Later in life he went bankrupt and died poor.

ROBERT GOULD SHAW (1837–1863) was a captain of the Second Massachusetts during the Civil War. He was assigned with raising the first regiment of African-American soldiers from a Northern state. Robert recruited and trained blacks from all over New England, and the regiment went into service in May of 1863. In July, he led an assault where one-third of the regiment died—including him. Thinking that they were insulting him, the Confederates buried him in the same grave as his men, but they weren't aware that he had grown up in a home that supported abolition. His parents believed their son would have wanted to be buried with the men he led.

ROBERT PENN WARREN (1905–1989) was the first poet laureate of the United States. Born in Kentucky, he graduated summa cum laude from Vanderbilt University, received a doctorate from Yale, then was a Rhodes scholar. He won the Pulitzer Prize for fiction for his novel *All the Kings Men*, and won two Pulitzer Prizes for poetry, first in 1958 and again in 1978. He is the only writer to have won for both fiction and poetry.

"Storytelling and copulation are the two chief forms of amusement in the South. They're inexpensive and easy to procure." —Robert Penn Warren

---

ROBINSON: from the English for Robin's son.

ROBINSON JEFFERS (1887–1962) got to live the life most writers dream of. He inherited money, quit his job, and wrote. He published more than twenty volumes of poetry and drama. His version of Euripides's *Medea* was a Broadway hit; his best-known poems are "Apology for Bad Dreams," "To the Stone-cutters," "Shine," and "Roan Stallion."

ROGER: from the German for acclaimed spearman. Rodger is an alternate spelling. Rogelio is the Spanish version; Rutger is Dutch. Rodge and Rog are short forms.

ROGER SHERMAN (1721–1793) was a signer of the Declaration of Independence as well as the Articles of Confederation and the Constitution. After his father died, Roger worked as a shoemaker to support his family; he educated himself by keeping a book near his bench and reading while he worked, and was admitted to the bar in 1754. He served in the Connecticut legislature and became the treasurer of Yale University. After the war he was elected to the U.S. Congress.

ROGER WILLIAMS (1603–1684) was one of the founders of Rhode Island and the founder of Providence. He made the state a haven for anyone persecuted for religious beliefs, including Quakers, Native Americans, and Jews (the first synagogue in America was built in Rhode Island). Roger was exiled from Massachusetts when he questioned the king's claim to the land: he asserted that the land belonged to the Indians.

ROMARE: from the Italian for from Rome.

ROMARE BEARDON (1911–1988) was an artist influenced by the Harlem Renaissance. His parents moved from North Carolina to Harlem, and their home became a meeting place for Aaron Douglas, Langston Hughes, Duke Ellington, and other luminaries. He studied at New York University and the Art Students League, and although he painted landscapes, he is best known for his collage paintings, using images cut from *Ebony* and the *Saturday Evening Post*.

"It is not my aim to paint the Negro in America in terms of propaganda. . . . [It] is to reveal through pictorial complexities the richness of a life I know." —Romare Beardon

---

RONALD: from the Scottish for advisor to the king. Reynold and Reginald are variations. Ron, Ronn, Ronny, and Ronnie are diminutives.

RONALD REAGAN (1911–2004) was America's fortieth president. He was a film actor whose best-known role was as George "the Gipper" Gipp in *Knute Rockne, All American*. He became president of the Screen Actors Guild, then served as governor of California before running for president in 1980. He was shot sixty-nine days after taking office, and although he was seriously wounded he recovered completely. He helped to bring about the end of the cold war.

ROY: from the French for king.

ROY CAMPANELLA (1921–1993) was a Hall of Fame catcher. One of "the Boys of Summer," he was part of the Brooklyn Dodgers dynasty that dominated baseball in the 1950s. The son of an Italian father and a black mother, Roy started his career in the Negro Leagues. Branch Rickey signed him, and he played for the Dodgers' Minnesota farm team before he was called up. In his first game, he hit two home runs. He was paralyzed in a car accident in 1958.

ROYALL: from the French for kingly.

ROYALL TYLER (1757–1826) was a newspaper columnist and playwright. He started as a lawyer working in John Adams's office, then joined the army. While stationed in New York City he saw a performance of *The School for Scandal*, which inspired him to write a comedy contrasting American and English behavior. *The Contrast* was a great success, and he went on to write several more plays, as well as a novel called *The Algerine Captive*.

RUFUS: from the Latin for red-haired.

RUFUS PUTNAM (1738–1824) is called the Father of Ohio. A soldier and pioneer, Rufus was born in Massachusetts. He taught himself surveying; during the French and Indian War he designed defenses on the Great Lakes, and during the Revolutionary War he designed breastworks in Boston and fortifications at West Point. After the war he and a group of veterans moved to Ohio to create settlements; he founded Marietta, Ohio, in 1788.

RUTHERFORD: from the English for cattle ford.

RUTHERFORD B. HAYES (1822–1893) was the nation's nineteenth president. He graduated from Harvard Law School and practiced law in Ohio, but when the Civil War started he joined the army as a major and discovered he loved military life. Wounded four times, he was promoted to major general, and later ran for public office. He was elected to Congress and served as governor of Ohio, and although he lost the popular vote in the 1876 presidential election, he carried the Electoral College.

★ ★ ★ ★ ★ ★ ★ ★ S ★ ★ ★ ★ ★ ★ ★ ★

ST. JULIEN: French for St. Julian. Julian is a variation on Julius, from the Greek for Jove's child.

St. Julien Ravenel (1819–1882) was a chemist and surgeon who invented the *Little David*, a torpedo boat used by the Confederates during the Civil War. His boat was fifty feet long, five feet in diameter, and powered by steam. A four-man crew navigated the vessel and was to abandon ship before it hit the target. After the war, he discovered phosphate deposits near his home in Charleston and used them to make fertilizer.

SAMUEL: from the Hebrew for God heard. Sam and Sammy are the diminutives.

Samuel Adams (1722–1803) was a signer of the Declaration of Independence and the Articles of Confederation. A brewery owner and prime instigator behind the Revolution, Samuel emerged as a leader of the revolt. He wrote essays whose goal was to inflame the colonists to resist the Crown, calling the Stamp Act outrageous and putting forth the notion of "no taxation without representation." He founded the radical secret society the Sons of Liberty, and served in the Continental Congress from 1774 to 1781. After the war he served as governor of Massachusetts.

Samuel Chase (1741–1811) was a signer of the Declaration of Independence. He protested the Stamp Act and was a delegate from Maryland to the First and Second Continental Congresses. He and the other delegates had been instructed not to vote for independence, but when it became clear that compromise with England was impossible, Samuel rode to Maryland and argued passionately and eloquently for liberty. Maryland approved a vote for independence thanks to Samuel's moving speeches. After the war, he served as a judge in Maryland and as a U.S. Supreme Court justice.

Sam Houston (1793–1863) was one of the more colorful characters in American history. A Virginia native, he spent time with the Cherokee as a boy, then fought with Andrew Jackson during the Creek Wars. He spent two terms in the U.S. Congress before becoming governor of Tennessee; he resigned and spent six years living with the Cherokee. By

1835 he was in Texas leading the revolution, and was the first president when Texas won its independence. After it became a state, he represented Texas in the U.S. Senate. The city of Houston is named in his honor.

SAMUEL MORSE (1791–1872) invented the telegraph. He graduated from Yale and then worked as an artist, painting miniatures and portraits. When his parents and wife all died within a short period, he traveled to Europe. On the ship home, a scientist mentioned that electricity could travel any distance instantly. It occurred to Samuel that signals could be made by interrupting the flow of electricity. He invented the relay, and then the telegraph, and received the patent in 1840. He was nearly bankrupt when Congress appropriated funds to build a telegraph line between Baltimore and Washington, D.C. On May 24, 1844, Morse sent his first message in the dot-and-dash code he devised: "What hath God wrought?"

SATCHEL: from the Latin for small valise.

SATCHEL PAIGE (1906–1982) was born Leroy Paige in Mobile, Alabama. With a fastball clocked at a blistering 103 miles per hour, Satchel is regarded as one of the greatest pitchers in baseball history. At age seven he earned tips carrying baggage at the train station; his nickname came from the device he rigged to help him. He started playing baseball when he was ten and was playing semipro ball by the time he was seventeen. His career spanned decades: he played in the Negro Leagues until 1948 and joined the Cleveland Indians when he was forty-two years old. Satchel was the first Negro League player voted into the Baseball Hall of Fame.

SCOTT: from the Old English for from Scotland. Scot is an alternate spelling.

F. SCOTT FITZGERALD (1896–1940), named Francis Scott Key Fitzgerald, was known always as Scott (or Scottie). Born in Minnesota, he went to school at Princeton, then joined the army and was sent to Alabama. He met his wife, Zelda Sayre, in Montgomery. Scott's first novel, *This Side of Paradise*, was published to great acclaim in 1920. His novel *The Great Gatsby* appeared in 1925; *Tender Is the Night* is a semiautobiographical depiction of Zelda's mental instability and his alcoholism. When his wife became institutionalized he went to Hollywood and became a scriptwriter.

SCOTT JOPLIN (1868–1917) created a uniquely American form of music: ragtime. He studied music as a boy, and as an adult played in bars and honky-tonks. Adapting the folk music and banjo playing he'd heard growing up, Scott developed a style that encompassed syncopated rhythms and a strong beat. In 1899 he published "The Maple Leaf Rag"; it sold more than half a million copies, and the steady royalty income allowed him to write—prolifically. His song "The Entertainer" was featured in the movie *The Sting*. Although he wrote opera and other types of music, he is associated today with ragtime.

SHERWOOD: from the Old English for bright forest.

SHERWOOD ANDERSON (1876–1941) was a brilliant storyteller. He grew up in Clyde, Ohio; the town figures prominently in his best works. As a young man he joined the army and fought in the Spanish-American War, then went into advertising. In 1912 he left his family and moved to Chicago to write. His masterpiece, *Winesburg, Ohio*, was published in 1919. *Dark Laughter* followed, and he used the royalties to move to Virginia and buy two newspapers, which he edited.

SIDNEY: from the French for Saint-Denis. Sid is the short form. Sydney is an alternate spelling.

SIDNEY BECHET (1897–1958) was a jazz virtuoso who played alto saxophone. The son of a musician, he grew up in New Orleans listening to blues, jazz, and ragtime. He met Louis Armstrong, toured Europe with the Southern Syncopated Orchestra of Will Marion Cook, and ended up settling in Paris. His recordings include "Wild Cat Blues," "Kansas City Man," and "Cake Walkin' Babies from Home" with Louis Armstrong. He played in Josephine Baker's Negro Revue and with Noble Sissle in Paris and New York.

SINCLAIR: from the French for Saint-Clair.

SINCLAIR LEWIS (1885–1951) was a Nobel Prize–winning novelist. Born in Sauk Centre, Minnesota, his vision of life in small-town America is reflected in his novels *Main Street*, *Babbitt*, and *Elmer Gantry*. Devastating satire tempered with poignancy is his hallmark. One of his last books, *It Can't Happen Here*, is about the rise of a dictator in the United States.

STANISLAUS: from the patron saint of Poland. Stash and Stan are the most common familiar forms. Stanley is from the Old English for stony meadow.

STAN MUSIAL (b. 1920), born Stanislaus in a Pennsylvania mill town, was one of the greatest hitters to play baseball. He spent his entire career, from 1941 to 1963, with the St. Louis Cardinals. He won seven batting championships, played in a record twenty-four All-Star Games, and had a career batting average of .331. He had great respect for his fans and would sign autographs for hours, and he was careful to consider his behavior in public because he felt he was a role model. When he left the diamond the Cardinals retired his uniform number.

STEPHEN: from the Greek for garland. Steven is an alternate spelling. Etienne is the French spelling; Esteban is Spanish; Stefan is common in Germany, Scandinavia, and Slavic countries. Stavros is a Greek variation. Steve is the most common short form.

STEPHEN AUSTIN (1793–1836) was a pioneer who helped to settle Texas. He led more than twelve hundred settlers to the Brazos and Colorado Rivers, mapped and surveyed a significant portion of the area, and acted as a liaison with the Mexican government. He was arrested in Mexico City in 1833 on charges of sedition and went to prison; when he was released, war in Texas had broken out. After Texas won its independence he served as Sam Houston's secretary of state.

STEPHEN CRANE (1871–1900) lived just twenty-eight years before he died of tuberculosis, but in his short life he wrote one of the greatest war novels ever. Born into a family of writers, Stephen was ghostwriting books for family members when he was sixteen. He wrote *Maggie: A Girl of the Streets* when he was in college, and at age twenty-one wrote *The Red Badge of Courage*; he had not yet seen war. Later, he went to Greece as a war correspondent, then covered the Spanish-American War in Cuba.

STEPHEN HOPKINS (1707–1785) was a signer of the Declaration of Independence; he was the second-oldest signer, after Benjamin Franklin. A Rhode Island native, Stephen served in the House of Representatives from 1741 until 1756, when he became governor of Rhode Island. He introduced the first antislavery bill in the country and freed all of his slaves. In addition, he founded Providence's public library and served as chancellor of Rhode Island College (now Brown University).

SYLVESTER: from the Latin for woodsman. It is a modern variation on Silvanus and Silas. Sylvestre is the French form. Sly is the nickname.

SYLVESTER HOWARD ROPER (1823–1896) was an inventor. He started tinkering with steam-powered vehicles in the mid-1850s, and in 1865 he built a motorcycle—the first two-wheeled vehicle powered by a two-cylinder, coal-fueled steam engine, controlled by a throttle on the handgrip. He also invented an early version of the motorcar in 1866. His motorcycle is on display at the Smithsonian Institution.

★ ★ ★ ★ ★ ★ ★ ★ **T** ★ ★ ★ ★ ★ ★ ★ ★

TED: a nickname for Theodore, Edwin, or Edward.

TED SHAWN (1891–1972) is considered the father of modern dance. Named Edwin Myers Shawn at birth, he began dancing when he was nineteen as a form of physical therapy after a debilitating illness. It became his passion. In 1914 he met and married Ruth St. Denis. The two formed the Denishawn Company and School, one of the first of modern dance. He was a mentor to Martha Graham, and he taught Alvin Ailey, Merce Cunningham, and Robert Joffrey as well.

TENNESSEE: from the Southern state.

TENNESSEE WILLIAMS (1911–1983) was the pen name of Thomas Lanier Williams. One of America's great playwrights, he started writing at age eleven when he received a typewriter as a gift. A native of Mississippi, Williams used the South almost as a character in his plays, not just as a setting; his older sister's mental instability was also a theme. *The Glass Menagerie* was his first Broadway success and the winner of the New York Drama Critics' Circle Award. *A Streetcar Named Desire* garnered a Pulitzer Prize, as did *Cat on a Hot Tin Roof*.

THELONIOUS: of unknown origin.

THELONIOUS MONK (1917–1982) was called the Founding Father of Modern Jazz. He began playing piano professionally by age thirteen, and in the 1940s he started playing bebop, which he adapted into an eccentric, almost jarring style of jazz. His recordings for Blue Note are now considered classics; "Round Midnight" is his most famous work.

THEODORE: from the Greek for gift of God. Teodor is Spanish; Teodoro is Italian and Portuguese, and Fyodor is Russian. Ted and Teddy are the diminutives.

THEODORE ROOSEVELT (1858–1919) was the twenty-sixth president of the United States; he was sworn in after President William McKinley was assassinated. A hero during the Spanish-American War, Teddy served as governor of New York. An avid outdoorsman, he started the national parks system (and when he spared two bear cubs on a hunting trip, toy "Teddy Bears" became popular). He was also a trustbuster, and started construction of the Panama Canal. He won the Nobel Peace Prize for his role in ending the Russo-Japanese War.

"Speak softly and carry a big stick." —Theodore Roosevelt

THEODORE WILLIAMS (1918–2002) was known as Ted, the Kid, or the Splendid Splinter. The greatest hitter in baseball, Ted Williams of the Boston Red Sox worked to perfect his swing with a scientific methodology. He studied its arc, force, and his stance, and was the last hitter to end the season with a batting average over .400—his was .406. He fought in World War II and Korea, but still won two of baseball's Triple Crowns, two Most Valuable Player awards, and six American League batting championships, and hit 521 home runs.

"It was the center of my heart, hitting a baseball." —Ted Williams

THOMAS: from the Aramaic for twin. Tomás is the Spanish spelling; Tavish may be an Irish variation. Tom, Tommy, and Thom are nicknames.

THOMAS ALVA EDISON (1847–1931) received 1,093 patents in his life, more than any other individual. Of his inventions, the two he is most remembered for are the incandescent lightbulb and the phonograph. He contracted scarlet fever when he was fourteen; it left him completely deaf in one ear and 80 percent deaf in the other. With only three months of formal schooling, Edison became a telegraph operator. One of his first inventions was an automatic telegraph repeater. His first patent was for an electric voting machine. He also invented a stock ticker for Wall Street and the mimeograph machine, the fluorescent light, the alkaline battery, and a motion picture camera. His inventions were also used by others—the telegraph transmitter in telephones, and a means of telegraphing aerial signals in radios.

"Genius is 1 percent inspiration and 99 percent perspiration." —Thomas Edison

THOMAS JONATHAN JACKSON (1824–1863) is better known as Stonewall. General Jackson got his nickname during the First Battle of Bull Run. The rebels were under fire from Union troops, but were rallied with the cry "There is Jackson, standing like a stone wall." Born in Virginia, Jackson was orphaned and raised by his uncle; he graduated from West Point and joined the Confederate army when Virginia seceded. A Confederate hero, he fought sixty thousand federal troops with sixteen thousand men at Cross Keys; he drove the Union from the field at the Second Battle of Bull Run. He was injured at Chancellorsville and his arm was amputated, but he developed pneumonia and died.

THOMAS JEFFERSON (1743–1826) was America's third president. The author of the Declaration of Independence, Jefferson's influence on our country cannot be understated. A brilliant man, he graduated from the College of William and Mary when he was seventeen. He was a fierce advocate of separating from Britain and was part of the Continental Congress. He was governor of Virginia and ambassador to France, and as president he doubled the size of the United States with the Louisiana Purchase. He founded the University of Virginia, and his personal library became the core of the Library of Congress.

THOMAS NELSON, JR. (1738–1789) was a signer of the Declaration of Independence. A wealthy merchant, he became a commander in chief of the armed forces from Virginia. He used his own money to equip a cavalry, donating his horses to the army, feeding the militia, and sending his slaves to work the farms of men who were fighting. When the British commandeered his home to use as barracks, he ordered his men to shell it.

THORNTON: from the English for town of thorns.

THORNTON WILDER (1897–1975) is the only writer to win the Pulitzer Prize for both fiction and drama. He was born in Wisconsin but moved to China as a teenager when his father served as U.S. consul. He served in the Coast Guard during World War I and in Africa and Italy during World War II. *The Bridge of San Luis Rey* won him his first Pulitzer, in fiction; *Our Town* was a sensation on Broadway in 1938 and netted him his second; his third came for *The Skin of Our Teeth*. His play *The Matchmaker* was turned into the musical *Hello, Dolly!*

THURGOOD: from the Norse for Thor is divine.

THURGOOD MARSHALL (1908–1993), a civil rights lawyer who became a U.S. Supreme Court justice, was the son of a schoolteacher and a waiter. He graduated cum laude from Lincoln University and studied law at Howard University, then became a lawyer for the NAACP and in 1939 was director of its Legal Defense Fund. He won twenty-nine of the thirty-two civil rights cases he argued before the Supreme Court;

his most famous was *Brown v. Board of Education*. He was nominated to the Supreme Court in 1967 by Lyndon B. Johnson, and although Southern senators fought his nomination, he became the first black American Supreme Court justice on October 2, 1967.

TIMOTHY: from the Greek for God's honor. Timo is a Spanish variation; Tighe is Gaelic. Tim and Timmy are nicknames.

TIMOTHY DWIGHT (1752–1817) was a president of Yale University. He was a prodigy and could have gone to college when he was eight, but didn't enroll until he was thirteen. During the Revolutionary War he served as chaplain to the Connecticut Continental Brigade, and after the war he founded a school for boys *and* girls; later he gave his support to a school that taught black women how to read.

TIMOTHY O'SULLIVAN (1840–1882) was one of the first professional photographers. He was a field photographer during the Civil War; his poignant photographs of the dead at Gettysburg, Bull Run, and Appomattox are heartrending. After the war he went west with several geographical surveys. He took the first-ever photographs of the inside of a mine, photographing the Comstock Lode using magnesium flares. Hauling a twenty-by-twenty-four-inch view camera, he traveled all over the West and to Panama. Some of his most famous pictures are of the abandoned pueblo at Canyon de Chelly in Arizona.

TOWNSEND: from the English for town's end or boundary.

TOWNSEND HARRIS (1804–1878) established the first commercial ties between the United States and Japan. He ran an importing business with his father and brother. In the 1840s he joined the New York Board of Education; as its president he founded the New York Free Academy, which exists today as the College of the City of New York. When Japan established relations with America he became the first consul to Japan, working to secure American trade and diplomatic relations.

TRUMPETER: from the English for trumpet player.

TRUMPETER ISAAC PAYNE (1854–1904), a black Congressional Medal of Honor winner, was a Seminole Indian scout. He enlisted in the army when he was seventeen, and earned the medal on April 25, 1875. Except for brief periods between reenlistments, he served in the military until 1901. After he left the army he lived with his family at the Seminole-Negro Indian Camp until his death.

★ ★ ★ ★ ★ ★ ★ ★ **U** ★ ★ ★ ★ ★ ★ ★ ★

ULYSSES: the Latin variation on Odysseus, from the Greek for wrathful.

ULYSSES S. GRANT (1822–1885) was America's eighteenth president. A graduate of West Point, he served at isolated army posts, away from his beloved wife, Julia, until he resigned from the army in 1854. He was working as a clerk in a store when the Civil War broke out. He became a colonel in the Twenty-first Illinois, then was promoted to brigadier general. He captured Forts Henry and Donelson, then went on to crush the Confederate forces at Vicksburg, Gettysburg, and Chickamauga. After the war ended he ran for president and won handily.

UPTON: from the English for upper town.

UPTON SINCLAIR (1878–1968) was a muckraking novelist. Born in Baltimore, he attended City College in New York and studied law at Columbia University; he wrote adventure stories to support himself. His book *The Jungle* was published in 1906; it is a scathing indictment of the filthy conditions in the meatpacking industry. An uproar ensued, and the Pure Food and Drug Law was passed as a result of his exposé. He went on to write more than ninety books and earned more than $1 million, but he gave most of it away. In 1942 he won a Pulitzer Prize for his novel *Dragon's Teeth*.

★ ★ ★ ★ ★ ★ ★ ★ ★ V ★ ★ ★ ★ ★ ★ ★ ★ ★

VACHEL: from the French for young steer.

VACHEL LINDSAY (1879–1931) was an American version of the medieval bards. He walked the country reciting his poetry aloud, trading his poems for meals. As his popularity grew, people would chant the refrains with him at his recitals. His best-known poems are "The Congo," which has a jazzlike meter, "The Golden Whales of California," and "Abraham Lincoln Walks at Midnight." His poems have been collected into a volume entitled *General William Booth Enters into Heaven*.

VIRGIL: from the Latin for staff bearer.

VIRGIL THOMSON (1896–1989) was a Pulitzer Prize–winning composer. As a five-year-old he began to study music, and was performing professionally when he was twelve. He moved to Paris in the 1920s and studied with Nadia Boulanger. While there he became friends with Erik Satie, whose belief that the hallmarks of music should be simplicity and humor influenced Virgil's later work. He collaborated with Gertrude Stein; he wrote the music and she the librettos for two operas. Later he wrote film scores, and acted as the music critic for the *New York Herald Tribune* from 1940 to 1954.

WALKER: from the English for cloth washer.

WALKER EVANS (1903–1975) was a photographer whose images documented the Great Depression and the ordinary lives of ordinary Americans. He left St. Louis, Missouri, in the 1920s to become a writer in Paris, but after failing he returned to the United States and discovered photography. He worked with the Farm Security Administration on a study of poverty in the 1930s, and in 1936 he collaborated with James Agee on the seminal *Let Us Now Praise Famous Men*. His beautiful large-format photographs capture landscape and architecture, people at work and at play.

WALLACE: from the Scottish for Welshman or foreigner.

WALLACE STEVENS (1879–1955) wrote some of the best, and best-known, poems of the twentieth century. "Sunday Morning," "The Emperor of Ice Cream," and "Thirteen Ways of Looking at a Blackbird" are just a few of the more than four hundred poems he penned. His first book, *Harmonium*, came out when he was forty-four; his second came out twelve years later. *Auroras of Autumn* won the Bollingen Prize, and *Collected Poems* won the Pulitzer and the National Book Award.

"One writes poetry because one must." —Wallace Stevens

WALTER: from the German for ruler of the people. Walther is an alternate spelling; Walt and Wally are nicknames.

WALTER REED (1851–1902) was a doctor whose work helped to eradicate yellow fever. He earned two medical degrees, both before he was nineteen; at age twenty-four he enlisted in the U.S. Army Medical Corps. He spent eleven years at frontier posts, then went to Washington, D.C., to teach at the Army Medical School. During the Spanish-American War soldiers developed yellow fever; many died. Walter Reed helped to develop a vaccine that played a crucial role in eliminating the disease. Walter Reed Hospital in Washington, D.C., is named in his honor.

WALT WHITMAN (1819–1892) called himself a poet of the people. He wrote one book, *Leaves of Grass*, but revised it nine times. The first edition appeared in 1855 and contained "Song of Myself," "I Sing the Body Electric," and "There Was a Child Went Forth." The "Death Bed" edition came out in 1892 and is the one most readers know today. His elegy to Abraham Lincoln, "When Lilacs Last in the Dooryard Bloom'd," was written late in 1865.

"I believe a leaf of grass is no less than the journeywork of the stars."
—Walt Whitman

WARREN: from the German for general or authority.

WARREN G. HARDING (1865–1923) was the twenty-ninth president of the United States. He had been a newspaper owner who was involved in local politics in his home state of Ohio. Helped by his ambitious wife, Florence, he ran for president and won the largest popular majority in history. As president, he ended the twelve-hour workday in the steel industry, commuted prison sentences of World War I objectors, devised programs to help farmers, and, recognizing the popularity and importance of the automobile, increased spending on highways. Although he was honest, his friends in the oil business were less than ethical. At a loss to stop the brewing Teapot Dome scandal, Harding suffered a fatal heart attack and died while in office.

WASHINGTON: a surname used as a first name, often in honor of George Washington.

WASHINGTON IRVING (1783–1859) wrote stories that have become part of America's heritage. A native of New York City and the youngest of eleven, Washington started writing as a teenager. His send-up of New York under the Dutch won him a following, but it wasn't until he was in his mid-thirties that he decided to make a living as a writer. *The Sketch Book* by "Geoffrey Crayon" included three short stories that catapulted him into the pantheon: "Rip Van Winkle," "The Spectre Bridegroom," and "The Legend of Sleepy Hollow," a tale of Ichabod Crane and the Headless Horseman.

WASHINGTON AUGUSTUS ROEBLING (1837–1926) was the mechanical genius behind the Brooklyn Bridge. He went to Rensselaer Polytechnic Institute, then went to work with his father, the premier builder of suspension bridges in the country, and helped build the Allegheny River

Bridge in Pittsburgh and the Cincinnati Bridge across the Ohio River. His father died shortly before they began work on the Brooklyn Bridge, so Washington oversaw its construction. Three years into the project he suffered the bends; he was disabled and in chronic pain, and supervised the work using a telescope from a house in Brooklyn.

WENDELL: from the German for wanderer.

WENDELL BERRY (b. 1934) is called the Prophet of Rural America. A native of Kentucky, he attended the University of Kentucky, then won a fellowship to study creative writing at Stanford. He returned to Kentucky in the 1960s and lives on farmland that has been in his family for generations. A conservationist and environmentalist, Berry has written more than thirty books. *The Unsettling of America: Culture and Agriculture* is a critique of the rise of agribusiness at the expense of family farms. *Given* is a collection of poetry.

"The most alarming sign of the state of our society now is that our leaders have the courage to sacrifice the lives of young people in war but have not the courage to tell us that we must be less greedy and wasteful." —Wendell Berry

---

WILBUR: from the German for unmoving fortress.

WILBUR WRIGHT (1867–1912), with his younger brother, Orville, built the first airplane. A high school dropout, Wilbur was brilliant. His father said of him, "In memory and intellect, there was none like him. He systemized everything." Wilbur and Orville opened a bicycle repair shop, and they used their income to finance their research of flying machines. They made gliders and tinkered with wing designs, and by the fall of 1903 had built a plane that was propelled by an engine. The two went to the Outer Banks of North Carolina and on December 17, 1903, with Wilbur at the controls, their plane took off, flew, and landed four times; the longest flight was 852 feet. Wilbur died of typhoid fever in 1912. Their plane is exhibited at the National Air and Space Museum in Washington, D.C.

WILLIAM: from the Old German for determined protector. Wilhelm is a German form; Willem is Dutch; Guglielmo is Italian; Guillaume is French; Guillermo is Spanish, and Liam is the Gaelic variation. Nicknames include Bill, Billy, Will, Willy, Willie, Wills, and Wim.

WILLIAM BEEBE (1877–1962) was an oceanographer who explored the sea in a bathysphere. He wanted to study sea creatures that lived at extreme depths, but ocean pressure limited the depths that humans could withstand. In 1929 William used a round metal sphere to dive 800 feet—175 feet deeper than anyone had before. He descended to 1,426 feet on his next dive, and in 1934 he descended to 3,028 feet—a dive record that was not broken until 1949. He discovered hundreds of sea animals.

WILLIAM HARVEY CARNEY (1840–1908) was the first black man to win the Congressional Medal of Honor. A member of Company C in the Fifty-fourth Massachusetts Infantry, he was at Fort Wagner on July 18, 1863. The color bearer was wounded when the Fifty-fourth began its advance. William grabbed the flag and moved to the front of the column and made it to the fort's entrance. He was surrounded by Confederates and was wounded several times, but he refused to give up the flag. When he died, flags at the Massachusetts State House were flown at half-staff; Sergeant Carney is the only nonpresident to receive that honor.

WILLIAM CLARK (1770–1838) was the second half of the Lewis and Clark expedition. Born in Virginia, he served in the army under Anthony "Mad Anthony" Wayne. He resigned in 1796, and when Meriwether Lewis invited him to join his expedition to find a route to the Pacific Ocean, he leaped at the chance. The men complemented each other well: Lewis was the politically connected intellect who would write the account of their trip; Clark was a leader and an outdoorsman as well as a mapmaker. They began their journey on May 14, 1804, and in 1805 they met up with Sacagawea, the sister of a Shoshone Indian chief, who acted as their guide.

WILLIAM JEFFERSON CLINTON (b. 1946) was the forty-second president of the United States. He decided he wanted to go into politics in 1963 when he met John F. Kennedy. He attended Georgetown University, then attended Oxford University as a Rhodes scholar before attending Yale Law School, where he met his wife, Hillary Rodham. They returned to Arkansas, where he became governor (the youngest in the state's history); he lost his bid for reelection, but won again in 1982. Clinton's administration saw great prosperity—low inflation, low unemployment rates, high home ownership, and a balanced budget. His second term was overshadowed by a sexual scandal that resulted in his impeachment, but he was acquitted by the Senate.

WILLIAM CODY (1846–1917) was known as Buffalo Bill. A scout, hunter, Pony Express rider, and star of a Wild West show, this Iowa native earned his name hunting buffalo for the Kansas Pacific Railroad crews. He was a scout for the U.S. Army and won the Congressional Medal of Honor. In 1883 he was the featured attraction in a Wild West show that toured for decades. By 1900 he was one of the most famous men in the world.

WILLIAM EDWARD BURGHARDT DUBOIS (1868–1963), known as W. E. B. DuBois, was born of French and African descent in Massachusetts. He attended Fisk, where he witnessed segregation and Jim Crow laws; Harvard, where he was the first black to earn a doctorate but had to live off-campus; and the University of Berlin. In 1903 he wrote the seminal work *The Souls of Black Folk*; in 1909 he helped to found the NAACP. He spent the rest of his life as an advocate for peace and racial equality, but had problems with the FBI.

"The problem of the twentieth century is the problem of the color-line."
—W. E. B. DuBois

WILLIAM FAULKNER (1897–1962) was one of the great Southern voices of the twentieth century; he wrote such novels as *The Sound and the Fury*, *As I Lay Dying*, and *Absalom, Absalom!*, as well as dozens of short stories. In his third novel, *Sartoris*, he created a fictional county in Mississippi; Yoknaptawpha and its residents figured prominently in his subsequent books. His long, somewhat convoluted sentences stood in marked contrast to the prose of peers like Ernest Hemingway, but Faulkner nevertheless won a Pulitzer Prize for fiction, the Nobel Prize in Literature, and a National Book Award.

"The writer's only responsibility is to his art. He will be completely ruthless if he is a good one. . . . If a writer has to rob his mother, he will not hesitate; the 'Ode on a Grecian Urn' is worth any number of old ladies."
—William Faulkner, in *Writers at Work: The Paris Review Interviews*

WILLIAM LLOYD GARRISON (1805–1879) was a famous and influential abolitionist. He published an antislavery newspaper called the *Liberator*, and called attention to his causes by deliberately creating controversy: he publicly burned a copy of the U.S. Constitution, stating that it allowed slavery and that it was "a covenant with Death and an agreement with Hell." When slavery was abolished, he fought for rights on behalf of women and Native Americans.

"Our country is the world—Our countrymen are mankind." —motto of William Lloyd Garrison's newspaper, the *Liberator*

WILLIAM HENRY HARRISON (1773–1841) was America's ninth president and the first to die in office. A native of Virginia, he joined the army and went to fight Indians with Anthony "Mad Anthony" Wayne; after fighting on the frontier he became governor of Indiana Territory. He became a hero after fighting against the Indian chief Tecumseh at Tippecanoe. He barely won the popular vote for president, but he carried the Electoral College—and died of pneumonia less than a month after his inauguration.

WILLIAM MCKINLEY (1843–1901) was the twenty-fifth president of the United States. A native of Ohio, he studied law and became active in state politics, first as a congressman and then as governor. He defeated William Jennings Bryan in the presidential race, and after the Spanish-American War he annexed Puerto Rico, Guam, and the Philippines as U.S. territories. He defeated Bryan handily in his bid for re-election, but he was assassinated by an anarchist in Buffalo, New York, less than a year into his second term.

WILL ROGERS (1879–1935) was America's "cowboy philosopher." Born of mixed Indian ancestry in Oklahoma, Will was an expert horseman. He started as a rancher but then joined the circus, first in South America and then with the Ziegfeld Follies. Performing as Cherokee Bill, his act combined maneuvers with horse and lasso with folk wisdom and wit, and soon he was writing a newspaper column and books, as well as appearing on radio and in movies.

"I have never met a man I didn't like." —Will Rogers

WILLIAM TECUMSEH SHERMAN (1820–1891) was a Civil War general for the Union. He graduated from West Point in 1840 and served in the Second Seminole War and the Mexican War before resigning in 1853. He returned to service in the Civil War, fighting with Ulysses S. Grant at nearly every major battle. He had four horses shot out from under him at Shiloh, and after capturing and burning Atlanta in September of 1864, he and sixty-two thousand men began their march to the sea, burning houses, fields, and forests on their way. He captured Savannah in December, and it was the only place in his path that he did not burn to ash and rubble—he left it untouched at Mary Todd Lincoln's request.

WILLIAM HOWARD TAFT (1857–1930) was America's twenty-seventh president. He was born in Ohio and became a judge in the superior court; in 1890 he was appointed solicitor general of the United States. William McKinley made him civil governor of the Philippines, and under Theodore Roosevelt he was secretary of war. He defeated William Jennings Bryan in the 1908 presidential election. He was defeated when he ran a second time, but was appointed to the Supreme Court in 1921.

WINSLOW: from the English for hill.

WINSLOW HOMER (1836–1910) was a self-taught painter who is best remembered for his seascapes off the Maine Coast. He began his career as a lithographer's apprentice, then went to the front lines of the Civil War as an artist for *Harper's Weekly*. His paintings from the conflict, *Sharpshooter on Picket Duty* and *Prisoners from the Front*, were painted after the war. By the 1870s he was painting scenes of children and farm life; *Snap the Whip* is from this period. He then moved to Maine, where he painted watercolors, such as *Mending the Nets*, *Eight Bells*, and *Gulf Stream*.

WILSON: from the English for Will's son. Willson is an alternate spelling; Will and Wills are nicknames.

WILSON BROWN (1841–1900) was a black American who won the Congressional Medal of Honor. He enlisted in the navy and served aboard the USS *Hartford* in the Civil War. When the *Hartford* led a fleet of fourteen ships past the guns in three separate forts into Mobile Bay, Landsman Brown was one of the men working the shell whip when an enemy shell exploded. Four men were killed, and although Wilson was knocked unconscious, he came to and crawled from under bodies to return to the shell whip for the rest of the battle.

WOODROW: from the English for row of houses by the woods. Woody is the familiar form.

WOODROW WILSON GUTHRIE (1912–1967) was known to all as Woody. A folk singer, wandering minstrel, and "balladeer of the Dust Bowl," Woody left his home in Oklahoma for Texas and then California. He rode the rails, lived in hobo camps and lean-tos, and spoke with factory workers and migrant farm laborers, turning what he heard and saw into songs. In 1940 he moved to New York City, where he began to record his songs. "This Land Is Your Land," "Roll On, Columbia," and "Bound for Glory" became anthems for the protest movements in the 1960s and influenced a new generation of musicians, including Bob Dylan and Phil Ochs. Woody Guthrie was inducted into the Rock and Roll Hall of Fame in 1988.

WOODROW WILSON (1856–1924) was the country's twenty-eighth president. The son of a Presbyterian minister, Wilson was born in Virginia and went to Princeton and Johns Hopkins, where he earned his Ph.D. He returned to Princeton as a professor and eventually became the university's president. He ran for governor of New Jersey and then for the presidency. He described the United States' entry into World War I as necessary to make the world safe for democracy; after the war he helped to negotiate the Treaty of Versailles and worked to establish the League of Nations. He suffered a debilitating stroke while he was in office; his wife, Edith, took an active role in his care, carefully screening visitors and documents and having an influence on the rest of his term.

WYATT: from the Old English for war strength. Wiat and Wiatt are alternate spellings; Wye is a variation.

WYATT EARP (1848–1929) was born in Illinois, but his name is synonymous with the Wild West. He left home in 1864 and eventually became deputy marshal of Wichita and Dodge City, then chased cattle rustlers to Texas, where he met Doc Holliday. He went to Arizona as a prospector, but when he came to the outlaw town of Tombstone he, his two brothers, and Doc Holliday had a shoot-out at the O.K. Corral with the Clanton Gang. Wyatt went on to build a fortune, and became a living legend.

★ ★ ★ ★ ★ ★ ★ ★ **Z** ★ ★ ★ ★ ★ ★ ★

ZACHARY: a variation on Zachariah, from the Hebrew for God remembered. Zack, Zac, and Zeke are nicknames (Zeke is sometimes used with Ezekiel).

ZACHARY TAYLOR (1784–1850) was America's twelfth president. A native of Virginia and the son of a lieutenant colonel who had fought with George Washington, Zachary was a career military man. Called Old Rough and Ready, Taylor fought Tecumseh and Black Hawk and in the Mexican War. When he won the presidency, Southerners thought he would support slavery, but he opposed it in New Mexico and California. When Southern senators threatened to secede, Taylor threatened to hang traitors and vowed to hold the nation together by force. He died in office after contracting food poisoning.

ZANE: a variation on John.

ZANE GREY (1872–1939) invented the Western novel. Of the eighty-nine books he wrote, fifty-six are set in the West, and forty-six were made into movies. Born in Zanesville, Ohio, he went to dental school on an athletic scholarship, then opened a practice in New York City. He wrote at night and sold his first story in 1902. After meeting a man named Buffalo Jones and visiting a ranch in Arizona, he wrote his first Western, *The Heritage of the Desert*. His best-known book is *Riders of the Purple Sage*.

ZEBULON: from the Hebrew for exalted.

ZEBULON MONTGOMERY PIKE (1779–1813) was an explorer. He was born in New Jersey and joined the army. He was sent to what is now Minnesota to find the headwaters of the Mississippi River, which he mistakenly identified as Leech Lake; he also bought 100,000 acres from the Sioux and founded the city of St. Paul. He was sent on a secret mission to explore Spanish lands; in Colorado he attempted to climb a "great peak" that is now named for him. Later, he and his party got lost searching for the Red River and were captured by the Spanish. When he was released he wrote about his journey and became famous.

ZOOT: American jazz slang for cool.

ZOOT SIMS (1925–1985) was born John Haley Sims. He grew up in a vaudeville family, playing clarinet and drums, but was inspired by Lester Young to switch to tenor saxophone when he was thirteen. By the time he was fifteen he was playing professionally, and at eighteen he had joined Benny Goodman's band; he played with Goodman for thirty years, and also sat in with Woody Herman, Buddy Rich, Artie Shaw, Stan Kenton, and Al Cohn. He was famous for his dry wit. When he met Italy's top jazz player, who was also Benito Mussolini's son, he shook the man's hand and said, "Sorry to hear about your dad."

About the Author

CHARLOTTE DANFORTH is a professional copywriter and author of nonfiction books. Formerly an assistant professor of English literature, she holds a master's degree from Rutgers University and was awarded a National Endowment for the Humanities Fellowship. Her large extended family has lived in northeastern Pennsylvania since the Revolutionary War. Charlotte currently lives in a 150-year-old farmhouse with two dogs and many cats.